Enriching Curriculum for All Students

▶ ▶ ▶ ▶ ▶ ▶ ▶ ▶ ▶ ▶

Joseph S. Renzulli

Foreword by Howard Gardner

SkyLight
Professional
Development

Arlington Heights, Illinois

The work reported herein was supported under the Educational Research and Development Centers Program, PR/Award Number R206R50001, as administered by the Office of Educational Research and Improvement, U.S. Department of Education. The findings and opinions expressed in this publication do not reflect the position or policies of the National Institute on the Education of At-Risk Students, the Office of Educational Research and Improvement, or the U.S. Department of Education.

Enriching Curriculum for All Students

Published by SkyLight Professional Development
2626 S. Clearbrook Dr., Arlington Heights, IL 60005
800-348-4474 or 847-290-6600
Fax 847-290-6609
info@skylightedu.com
http://www.skylightedu.com

Director, Product Development: Carol Luitjens
Acquisitions Editor: Sue Schumer
Editor: Andrea Coens
Project Coordinator: Anne Kaske
Cover Designer and Illustrator: David Stockman
Book Designer: Bruce Leckie
Production Supervisor: Bob Crump

LCCCN 00-107341
ISBN 1-57517-354-9

2787-V
Item Number 2156
Z Y X W V U T S R Q P O N M L K J I H G F E D C B A
 08 07 06 05 04 03 02 01 00   15 14 13 12 11 10 9 8 7 6 5 4 3 2 1

This book is dedicated to my uncle and lifelong friend
Bruno Ferrer Renzulli
Who has taught me far more about life, love, and learning
Than I can ever hope to teach to others.

J.S.R.

A rising tide
lifts all ships.

Contents

Foreword

Many of us carry around two apparently contradictory notions. On the one hand, we believe that individuals have different talents and can develop these potentials to a high degree. On the other hand, we also believe that there is a single ability called "intelligence"; that we are born with it; and that people can be arrayed in bell-shaped curve fashion, in terms of their respective intellectual capacities, promise, and limitations.

These tensions are reflected in school programs and philosophies. Some programs are designed to help individual students realize their particular talents, while others pick out those with high psychometric intelligence and mete out enriched or advanced work. Educational bodies differ as well in their attitudes toward scarce resources: some favor supporting the disadvantaged, some favor supporting the gifted, and others seek to mainstream students as much as possible.

What to do midst such a welter of messages? For many years, Joseph Renzulli and his colleagues at the National Research Center on the Gifted and Talented have been developing a coherent approach to education, one that recognizes the distinct talents of individuals and at the same time attempts to share educational resources with the widest swathe of the population. The Renzulli group has not only undertaken the challenging work of crafting an integrated approach; it has also tried out that approach in many settings.

In this book, readers can gain familiarity with the key ideas of the Schoolwide Enrichment Model, including strategies and practices that can help all students succeed. When this approach is adopted, students have an opportunity to identify their talents and to develop them through participation in enrichment clusters. Moreover, they gain insights into the unique operations of their own minds. Teachers have the opportunity to integrate the approach into their curriculum so that they do not have to shift lessons radically or add to their already busy weeks.

Faculties learn about the management structures that can help bring about a reorientation of, and improvement in, their school. Schools become places where talents are recognized, developed, and marshaled for the good of the wider society.

It would be disingenuous to claim that such transformations are easy to achieve. They are not: they require will, determination, leadership, toughness, and vision. In *Enriching Curriculum for All Students,* Renzulli introduces his vision and then explains how to implement the model. Renzulli and his colleagues have devoted much effort to helping faculties and schools "walk the talk" of schoolwide enrichment.

Theories abound about human potential, talent development, and multiple intelligences. To acknowledge the opposite rhetoric, theories abound as well about selection, the power of the bell curve, and the hegemony of genetics. But such theories are not merely theories; they carry within them definite value systems about the kind of society we wish to become and the kinds of attitudes that we assume toward our fellow humans. I have no hesitation in voting for the ideas expressed in this book and the ensemble of practices that can help bring his vision to life.

—HOWARD GARDNER

Introduction

▶   ▶   ▶   ▶   ▶   ▶   ▶   ▶   ▶   ▶

This book is a practical, research-based guide and set of strategies for educational decision makers who are serious about transforming the quality of education in their schools. This plan, the Schoolwide Enrichment Model (SEM), has demonstrated its effectiveness in a wide variety of schools across the United States, Canada, and several nations overseas—with widely differing students. In addition, the SEM has benefited from extensive field testing and refinement since the late 1970s—reaping the beneficial results of empirical, field-based studies that are enjoyed by few other school improvement plans, models, or proposals.

How does the Schoolwide Enrichment Model differ from other models and proposals for school change? First, it is intensely practical, respecting the daily realities of school life and the structures within which schools function. Second, it empowers teachers to do what they were hired to do: teach and teach well. Third, when implemented correctly, it acts as a catalyst for broad-based school improvement originating *within* the school—which is the fulcrum for any concerted action and change. This plan is designed for use in general education, but it is based on a large number of instructional methods and curricular practices that had their origins in special programs for high-ability students.

While it is not a blueprint for school improvement to be followed with slavish devotion, the Schoolwide Enrichment Model offers a comprehensive set of specific strategies that will increase student effort, enjoyment, and performance and also increase teacher satisfaction and efficacy. These strategies also can be used to integrate a broad range of advanced learning experiences and higher-order thinking skills into any curricular area, course of study, or pattern of school organization.

An Overview of School Improvement Efforts

CHAPTER 1

WHO BENEFITS FROM GOOD SCHOOLS?

Why are the nation's schools in such critical need of a school improvement plan like the Schoolwide Enrichment Model (SEM)? The answer to that key question is remarkably simple: Everyone benefits from high-quality schools. It is not an overstatement to emphasize that literally everyone has a stake in schools that provide all of our young people with a high-quality education. The list of individual and group benefits to our society and to our nation is clear:

- Professional educators at all levels benefit when the quality of schools for which they are responsible results in respect for their work and generous financial support for the educational enterprise.
- Young people benefit when their different learning styles, interests, and ambitions are respected and responded to properly by schools and educators.
- Parents benefit when their children are prepared to lead happy and successful lives.
- Employers and colleges benefit when they have access to people who are competent, creative, and effective in the work they do and in higher educational pursuits.
- Political leaders benefit when good citizens and a productive population contribute to a healthy economy, a high quality of life, and respect for the values and institutions in a democracy.

> Young people benefit when their different learning styles, interests, and ambitions are respected and responded to properly by schools and educators.

At their best, schools create and re-create a successful modern society. In the twenty-first century, the need for an accomplished and prepared citizenry is almost beyond current imagination. As schools currently exist, however, far too many of tomorrow's citizens will not be prepared for the challenges that await them if we do not take practical, yet visionary action to bring about real and lasting school change.

THE PROBLEM WITH THE NATION'S SCHOOLS

Although it would be difficult to find anyone who does not want good schools, the United States is plagued by a widespread "school problem." While the benefits of high-quality schools are clear, the nation's school problem is also painfully apparent. This malaise is evidenced by a lack of public confidence in the nation's schools and concern about whether US students can compete favorably with their peers in other developed nations. While many parents report they are pleased with their local public schools, just as many opt out of the system in favor of an alternative, publicly funded or private. Anyone who has attended a local school board meeting has witnessed, first-hand, acrimonious exchanges between and among board members, parents, and teachers—exchanges that reveal the frustration and impotence many stakeholders experience when dealing with public education. And parents of poverty may feel particularly helpless as they watch their children consigned to low-end instruction, falling further and further behind, with little chance to advance from the constraints of their family's socioeconomic status.

The symptoms of this school problem include the spread of a culture of negativity, public dissatisfaction, and external input into school change, specifically:

- A mounting lack of public confidence in schools and the people who work in them.
- Drastically limited financial support for education.
- General public apathy or dissatisfaction with the quality of education our young people experience.
- Pervasive parental hopelessness regarding public education's ability to advance high-poverty children into bright futures.
- Middle-class discontent with public schools, perhaps for the first time in our nation's history, which has led to active exploration of government-supported alternatives such as vouchers and tax credits for private schools, home schooling, charter schools, and summer and after-school programs that enhance admission to competitive colleges.
- A general belief that school problems are too large to be overcome.

A great deal has been written and said about America's school problem. With such scrutiny of the problem, why have US schools remained so resistant to change? It has been said that a school in the year 2000 bears a strong resemblance to a school one hundred years ago. Yet our society has transformed itself—and schools are the one institution that has not kept up.

WHY HAVEN'T SCHOOLS IMPROVED?

If previous school improvement efforts were as effective as their promotional literature and proponents would suggest, there would be no need for the SEM. But the history of education reform in the United States has shown that schools are remarkably resistant to change. In the current era of school improvement and education reform, there are several reasons that, independently or in tandem, effectively keep schools from improving themselves. These reasons include:

- Numerous school reformers and outside consultants who tout school improvement plans but cannot produce compelling evidence of success.
- Accountability plans intended to improve student achievement—at the cost of school staff being excluded from the planning process that resulted in the accountability plan.
- School reform proposals and plans that, while well intentioned, are not rooted in classroom practices.
- Test-driven decision making that imperils creativity, initiative, and student engagement.
- A proliferation of external-to-the-school stakeholders who intend to change schools *without* the involvement and wisdom of the people who work day-to-day with students.

We now turn to a brief discussion of the main reasons why schools, with notable exceptions, remain mired in practices that do not satisfy any thoughtful participant.

Improving Schools from Outside: An Exercise in Futility

First, the current overabundance of "school reformers" and consultants has resulted in nothing less than a new species that attempts to improve schools from *outside* the schools themselves—a key reason why previous school improvement efforts have not succeeded. These individuals and groups are *external* to an effective school improvement process; as such, they are ineffective or actually detrimental. This species typically inhabits institutions of higher education, federal and state educational agencies, consultant hutches, and, occasionally, the central offices of school districts. Noticeably absent are school personnel who are expected to carry out recommended practices, the students upon whom the practices are targeted, and parents who are the proxy holders of their children's education. These consultants typically do not plan concerted follow-up to their motivational workshops, nor do they observe classrooms in action. School staff who must submit to lectures and exhortations about the inadequacies of their practice become cynical about each new wave of reform (particularly when they try the reform and find it is ineffective, impractical, and does not consider the day-to-day realities within which they must work.)

A brief tour of past innovations is discouraging to anyone interested in education. Progressive education, programmed instruction, discovery learning, open education, and a host of other "innovations" lie battered and broken on the roadside of educational reform. Goodlad (1984) and other analysts tell us that in spite of massive efforts and billions of dollars expended to bring about significant changes in the education process, present-day schools bear a striking resemblance to the structure of education at the turn of the twentieth century. Whole-group instruction, prescribed and didactic curriculum, and an emphasis on basic skills and minimum competencies have turned our schools into dreary places that cannot begin to compete with out-of-school interests, extracurricular activities, and endless hours in front of the television set.

Accountability Plans

Second, accountability plans will not necessarily improve schools and can actually have a detrimental effect. This can be seen nationwide through the presence of state-level testing programs that are intended to prod schools and teachers into "accountability" for student achievement; they do not improve schools. Instead, the well-documented results of increased testing include:

- More pressure on teachers to concentrate on basic skills.
- A slow-but-steady movement toward a national, one-size-fits-all curriculum.
- An externally sanctioned ethos that encourages admittedly poor teaching practices.
- A group-think mentality about teaching that results in homogenized instruction; this instruction discounts students' talents, interests, and potential.

In addition, high-stakes testing programs have created an irony: Those students whose socioeconomic status is lowest—those who traditionally have scored lower than the general population—end up receiving ever-increasing amounts of drill on the low-level skills that these tests measure. This practice is inconsistent with current reform that warns us about our post-industrial society's need for creative thinkers and problem solvers. Some reports do, indeed, tell of test score increases resulting from highly regulated compensatory programs. However, these reports do not mention some significant outcomes:

- Concomitant increases in dropout rates.
- The lack of preparedness for anything but the lowest-level jobs.
- No increases in the percentages of students who can perform at the highest levels of reading, mathematics, and science.

- Little to no increase in the number of disadvantaged students entering higher education (Educational Testing Service 1991).

These reports also do not mention how low-achieving students sometimes are excluded from post-testing because they have been declared learning disabled or in need of other forms of special education. This is particularly critical at a time when the population of language minority students is on the dramatic upswing; too many of these students are excluded from large-scale assessments, become discouraged, and drop out of school entirely in unacceptably high numbers (Lockwood and Secada 1999).

Test-Driven Decision Making

Third, testing not only has failed to improve schools, it has actually been counterproductive. Consider the almost schizoid policies that have resulted from test-driven decision making. Schools with large numbers of low-scoring students routinely receive additional funding through compensatory education programs. A worst-case scenario is that school districts actually profit from poor performance by receiving increased funds. Some recent policies, on the other hand, are offering financial rewards for improved test scores. Since socioeconomic level is the only consistent factor that correlates with test scores, this practice may become yet another way of punishing young people because their families' socioeconomic status is low.

External Stakeholders

Finally, and perhaps most surprisingly, parents, school boards, and central office administrators cannot change schools. These groups are essential players in the overall process of school improvement, but without the genuine participation of principals and teachers, these groups play the same role as that of the state agencies and external regulations discussed earlier. And even principals and teachers cannot change schools unless they are willing to co-operate with one another and to compromise when differences of opinion occur. In this day of job actions, work-to-rule, involuntary transfers, and placing "a letter in your file," almost everyone who works in schools knows that maintaining the status quo may not be the best way to serve all of our students, but it certainly is the easiest way to survive complex and bureaucratic organizations.

LESSONS LEARNED FROM FAILED SCHOOL IMPROVEMENT EFFORTS

Failed attempts to improve schools have taught us a great deal about what to avoid. These are lessons that have been put to use in the Schoolwide Enrichment Model. There are two additional overarching reasons why effective, student-centered teaching techniques are not used as often as they should be by experienced teachers.

External Regulations

The first reason is a proliferation of external regulations designed to increase accountability, and that are subtly but powerfully enforced by standardized tests. These tests are "the elephant in the room" of school improvement, and their influence has become so pervasive that various plans have been put forward to link teacher evaluations with test scores. In keeping with the gentle but evolutionary approach to change recommended in this model, we are not proposing the elimination of standardized tests as part of the criteria by which we should examine the quality of learning that takes place in a school. We need to know how well our students are progressing on commonly agreed-upon goals, but it is equally important for teachers to be a part of the decision making process that determines both the goals and *the full range of criteria* that can be used to evaluate progress toward these goals.

Professionals are people who make decisions rather than receive orders about the work that they do. If we want teachers to be enthusiastic participants in school improvement activities, it is essential that school governance models allow for shared decision making on goals and evaluative criteria as well as the teaching and curricular practices that are the means for achieving goals. The first step toward achieving true teacher professionalism, therefore, is to invite teachers into the decision making process as equal partners with administration on the most important decisions to be made.

The scarcity of high-quality teaching practices is related to the issue of external regulations and accountability, but it is manifested in the relationships between administrators and teachers, which frequently become adversarial. Decay in the quality of these relationships is the inevitable result of both top-down decision making and a failure on the parts of teachers and administrators to communicate effectively about their respective problems and agendas.

Traditional approaches to professional development illustrate the "us-and-them" attitude that is almost universal between and among teachers and administrators. The process customarily begins with knowledge about a particular idea, teaching technique, or curricular package that is obtained from one or a combination of three sources: professional reading, attendance at professional meetings, or directives received from state agencies and passed down from central administration. Occasionally, the idea may originate with teachers, but in order for the idea to move forward, approval must be obtained from building and/or district level decision makers. Teacher-initiated ideas are more likely to gain approval for what might be called microskill improvements, and what follows is yet another replay of "the workshop game." A one-shot workshop is arranged on a specific topic such as thinking skills, assertive discipline, time management, or a broad range of make-it-and-take-

> . . . it is essential that school governance models allow for shared decision making on goals and evaluative criteria as well as the teaching and curricular practices that are the means for achieving goals.

it activities that teachers can use with their students. The salient features of microskill workshops initiated by teachers is that they pose little or no threat to the status quo, and although they may improve individual teaching skills, they seldom have a major or lasting impact on policy or new directions for a school district.

Major or macrochange initiatives follow a different pathway. State-level directives or guidelines are usually the trigger for adopting a systemic change initiative, and central office administrators are almost always the initiators. When a plan is adopted for a comprehensive school improvement process (with or without input from teacher members of a district-level committee), a different workshop scenario is played out. Following introductory remarks about the importance of the topic, the school or district's commitment to implement whatever is being considered, and the marvelous credentials of the visiting speaker(s), the initiators make a graceful exit from the workshop situation and the excruciating details of implementation. Teachers who are expected to put the new initiative into practice often feel put upon by yet another top-down educational innovation and a lack of support in terms of both time and resources to put the practice into action. Their feelings of alienation from the decision making process frequently result in minimal compliance, passive resistance, and a this-too-shall-pass attitude. Administrators usually respond to these attitudes by raising the stakes in the accountability game, and test scores become an enforcer that further widens the gulf between teachers and administration.

Alienation Among Teachers

A second reason why high-quality teaching techniques are not easily applied is that the present structure of schools has cut most teachers off from the kinds of professional improvement that can be derived from colleagues as well as the kinds of growth that result when professionals consult with one another. If we observe other groups of professionals at work—physicians, engineers, plumbers, or any other client-serving group—they talk to one another about problems in need of solution. The teaching profession, on the other hand, has evolved into a very private set of behind-closed-door domains and competencies. Barth (1990) compares the work of teachers with the parallel play that takes place between toddlers playing at opposite corners of the same sandbox, and describes the taboo in teaching that prevents one teacher from observing another teacher at work or the taboo of sharing craft knowledge with one another. He reported that when teachers do interact with one another, the conversation often focuses on criticism of colleagues or administrators rather than the sharing of extraordinary insights or rich experiences.

Breaking down both the structural isolation of teachers' work and the us-and-them attitude that currently exists between teachers and administrators are major parts of the professionalism goal of SEM. This task must be approached in a systematic and nonthreatening manner, and it must extend beyond the usual practice of parading one visiting speaker after another through the time blocks devoted to staff development.

HOW TO IMPROVE SCHOOLS: THE SCHOOLWIDE ENRICHMENT MODEL

The only way to improve schools in substantial and lasting ways is to change classroom practices. For this reason, the School Enrichment Model focuses on the act of learning as it takes place in classrooms where teachers, students, and curriculum interact with one another. And it is also for this reason that schools can change only from within. School systems at large can be improved only to the extent that classrooms change, and classrooms can change only when individual school principals and faculties dedicate themselves to specific, research-based plans that have shown their effectiveness.

In other words, schools change one at a time. And they change only as a result of what people inside a given school do with their students and with each other. It is for this reason that the main audience for this book is the "nuclear school family." The principal and faculty are key players in this family, but parents and students are also important members without whom a nuclear school family cannot exist.

HOW THE SCHOOLWIDE ENRICHMENT MODEL IS DIFFERENT

The Schoolwide Enrichment Model differs from other school improvement reforms in key ways. Although other educational reforms have their own merits, they tend to focus on changing the school from the outside, ignoring three crucial points that are the heart of the Schoolwide Enrichment Model. These three points include: (1) the central role of learning, (2) the issue of time, and (3) a gentle and evolutionary approach to the process of school improvement.

The Central Role of Learning

Improving schools must begin by placing the *act of learning* at the center of the change process. Organizational and administrative structures such as site-based management, school choice, ungraded classes, parent involvement, and extended school days are important considerations, but they do not address directly the crucial question: How can the act of learning be improved?

An act of learning takes place when three major components interact with one another in a way that produces the intellectual or artistic equivalent of spontaneous combustion. These three components are a teacher, a learner, and the

The Act of Learning

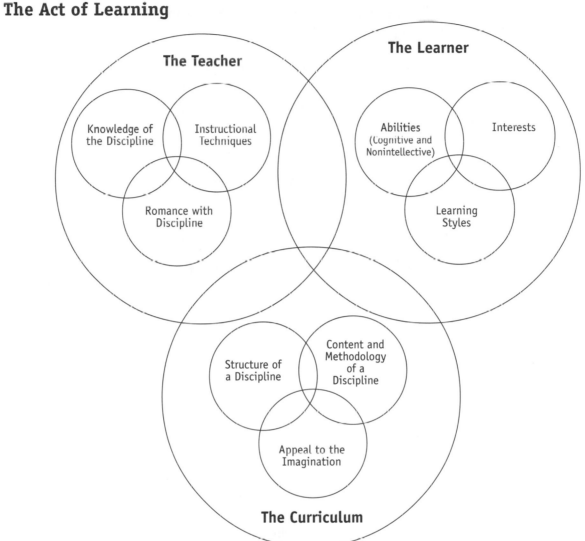

Figure 1.1

material to be learned (i.e., curriculum). A figural representation of an act of learning is shown in Figure 1.1.

Each of these three major components of an act of learning has its own important subcomponents, which include the following:

The Teacher

- The teacher's *knowledge of the discipline* needs to be ascertained.
- The teacher's *familiarity and comfort level with various instructional techniques* must be clear.
- The teacher's *ability to develop a "romance" with the material* being taught must be determined.

The Learner

- The learner's *abilities and current achievement level* in a particular content area must be examined.
- The learner's *interest in the topic* must be assessed (along with ways in which current interests can be enhanced and new interests developed).
- The learner's *preferred styles of learning* must be assessed (those learning styles that will improve the learner's motivation to pursue the material being studied).

The Curriculum

- The curriculum's *structure* must be examined.
- The curriculum's *content and methodology* for the particular discipline need to be gauged.
- The curriculum's *appeal to students' imagination* must be ascertained.

The intersecting circles in Figure 1.1 show *dynamic interactions* rather than linear relations between and among the components. This representation of the act of learning does not assume equity among all components and subcomponents. The circles undoubtedly vary in size from one learning situation to another, and variations exist even within a single learning situation. But the theory that is summarized in this diagram (Renzulli 1992) does argue that all acts of learning can be optimized by organizing experiences that result in interaction among the several parts of this conception of the learning process.

The Structured to Unstructured Continuum of Learning and Teaching

All learning and teaching exists along a continuum ranging from highly structured situations to situations that are totally unstructured. The structured end of the continuum consists of prescribed material based largely on the use of predetermined textbooks and didactic teaching methods. Structured learning almost always is geared toward carefully specified student outcomes, such as content mastery. Although attention has been given in recent years to process outcomes such as thinking skills, structured models of learning continue to be the predominant method of instruction used in most classrooms. Pressures placed upon schools and teachers to raise scores, and test score comparisons between and among schools, districts, and states have increased the emphasis on mastery and outcome-based models. These pressures have resulted in squeezing less structured learning activities out of the curriculum.

Although a certain amount of structured learning has its value in the curriculum, schools dominated by such approaches are mechanistic, dreary places. In short, schools dominated by structured learning have lost sight of innumerable opportunities to make classrooms inviting places that students *want* to be, places that have at least some of the excitement and challenge typically found in club programs, self-selected extracurricular activities, or "on the street."

Other evidence shows that learning environments that are structured to produce high achievement can actually produce the exact opposite. In spite of the billions of dollars that have been spent on highly structured compensatory education programs designed to improve the achievement of at-risk students, test scores have shown negligible gains, dropout rates in our inner cities continue to climb, SAT scores are at their lowest levels in decades, and international comparisons place the achievement of US students at or near the bottom of most of the industrialized nations (Applebee, Langer, and Mullis 1989; Educational Testing Service 1991; Singal 1991; Stevenson, Chen, and Lee 1993; Stevenson, Lee, and Stigler 1986).

Enrichment Learning and Teaching

The Schoolwide Enrichment Model provides a strong alternative to an over-regulated, structured curriculum through a method of schooling known as *enrichment learning and teaching*. This perspective is based on the knowledge that the role of the learner is central to effective growth, both in terms of achievement and the motivation to put forth one's greatest effort. All learning improves under the following circumstances:

> . . . the role of the learner is central to effective growth, both in terms of achievement and the motivation to put forth one's greatest effort.

- Schools are perceived as enjoyable, relevant, friendly places where students have some role in deciding what they will learn and how they will pursue topics in which they may have a special interest.
- Teachers can create effective learning environments, balancing structured teaching with less structured and more personalized experiences, using student interests and learning styles as points of departure for classroom activities.
- At least some of the prescribed curriculum is replaced with self-selected, open-ended, real-world problems that allow students to assume roles as first-hand investigators.
- Teacher- and textbook-dominated activities are replaced with group investigation models of learning.
- Alternative scheduling procedures are chosen, such as cross-grade grouping, interest and common-task grouping, and specially designated time blocks during which the *highest* premium is placed on talent development and creative productivity.
- Traditional testing and grading procedures are expanded to include authentic assessment techniques such as product evaluation and feedback procedures, post-learning analysis sessions, portfolio review and analysis, and portfolio "engineering" (i.e., taking specific steps to guarantee that student products are carried forward to subsequent teachers, college admission officers, and prospective employers).

The Schoolwide Enrichment Model's approach to learning follows the ways in which learning takes place in the natural (i.e., nonschool) environment. In almost all fields except pedagogy, scientists look to nature for the solutions to complex problems. *Learning is a natural phenomenon*, and, thus, the concept of enrichment learning and teaching is based on organized common sense about how people learn naturally.

The Issue of Time for Students and Teachers

Students' Time

Although schools without schedules probably would be chaotic, there is an almost universal pattern of school organization—one which makes it difficult to make even the smallest changes in the overall learning process. The major content areas (Reading, Mathematics, Language Arts, and Social Studies) are taught on a regular basis, five days per week. Other subjects (sometimes called "the specials"), such as Science,[1] Music, Art, and Physical Education, are generally taught once or twice a week. Even the slightest hint about possible variations is met with a storm of protest from administrators and teachers: "We don't have time now to cover the regular curriculum." "How will we fit in the specials?" "They keep adding new things [Drug Education, Health Education, etc.] for us to cover."

Because so many educators do not question the elementary and secondary school schedule, they have forgotten that college-level schedules—with more advanced and challenging material—use a three day (and sometimes even two day) per week schedule of classes. And US adherence to the more-time-is-better argument fails to take into account research that shows quite the opposite. For example, international comparison studies report that eight of the eleven nations that surpass US achievement levels in mathematics spend less time on math instruction than do American schools (Jaeger 1992).

Some current reform proposals have recommended changes in the school schedule, but most of these proposals suggest extending the school day and year. These recommendations ignore the fact that extending school time *without primary attention to the quality of learning* will only increase the number of students who refuse to learn because of their boredom with both content and pedagogy.

The scheduling modifications recommended by the Schoolwide Enrichment Model guarantee that some time will be available in each school week during which enrichment learning and teaching will take place. Not only do students benefit from this more flexible approach to learning, but teachers benefit as well.

Teachers' Time

School improvement is directly affected by the amount of time that teachers can work collaboratively with one another. School improvement studies have shown that the ways in which teacher time is utilized are more important than equipment, facilities, or staff development, and that successful schools are distinguishable from unsuccessful ones by the frequency and extent to which teachers discuss practice, collaboratively design materials, and inform

> . . . extending school time *without primary attention to the quality of learning* will only increase the number of students who refuse to learn because of their boredom with both content and pedagogy.

and critique one another (Raywid 1993). Fullan and Miles (1992) report that the ways in which teacher time is used is the major issue in every study of school improvement that has appeared during the last decade. International studies by Stigler and Stevenson (1991) report that in highly effective Asian schools, teachers spend 30 to 40 percent of their school hours in activities other than teaching.

In a study dealing with how schools are finding the time for teachers to work collaboratively, Raywid (1993) describes fifteen examples of specific methods through which time can be made available. These examples fall into three general categories: taking time from that which is now scheduled for instruction or staff development; adding time to the school day and/or year; and altering staff utilization patterns. The fifteen examples that Raywid provides are both creative and feasible. For example, a school district in New York reallocated time from staff development days in such a way that two-hour collaborative sessions for teachers were made available every two weeks throughout the school year. Some schools used time gained when students were involved in community internship activities; and others trimmed some instructional time in exchange for voluntary contributions of equal amounts of teachers' time.

The challenge of reallocating even small proportions of teachers' time is fraught with bureaucratic regulations, collective bargaining issues, and the willingness of teachers to make adjustments in what has become a very standardized way of viewing their work. It is clear that everyone has to to give a little and to compromise on vested interests in order for collaborative time for teachers to be made available. Current school schedules and work rules were not divinely inspired; therefore, they should be open to the kinds of examination that allow both imagination and experimentation to be brought to bear on the process of modifying them.

A Gentle and Evolutionary Approach to School Improvement

The change process recommended in the School Enrichment Model begins with an examination of the major factors that affect the quality of learning in a school (see Figure 1.2). These factors exist along a continuum of internal (to the school) to external factors. Each factor is interdependent with the others. For example, an internal factor such as the building principal may be externally influenced if the principal is assigned by central administration; and an external factor such as a state regulation may be internally influenced by the ways in which it is interpreted (or possibly ignored) by teachers and administrators. All of these factors have three salient characteristics. First, they are always present, and regardless of micro or macrochange initiatives, they will always be present. Second, each factor exists along a continuum of negative to positive influence on the quality of learning that takes place within

Factors Affecting the Quality of Learning

Low Quality ⟶ High Quality

Internal

Teachers
Principal
Parent Involvement
The School Building
Special Services
The School's Collective Self-Concept
Textbooks
The Curriculum
Standardized Tests
Central Administration
The Board of Education
The Budget
Latest Innovation(s) Adopted
Latest Application of Beliefs on Grouping
Collective Bargaining Agreements
State Regulations

External

Figure 1.2

a given school. Third, each factor goes through a process of change, for better or worse.

How does the Schoolwide Enrichment Model play out in the daily life of the school? The SEM applies its strategies and services to the givens of school life. It is not practical to eliminate textbooks, standardized tests, or recently adopted initiatives such as heterogeneous grouping or standards-based educational models. But the SEM does insist on modifying and adapting the factors in Figure 1.2 in ways that will help to accommodate individual students' interests, abilities and learning styles. In chapter 4 we will discuss a SEM component called *curriculum compacting* that provides a research-proven method for modifying the regular curriculum for students who have already mastered prescribed outcomes.

A Realistic Approach to School Improvement

Schools are bombarded with proposals for change. These proposals range from total, systemic reform to tinkering with bits and pieces of specific subjects and teaching methods. Often the proposals are little more than lists of intended goals or outcomes, but limited direction is provided about *how* these outcomes can be achieved; even less information is provided about the effectiveness of recommended practices in a broad range of field test sites. Worse are the mixed messages that policymakers and regulators broadcast to schools at an unprecedented rate, messages that are often incompatible with one another.

The cost of trying to improve schools in these ways is high both in dollars and human resources. Schools spend approximately half a billion dollars annually on standardized testing (Paris, Lawton, Turner, and Roth 1991), and approximately 100 hours of class time are spent practicing for and taking tests (Smith 1991). The demands placed on schools for increased testing also increase the likelihood that schools will continue to offer a curriculum that prepares students for nonexistent factory work rather than one that prepares students for the modern, complex, and rapidly changing technological world (McCaslin and Good 1992).

For at least four reasons, the SEM has experienced success in widely differing settings. The satisfaction of teachers, students, and parents can be documented through evaluation and research studies, commendations by educators using the model, and site visits to places where the model is used.

Practicality and Existing Know-How

The SEM has been successful because of its clarity, practicality, and flexibility. The roles and responsibilities of participating teachers, students, and administrators are easy to learn and are described in ways that avoid complex language or ponderous rhetoric. And although the model is directed toward a small number of common goals, each school is encouraged to develop its own unique program within the framework of general goals, guides, and how-to information. Indeed, this flexibility has produced numerous examples of local pride and ownership, and it also has generated many practitioner-developed contributions to the model that have been shared locally and nationally. This type of model-based sharing has expanded the know-how available to networking users of the model, and it has served as a source of motivation for the professionalism objective described in chapter 2.

In order for a model to work, it must be based on sound ideas and research, and every idea must be backed up with practical information, strategies, service delivery components, and materials. The following list represents categories of the broad array of service delivery components that we have developed and field-tested over the years:

- Print and video staff development materials
- Planning guides and worksheets for each major component of the model
- Instruments for assessing students' strengths, interests, and learning styles

- Procedures for developing schoolwide enrichment teams
- A slide presentation and script for parent orientation
- A taxonomy of specific thinking skills
- Guidelines for preparing interest development centers
- Procedures for developing a scope and sequence for thinking skills
- A directory of within- and across-discipline enrichment materials
- A directory of "how-to" books for first-hand investigative activities
- Sample letters, memos, and pamphlets for parents, students, and faculty
- Guidelines for developing a faculty/community mentor system
- Procedures for establishing a student "research foundation"
- A set of slides and script to train students in the investigative process
- Planning worksheets and documentation forms
- A community resources survey and classification system
- Easy-to-understand charts, diagrams, and summary sheets that facilitate staff development and student and parent orientation
- Evaluation forms and instruments for each major component of the model
- A residential summer staff development institute for advanced training and the training of trainers
- A national network and directory of school districts using the model
- A directory of practitioner consultants who have extensive experience in using the model
- Technical reports verifying the research base underlying the model

Underlying Theory and Research

A second reason for the success of SEM has been the practicality of the theory underlying the model and the research that has been carried out over the years to support various aspects of the model. The underlying theory is divided into two dimensions. The first dimension focuses on a broadened conception of human potential and creative productivity (Gardner 1983; Renzulli 1977a, 1985); the second dimension concentrates on pedagogical issues that are related directly to improving high-level acts of learning.

Most proposed changes in educational systems are implemented because of good intentions and desperate needs for improvement in the status quo. We have taken the time over the years to examine the effectiveness of the model in a broad range of school settings (Renzulli and Reis 1994), and this research has been summarized in Appendix A. We have also compiled numerous examples of program materials and documents that point out a broad variety of implementation activities in districts with widely differing demographic characteristics.

> A second reason for the success of SEM has been the practicality of the theory underlying the model and the research that has been carried out over the years to support various aspects of the model.

Attractiveness to All Types of Schools

The third reason for the success of SEM has been the quality and commitment of educators who have implemented the model at the local level. For a variety of reasons, the model has attracted energetic teachers and administrators who believe that schools can be more effective and caring places. Many of these persons first became involved with the SEM because of their work in special programs for high-ability students. Initially, they were attracted to our written material and summer training programs at The University of Connecticut because of our concerns for equity as well as excellence in learning and teaching, and because of the flexible and commonsense features of the model. We have always advocated serving larger proportions of the school population than those served in traditional programs for the gifted. And as the model evolved toward more specific recommendations and procedures for total school enrichment, most of these people continued with us and even became emissaries for change in their local districts. Whereas our annual summer institute formerly attracted only persons who were employed as teachers of the gifted, in recent years the majority of persons attending have been general classroom teachers and administrators. We attribute this shift to both the activism of our emissaries and the growing national concern for using the technology of gifted education to improve the quality of schools at large.

Concern for At-Risk Populations

A final reason for the growing popularity of the Schoolwide Enrichment Model is our concern for providing special enrichment opportunities for students from low socioeconomic backgrounds and for students who show potentials for superior performance in areas that are not easily assessed by traditional ability measures. Low achievement among economically disadvantaged students represents the single most glaring failure of our educational system. The lack of results from years of compensatory programs and expenditures of billions of dollars have caused a small but growing number of educators at all levels to realize that we must explore alternatives to traditional remedial models. These models have grossly underestimated the potentials of poor children—one of our most important natural resources.

Theories are emerging regarding the underachievement of high-ability urban youth. Ogbu (1974, 1985, 1987, 1991) argues that two types of minorities—immigrant and involuntary—enter differentially into the process of schooling. Accordingly, he believes these students' academic achievement is affected differentially. He concludes, " . . . neither the core curriculum approach nor the multicultural education approach will appreciably improve the schooling performance of some minority groups until they and other school interventions, innovations, and reforms are informed by an understanding of *why* children from specific minority groups are experiencing learning and performance difficulty" (Ogbu 1992, 7).

OPENING THE SCHOOL DOOR TO IMPROVEMENT THROUGH ENRICHMENT

Many educators and educational reform leaders have a negative attitude toward special programs for the gifted. This attitude has created barriers toward the broader implementation of any set of ideas with gifted roots. Overt charges of elitism have been directed toward a field that historically has found its greatest support in school districts that serve the white middle class. Some of these criticisms are not unfounded. Quota requirements for the funding of special programs and identification guidelines that are predominantly based on ability test scores are still in effect in most states, and the conservative branch of the field's leadership continues to argue for restrictions on the number of students identified as the "truly gifted." Conservatives in the field also look with suspicion on identification procedures that are alternatives to IQ scores, and models such as SEM have been viewed with particular scorn by gifted education conservatives because they believe the concept of giftedness has been watered down. The conservative leadership also has criticized our more flexible approach to identification because *our* advocacy for developing thinking skills in all students is viewed as a usurping of their early discovery of the process models.

All of these forces act against the provision of special enrichment opportunities for students who are from low socioeconomic backgrounds or students who show potentials for superior performance in areas that are not as easily assessed as those areas measured by traditional ability tests. These same forces also limit the opportunities of females in areas such as mathematics, science, and engineering. Compounding the problem is the slow but certain movement toward a test-driven, basic skills curriculum that has gained a strong foothold in many states. This movement (primarily directed toward raising scores on state and national wall charts) is already resulting in cutbacks in library and media programs, arts programs, extracurricular activities, and just about anything else that makes school an enriching and inviting place. Increasing test scores is, indeed, an important national priority, and a goal of the SEM. But thirty years of federal and state support for compensatory education has produced negligible results, and students at risk have been the major victims of this "drill-and-kill" approach to learning. It is the children of the poor who suffer most from declining enrichment opportunities. It is the families of these young people who cannot afford the computer camps, the dance or art lessons, the well-stocked home bookshelves, the summer on-campus science programs, and the SAT prep courses that the middle class uses to compensate for unchallenging schools.

Because so much of the reform movement currently exists in words rather than in deeds, the reformers themselves are already locked in deadly, albeit rhetorical, battles about school improvement. The SEM is a systemic approach to general school improvement because it is based on a model for learning that cuts across all activities that take place in a school. It is purposefully designed to create such an environment by blending the kinds of activities that promote challenge, effort, and enjoyment into the entire curriculum. These types of activities have been used for years in special programs, and they can be applied easily to general education if we can pry open the door of entrenched school curriculum and governance.

ENDNOTE

1. It is interesting to note that our national commitment to the improvement of science scores has not elevated courses in science to five-day-per-week status in most elementary and middle schools.

An Overview of the Schoolwide Enrichment Model

▶   ▶   ▶   ▶   ▶   ▶   ▶   ▶   ▶   ▶

THE GOALS OF SCHOOLWIDE ENRICHMENT

The Schoolwide Enrichment Model (SEM) has been described in various ways by a myriad of people who have used it, worked with it, and helped refine it to its current state of effectiveness. Although one commentator referred to it as "elegant common sense," the SEM actually is an empirically tested and carefully chosen blend of research and proven practices, with five main goals.

> Schools should be enriching places, where the mind, spirit, and values of each student are expanded and developed in an atmosphere that is enjoyable, interesting, and challenging.

> ▶ ▶ GOAL 1 ▶ ▶
>
> To develop the talent potentials of young people by (a) systematically assessing strengths, (b) providing enrichment opportunities, resources, and services to develop the strengths of all students, and (c) using a flexible approach to curricular differentiation and the use of school time.

A Focus on Talent Development

Schools should be enriching places, where the mind, spirit, and values of each student are expanded and developed in an atmosphere that is enjoyable, interesting, and challenging. While knowledge acquisition is unquestionably an important educational goal, other goals such as know-how, creativity, self-fulfillment, and wisdom are equally significant. Schools should not be places where young people merely learn what is already known. Instead, schools should seek a higher mission: creating learning environments in which the knowledge that students bring to school with them is valued. This student-owned knowledge should be viewed as a stepping stone to the creation of new knowledge, to the solutions of unsolved problems, and to invention, artistic production, and examination of ways to improve the quality of life.

Programs such as 4-H, Junior Achievement, the Foxfire Program, Future Problem Solving, Invent America, and a broad range of extracurricular activities consistently have demonstrated that when the application of knowledge is coupled with the acquisition of knowledge, school problems are solved, or at least minimized. Observation of 4-H students at work, or of a school newspaper staff rushing to publish the next edition, allow us to see genuine motivation, engagement, and involvement, as well as cooperativeness, enjoyment, and purpose. These examples of students at work represent the kinds of authenticity in learning that have eluded so much of traditional schooling. These activities also frequently span students' age levels, socioeconomic backgrounds, demographics, and ability levels.

Goal 1 is targeted directly toward a *qualitative* change in schools. It is based on a reconceptualized role of the teacher, the curriculum, classroom organization and management, and, most of all, the role of the student. These reconceptualized roles are neither new nor abstract. They have occurred in learning situations throughout history, in classrooms and nonschool learning situations, in extracurricular activities, and in apprenticeships and on-the-job training experiences. We have seen increases in these changing roles of teachers and students as a direct result of applying SEM to a variety of school situations; we know from our field testing of the SEM that this model can fortify a proposal for school change. A goal that focuses on developing talent potentials is not an educational revelation, but the traditional achievement goal always has held supremacy. By making this objective the centerpiece of SEM, we emphasize that what has occurred in the past—a series of scattered, random, and infrequent examples of enriched learning—has the potential to become standard operating procedure for the majority of schools that make a commitment to this plan.

> ▶ ▶ GOAL 2 ▶ ▶
> **To improve the academic performance of all students in all areas of the regular curriculum and to blend into the standard curriculum those activities that will engage students in meaningful and enjoyable learning.**

Indicators and Reasons for Declining Academic Performance

The most obvious and publicized problem facing our schools is poor academic performance—especially the performance of students termed disadvantaged. Although recent studies have shown these students are making slow but steady gains on standardized tests, the scores for this population are still well below desirable levels. What is more, high school and college graduation rates have shown little or no increase over the past several decades. Improving the performance of disadvantaged students continues to be the single most important challenge facing our schools. There is, however, another crisis in American education that needs to be addressed.

The *overall* test scores for the nation at large have declined since their historic highs in the 1960s—despite modest achievement gains made by disadvantaged students. This overall decline can be explained by the fact that the performance of populations that traditionally have scored at higher levels has gone down. According to Herbert Rudman, an author of the Stanford Achievement Test, the highest-achieving students have shown the greatest decline across a variety of subjects as well as across age-level groups (Singal 1991). The most reliable international comparison studies[1] also paint a bleak picture of the achievement of American students. When compared with other industrialized nations, US students are at or near the bottom of almost every educational index imaginable, from academic areas to vocational studies.

If we are to understand these overall declines in school performance, we must examine some of the within-school factors that have influenced the achievement of students across the spectrum of socioeconomic groups. These factors include:

- The dumbing down of textbooks.
- Repetition in textbooks, which slows down learning.
- "Mentioning" in textbooks—a practice that focuses on coverage without depth and substance.

Because textbooks dominate the curriculum nationwide—and actually have created an informal national curriculum—they need to be considered carefully when implementing any school improvement plan, including the SEM.

> ▶ ▶ **GOAL 3** ▶ ▶
> **To promote continuous, reflective, growth-oriented professionalism on the parts of all school personnel.**

What Does It Mean to Be a Professional?

Schools are only as good as the people who work in them. This goal focuses on the crucial but elusive task of improving the professionalism of teachers, administrators, and other school personnel. It might be tempting to dismiss an objective about improved professionalism as idealistic but largely unachievable. However, this objective lies at the heart of school improvement. For this reason we must examine both failed attempts and promising approaches to professional improvement, and we must use our accumulated knowledge, experience, and wisdom to devise a practical plan to improve the professionalism of personnel in schools using the Schoolwide Enrichment Model.

Professionals are people within an occupational category who share a common body of knowledge and standards of practice that allow them to make decisions in the best interests of their clients. The work of true professionals is characterized by the regular use of judgment and nonroutine activities rather than mechanized or prescribed applications of duties. In order for true professionalism to be achieved, the individual and the institution within which the individual works must be amenable to change. Many reform proposals have recognized the importance of improved professionalism, but they have failed to respect the ground rules of professional work. In short, professionalism is a social contract that requires individuals to acquire and make use of certain competencies and ethics, but the contract also requires that the institution support the application of these competencies and ethics.

> ▶ ▶ **GOAL 4** ▶ ▶
> **To create a learning community that honors ethnic, gender, and cultural diversity; mutual respect and caring attitudes toward one another; respect for democratic principles; and preservation of the Earth's resources.**

Schools for a Better Society

Most people in the United States concur that schools should play a role in ameliorating important problems in our society. Our schools originally were invested with the obligation to teach the three Rs and to pass on the accumulated knowledge of the past. A rapidly changing world, dramatic changes in the job market, and a host of increasingly complex societal issues placed demands on the educational system that now require an expanded role for the schools. This role can be seen in the curriculum's inclusion of numerous issues that range from driver education and a "life adjustment curriculum," to concerns about war and peace, values and character, and sex and drug education. Each of these issues, and the efforts to address them through additions to the school curriculum, have kindled or rekindled the classic controversies between conservative and liberal ideologies. Although this goal does favor a broader set of beliefs about the role of the school, it is included as a major focus of the SEM because of the rapid changes taking place in our society and the declining well-being of young people in the United States.

Most people would agree that talent development and academic performance are the main responsibilities of schools. However, changes in family structures and a fast-track society have also placed a broader range of responsibilities on schools. Issues such as alarmingly high delinquency rates, substance abuse, racial disharmony, teenage pregnancy, intolerance, wasteful consumerism, and a lack of respect for our fellow human beings have resulted in a generation of young people who are experiencing psychological distress and social alienation as well as declining school performance. Many will argue that school is not the place to address such problems, but these problems and their by-products have ended up on the schoolhouse doorstep. Education alone cannot resolve these problems, but schools can play an important role in fostering the intelligence, persistence, and creativity necessary to bring about needed improvements in both the quality of life for young people and the improvement of the social institutions that are necessary for perpetuating our democratic society.

This goal is not intended to impose a set of political beliefs or social values on schools that use the SEM. But contemporary issues should be part of an enrichment program that attempts to bring relevancy and realness into the curriculum. At the same time, we also believe that local decision making must prevail as far as specific topic selection is concerned.

Because the focus of this model is on the act of learning, we will pursue this goal by concentrating on instructional methods that address more effectively the topics that schools select within broad parameters of this goal. We will also provide references to materials that are available for various kinds of enrichment experiences related to selected topics.

> . . . schools can play an important role in fostering the intelligence, persistence, and creativity necessary to bring about needed improvements in both the quality of life for young people and the improvement of the social institutions that are necessary for perpetuating our democratic society.

> ► ► **GOAL 5** ► ►
>
> **To implement a democratic school governance procedure that includes appropriate decision making opportunities for students, parents, teachers, and administrators.**

The Need for Democratic Governance

Educational leaders across the nation have recognized that decentralized management procedures are a major component of school improvement. This type of management, commonly referred to as site- or school-based management (SBM), has a long and successful history in the private sector. School-based management decreases centralized control and encourages high levels of involvement and control from the people who are closest to the creation of products and the delivery of services. Although this goal is evolutionary, maturing over a period of several years, it is essential for any real and lasting school improvement effort.

If a school decides to adopt this (or any other) model or school improvement initiative, the decision must be protected from the biases or predilections of the always-changing personnel who occupy district decision making positions. In one district with which we are familiar, a new assistant superintendent in charge of curriculum wiped out one of the most successful enrichment programs in the country because of a personality conflict with the program coordinator and her desire to assert authority. Efforts made by a majority of teachers to reinstate the program, including the support of highly satisfied parents in the community, were not strong enough to overcome the amount of power vested in a single person.

Democratic school governance represents a fundamental and systemic organizational change. Like all other changes of this magnitude, and especially changes that include a redistribution of power to make important decisions, the process must be approached with care and thoughtfulness. Training in management and decision making techniques must be provided to personnel who customarily have been in subordinate roles, just as central office personnel must learn to share power, knowledge, information, and opportunities to influence the reward structure of the school.

SCHOOL STRUCTURES AND THE SCHOOLWIDE ENRICHMENT MODEL

The School Enrichment Model implements the five goals through *the school structures* toward which these components are targeted and through two other factors—*the service delivery components* and *the organizational components*. These factors represent a three-way interaction between and among the components and the school structures, which are the settings where learning takes place. These interactions are depicted in the three-dimensional diagram in Figure 2.1.

The school structures are presented on the top of the diagram and the other two types of components are shown on the front and side dimensions of the figure. The school structures toward which the service delivery and organizational components are targeted include:

- The regular curriculum
- The enrichment clusters
- The continuum of special services

These structures will be described in the following section.

The Regular Curriculum

The regular curriculum consists of anything and everything that is a part of the predetermined goals, schedules, learning outcomes, and delivery systems of the school. The regular curriculum might be traditional, innovative, or in the process of transition, but its predominant feature is that authoritative forces (i.e., policymakers, school councils, textbook adoption committees, state regulators) have determined that certain outcomes should be the centerpiece of student learning.

The current emphasis on defining curriculum in terms of standards for content and performance is a favorable development. However, without safeguards, the standards movement could end up as another ill-fated regression

Schoolwide Enrichment Model

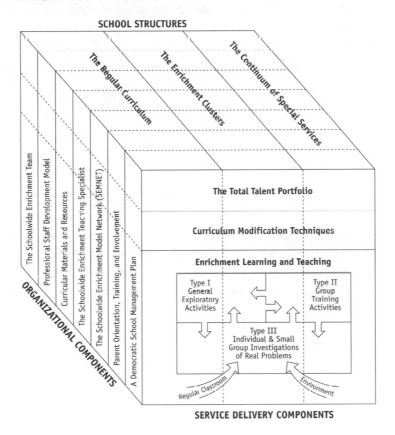

Figure 2.1

to a minimum competency, basic skills approach to learning. It is absolutely essential that the regular curriculum include within each unit of instruction systematic service delivery procedures for:

1. Adjusting levels of required learning so that all students are challenged.
2. Increasing the number of in-depth learning experiences.
3. Introducing various types of enrichment into regular curricular experiences.

The Enrichment Clusters

The second school structure toward which the SEM is targeted consists of a series of interest-based groupings called enrichment clusters. The enrichment clusters are nongraded groups of students who share common interests; they meet during specially designated time blocks to pursue these interests. The model for learning used in these clusters, which is described in chapter 5, is called enrichment learning and teaching. It represents a significant departure from traditional didactic approaches to instruction. Enrichment clusters cut across grade and ability levels, and they exist for various durations of time ranging from one semester to several years. Like extracurricular activities and programs such as 4-H and Junior Achievement, the main rationale for participation in one or more enrichment clusters is that *students and teachers want to be there.*

Selection of an enrichment cluster, however, is not random or spontaneous. Through the use of a SEM component called the Total Talent Portfolio (chapter 3), a systematic process helps students make meaningful decisions about clusters in which they might want to participate. A similar kind of interest assessment is used with teachers and other adults who might be interested in nurturing a cluster.

Developing Talents Through Multiple Enrichment Clusters

The organizational pattern for enrichment clusters is a programmatic application of Gardner's Theory of Multiple Intelligences (Gardner 1983) and Renzulli's (1978) earlier conception of a developmental theory of human potential. The clusters have been organized around the broad subject areas listed in the left-hand column of Figure 2.2 because they are more commonly used in schools and they are areas in which students usually develop special interests.

For example, it is much more likely that students will say: "We are interested in doing research on child abuse or toy safety" rather than, "We want to develop our logical/mathematical and task commitment skills." We view Gardner's intelligences and Renzulli's three sets of characteristics (Abilities, Task Commitment, and Creativity) as capacities to be developed and as factors that cut across the areas around which the clusters are organized.

How do enrichment clusters differ from traditional patterns of grouping students for special activities? These clusters differ in the following four ways:

1. Interests and learning styles—rather than ability—are major considerations for participation in a particular cluster.
2. All students are involved in clusters; the choice of an enrichment cluster(s) is student-determined.
3. Teachers select the clusters in which they would like to participate (individually and cooperatively with other adults).
4. The clusters are guided by an enrichment learning and teaching model rather than by most of the practices that characterize formal instruction.

In the right-hand column of Figure 2.2 are the names of enrichment clusters observed over the years in various schools using the SEM. Although they have been placed in categories according to general subject areas, an examination of the clusters' titles points out the interdisciplinary nature of several groups. An effort has been made to avoid academic terms such as "course" or "class." Similarly, the use of the term "club" has been avoided because we want to emphasize the professional nature of the work that will be pursued in the clusters.

Sample Enrichment Clusters

GENERAL AREAS	SPECIFIC EXAMPLES OF CLUSTERS
Language Arts, Literature, and the Humanities	The Young Authors' Guild The Poets' Workshop The African-American Literary Society The Investigative Journalism Group *The Quarterly Review of Children's Literature*
Physical and Life Sciences	The Save the Dolphin Society The Physical Science Research Institute The Mansfield Environmental Protection Agency The Experimental Robotics Team
The Arts	The Electronic Music Research Institute The Visual Artists' Workshops The Meriden Theater Company The Native American Dance Institute The Video Production Company The Young Musicians' Ensemble The Photographers' Guild
Social Sciences	The Hispanic Cultural Awareness Association The Junior Historical Society The Social Science Research Team The Torrington Geographic Society The Creative Cartographers' Guild
Mathematics	The Math Materials Publication Company The Math Mentors' Association The Female Mathematicians Support Group The Mathematics Competitions League The Math Puzzle Challenge Quarterly
Computers	The Computer Graphics Design Team The Computer Games Production Company The Computer Literacy Assistance Association The Creative Software Society The Desktop Publishing Company
Physical Education	The Experimental Games Research Team The Physiology of Sport Study Group The Physical Fitness Support Group The Institute for the Study of Multicultural Recreation
Industrial Arts/Home Economics	The Creative Furniture Design Company The Architecture for Learning Research Team The Experimental Dietary Group The Future Fashion Research Institute The Child Care Assistance Group

Figure 2.2

SkyLight Professional Development

Due to the traditional way that students view school, those students in enrichment clusters are likely to say that they want to learn about something on a particular topic. The closest parallel to this kind of choice can be found in students' verbal and nonverbal indicators related to participation in extracurricular activities. The extracurricular option is closer to the way in which students should be able to select enrichment clusters, even though there is still a certain amount of traditional predeterminism in students' selection of extracurricular activities.

The best way to understand an enrichment cluster is to view it in the same way that we view a research laboratory, small business organization, artists' guild, or public service agency. These organizations have certain things in common that make them substantially different from the organization that we call a classroom. These include:

- Choice about the type of laboratory or agency in which one chooses to participate.
- A common interest and purpose that binds the group together and that is directed toward the production of a product or the delivery of a service.
- A division of labor in which everyone contributes in his or her own area of expertise and interest.

Although the multiple enrichment clusters are organized around traditional families of knowledge, there are also opportunities to form overlapping, interdisciplinary clusters. For example, students with interests in both electronics and music can combine efforts to form an electronic music cluster; students whose interests range across several topics (e.g., acting, writing, cinematography, costume design) can collaborate through the formation of a film or television production company.

Overlapping clusters have the potential to group students in the following ways:

- Spanning grade levels but linked by a common interest.
- Subdivided into smaller clusters that represent more specialized interests within the broader field of study.

When this type of arrangement is first brought to the attention of teachers and administrators, a few inevitable questions are raised: "Suppose there are more subgroups than there are teachers?" "What happens if some groups are very large and others only have a few students?" "This sounds like a good idea, but does it mean I will have to do extra preparation?" These are legitimate questions if we are thinking only in terms of the teacher-as-instructor and the student-as-lesson-learner, but the clusters offer opportunities for flexible roles.

The enrichment clusters are not intended to be the total enrichment program, but they are one of the major vehicles for pursuing Goal 1 of the SEM. The enrichment clusters are also vehicles for solid professional development.

They provide teachers with opportunities to participate in enrichment teaching and, subsequently, to analyze and compare this type of teaching with traditional methods of instruction. In this way, the cluster promotes a spill-over effect by encouraging teachers to apply some of these techniques to regular classroom situations.

Promoting Cooperativeness Through Enrichment Clusters

Enrichment clusters are excellent vehicles for promoting cooperativeness within the context of real-world problem solving, and they also provide superlative opportunities for promoting healthy self-concept. A major assumption underlying the use of enrichment clusters is that *every child is special if we create conditions in which that child can be a specialist within a specialty group.* Our experience has shown that common interests and goals related to product development produce much more effective groups than traditional age or ability grouping patterns, and they have the added advantage of creating situations in which authentic divisions of labor can take place. This type of working together to produce a meaningful, real-world product is a far cry from the contrived kind of cooperative learning that takes place when we ask groups of students to complete a worksheet or answer questions at the end of a textbook chapter.

> . . . common interests and goals related to product development produce much more effective groups than traditional age or ability grouping patterns, . . .

WHEN DO THE ENRICHMENT CLUSTERS MEET? Although enrichment clusters have proven to be remarkable vehicles for improving the quality of learning, they nevertheless do require some modest changes in the school schedule. Nothing substantially different will take place in classrooms unless specifically designated time blocks are made available for enrichment learning and teaching. However, it is crucial that changes be made with caution and forethought.

The requirements of the regular curriculum and entrenched instructional techniques are simply too powerful to legislate an immediate conversion to either a completely restructured schedule or a model that is based on enrichment teaching. Clearly, realistic approaches to change that have already produced demonstrated results are far more acceptable to educators and parents than wholesale attempts to change a system that has, over the years, become almost totally immune to large-scale change. What is more, the specificity of this approach provides opportunities to evaluate progress and make modifications according to feedback derived from specific learning situations, as well as a rationale for outward extensions based on demonstrated effectiveness.

Beginning school improvement with enrichment clusters makes sense for another reason: The activities that take place during the enrichment clusters provide an immediate vehicle for making young people want to go to school. It is well documented that most American students dislike school. Rising dropout rates, especially among urban and disadvantaged youth, bear stark testimony to the fact that our schools are viewed as dreary, unenjoyable, and uninviting places. While it would be easy to dwell on clichés about how *all* learning should be interesting, exciting, and enjoyable, this has been a largely elusive goal rather than a reality in many of our schools. Because of the premium that enrichment clusters place on self-selected, product-oriented activities and a learning environment that promotes cooperativeness and social interaction, we can give more young people a reason for wanting to go to school.

Certainly the SEM intends to improve general education by creating remarkably favorable and enjoyable learning environments in which teachers and students can experiment with and refine the strategies for enrichment learning and teaching. Our experience has shown that working in such an environment, even for relatively small amounts of time, eventually influences all instructional activities because it highlights the effectiveness, feasibility, and satisfaction that can be derived from engaging in a different "brand" of learning and teaching. In this regard, the enrichment clusters are viewed as learning laboratories that have wider application in general education for both students and teachers.

TIME-FINDING STRATEGIES FOR ENRICHMENT CLUSTERS. There are a number of ways to make time blocks available for enrichment clusters. Our preference is for these time blocks to be at least one-half of a school day and for the enrichment clusters to meet at least once a week. A number of patterns for such meetings are presented in Figures 2.3a–d.

Alternative Scheduling Plans: Typical Weekly Schedule

THE REGULAR SCHOOL SCHEDULE				
Monday	**Tuesday**	**Wednesday**	**Thursday**	**Friday**
1 Reading Math Language Arts Social Studies etc. . . .	2 Reading Math Language Arts Social Studies etc. . . .	3 Reading Math Language Arts Social Studies etc. . . .	4 Reading Math Language Arts Social Studies etc. . . .	5 Reading Math Language Arts Social Studies etc. . . .
8 Reading Math Language Arts Social Studies etc. . . .	9 Reading Math Language Arts Social Studies etc. . . .	10 Reading Math Language Arts Social Studies etc. . . .	11 Reading Math Language Arts Social Studies etc. . . .	12 Reading Math Language Arts Social Studies etc. . . .
15 Reading Math Language Arts Social Studies etc. . . .	16 Reading Math Language Arts Social Studies etc. . . .	17 Reading Math Language Arts Social Studies etc. . . .	18 Reading Math Language Arts Social Studies etc. . . .	19 Reading Math Language Arts Social Studies etc. . . .
22	23	24	25	26

Figure 2.3a

Figure 2.3a portrays one month of the typical "five-by-five" weekly schedule found in most schools. The five major subjects (reading, math, language arts, social studies, and science) ordinarily meet five days per week, and special subjects such as music, art, and physical education meet one or two times per week. Figure 2.3b presents a schedule in which one meeting of each major subject per *week* is "borrowed" from the regular schedule. This procedure yields one class meeting per *week* during which enrichment clusters take place. This approach is the least disruptive to the regular school routine, but it has the disadvantage of short time blocks and the types of discontinuity that

Alternative Scheduling Plans: One Enrichment Cluster per Week

THE PERIOD EXCHANGE SCHEDULE				
Monday	**Tuesday**	**Wednesday**	**Thursday**	**Friday**
1 **ENRICHMENT CLUSTER** Math Language Arts Social Studies etc. . . .	2 Reading Math Language Arts Social Studies etc. . . .	3 Reading Math Language Arts Social Studies etc. . . .	4 Reading Math Language Arts Social Studies etc. . . .	5 Reading Math Language Arts Social Studies etc. . . .
8 Reading Math Language Arts Social Studies etc. . . .	9 Reading **ENRICHMENT CLUSTER** Language Arts Social Studies etc. . . .	10 Reading Math Language Arts Social Studies etc. . . .	11 Reading Math Language Arts Social Studies etc. . . .	12 Reading Math Language Arts Social Studies etc. . . .
15 Reading Math Language Arts Social Studies etc. . . .	16 Reading Math Language Arts Social Studies etc. . . .	17 Reading Math **ENRICHMENT CLUSTER** Social Studies etc. . . .	18 Reading Math Language Arts Social Studies etc. . . .	19 Reading Math Language Arts Social Studies etc. . . .
22 Reading Math Language Arts Social Studies etc. . . .	23 Reading Math Language Arts Social Studies etc. . . .	24 Reading Math Language Arts Social Studies etc. . . .	25 Reading Math Language Arts **ENRICHMENT CLUSTER** etc. . . .	26 Reading Math Language Arts Social Studies etc. . . .
29 Reading Math Language Arts Social Studies etc. . . .	30 Reading Math Language Arts Social Studies etc. . . .	1 Reading Math Language Arts Social Studies etc. . . .	2 Reading Math Language Arts Social Studies etc. . . .	3 Reading Math Language Arts Social Studies **ENRICHMENT CLUSTER**

Figure 2.3b

result when there is a week between enrichment cluster meetings. In one middle school that experimented with this approach, the teachers said that by the time students got organized and settled down, the period was over.

Figure 2.3c presents a half-day-per-week approach. The instructional advantages of a longer time block are obvious, and this plan also allows time for students to rearrange their classroom environment so that it is more conducive to the type of work they are doing. For example, students in one enrichment cluster that produced a weekly newspaper transformed their room into

Alternative Scheduling Plans: Half Day per Week

HALF DAY ENRICHMENT CLUSTER SCHEDULE				
Monday	**Tuesday**	**Wednesday**	**Thursday**	**Friday**
1 Reading Math Language Arts Social Studies etc. . . .	2 Reading Math Language Arts Social Studies etc. . . .	3 ENRICHMENT CLUSTER Social Studies	4 Reading Math Language Arts Social Studies etc. . . .	5 Reading Math Language Arts Social Studies etc. . . .
8 Reading Math Language Arts Social Studies etc. . . .	9 Reading Math Language Arts Social Studies etc. . . .	10 ENRICHMENT CLUSTER Reading	11 Reading Math Language Arts Social Studies etc. . . .	12 Reading Math Language Arts Social Studies etc. . . .
15 Reading Math Language Arts Social Studies etc. . . .	16 Reading Math Language Arts Social Studies etc. . . .	17 ENRICHMENT CLUSTER Math	18 Reading Math Language Arts Social Studies etc. . . .	19 Reading Math Language Arts Social Studies etc. . . .
22 Reading Math Language Arts Social Studies etc. . . .	23 Reading Math Language Arts Social Studies etc. . . .	24 ENRICHMENT CLUSTER Language Arts	25 Reading Math Language Arts Social Studies etc. . . .	26 Reading Math Language Arts Social Studies etc. . . .
29 Reading Math Language Arts Social Studies etc. . . .	30 Reading Math Language Arts Social Studies etc. . . .	1 ENRICHMENT CLUSTER etc. . . .	2 Reading Math Language Arts Social Studies etc. . . .	3 Reading Math Language Arts Social Studies etc. . . .

Figure 2.3c

a "city room," complete with an editorial department, graphics center, layout section, and printing division. Students researched cardboard carpentry and made easily movable partitions. They received permission to bring extra computers and graphics design materials into the room; both these additions helped create an atmosphere that contributed to the overall professionalism and ambience of the cluster.

Figure 2.3d shows a weekly schedule in which one full day per week is devoted to enrichment clusters. Some clusters meet for an entire day, and

Alternative Scheduling Plans: Full Day per Week

THE PERIOD EXCHANGE SCHEDULE					
	Monday	**Tuesday**	**Wednesday**	**Thursday**	**Friday**
9:00 AM	Regular Class Day 1	Regular Class Day 1	The Enrichment Clusters Day	Regular Class Day 1	Regular Class Day 1
	2	2	All Day Cluster 1 / Half-Day Cluster 1	2	2
	3	3		3	3
	4	4		4	4
	5	5	Half-Day Cluster 2	5	5
	6	6		6	6
3:00 PM	7	7		7	7

Figure 2.3d

SkyLight Professional Development

others are organized so that students can participate in clusters that represent two areas of interest.

DEVELOPING THE "RIGHT" SCHEDULE: EXPERIENCE AND IMAGINATION. Each school must examine its own preferences and develop a schedule that accommodates local needs. Since all teachers, including special subject teachers, should be involved in the enrichment clusters, some accommodations need to be made in order to develop a mutually acceptable schedule. It might be necessary to double-up certain meetings of special subjects in order to provide equitable time for subjects that do not meet daily. The key issues regarding any modifications in the schedule are experimentation and imagination. Even issues such as the "required minutes game" (in states that regulate instructional time) can be overcome by simply allocating the time spent in a mathematics cluster, for example, to the total mathematics instructional time of a given school.

THE ROLE OF ADMINISTRATORS. Time after time, enthusiastic teachers who have expressed a strong commitment to adopt the SEM have expressed equally strong reservations because they feared administrative roadblocks. Arranging time blocks for enrichment clusters obviously requires a commitment from both central administration and building principals. The first question that administrators (and in many cases, teachers) inevitable raise is: "How can we cover the regular curriculum if we give up two or three periods a week?" The answer to this question could entangle us in endless dialogue and debate about larger issues such as the value of the five-day meeting schedule for basic subjects, how we determine the amount of time that should be devoted to any given subject, and the benefits that might be gained by substituting a small portion of regular subject meetings with enrichment opportunities.[2] Since there is no definitive theoretical or empirical rationale for the allocation of time to school subjects, we prefer to deal pragmatically with the time issue by recommending procedures for tightening up the regular curriculum, especially in the basic skill areas.

> The most effective and best-intentioned teachers cannot improve schools by themselves.

Will administrators be bold enough to exercise their authority over an issue that is clearly necessary for implementing a school change procedure? The most effective and best-intentioned teachers cannot improve schools by themselves. Changing complicated and often bureaucratized school systems requires a partnership in which persons in each role make a commitment to do something different within their respective domains of power and operation. Teachers need to extend themselves in order to deliver high-quality services associated with Goal 1 (as well as the other objectives) of this model. Principals and central office administrators need to extend themselves by supporting and assisting in the development of scheduling options necessary to allow the objective to commence. And superintendents and school boards need to extend themselves by obtaining waivers (when necessary) for state regulations that, in some cases, still specify instructional minutes per grade and subject.

The Non-Negotiables of Enrichment Clusters

There are only two non-negotiables regarding the scheduling of enrichment clusters:

1. *All* students should be involved in the enrichment clusters to keep the focus on talent development.
2. The time allocated to enrichment clusters must be respected on a par value with regular school subjects.

If this time block becomes a catch-all period for scheduling assemblies, taking school photographs, administering standardized tests, or making up classes that were missed because of snow days, students and teachers will learn quickly that talent development is not a highly valued part of the school's overall mission.

The Continuum of Enrichment Services

Types of Special Services

The third school structure targeted by the SEM includes a broad range of supplementary services. The continuum of special services encompasses enrichment and acceleration options that take place within or through:

1. Regular classrooms or clusters of classes from one or more grade levels during special grouping arrangements within classrooms, across grade levels, or in after-school and out-of-school programs.
2. Special schools such as magnet or high schools that focus on advanced learning opportunities in particular curricular areas.
3. Arrangements made for individual students at colleges, summer programs, internship opportunities, or special counseling services.

The continuum also ranges across both general and targeted groups of students. A general enrichment experience on a topic such as local history might be presented to all students at a particular grade level(s), or it might be provided on an invitational basis to students who have a special interest in history. In a later chapter we will discuss how general enrichment for all students serves as a stepping stone for more intensive follow-up on the parts of students who develop advanced interest in topics that were originally introduced through general enrichment.

Age and grade levels also play a role in making decisions about special services. Abilities, interests, and learning styles tend to become more differentiated among students and more focused on the parts of individuals as students grow older. There is, therefore, more justification for interest and achievement level grouping as students progress through the grades. It may be difficult to have a special class in mathematics, for example, at the primary or elementary grade levels. But a within-class cluster group or a nongraded cluster group of the highest achieving math students is one way of ensuring advanced levels of challenge for students with unusually high levels of achievement in mathematics. At the middle and secondary school levels, achievement in various subjects becomes more differentiated, and interests become more focused; thus, there is greater justification for advanced classes or special services such as a math club or a competitive math league group.

The nature of the subject matter and the degree to which classroom teachers can reasonably differentiate instruction also play a role in making decisions about grouping students for participation in activities on the continuum of special services. Subjects that are highly structured and linear-sequential in content (e.g., algebra, chemistry, physics) tend to be taught in a more unalterable fashion than subjects more conducive to variations in speed and level. Language arts and social studies, for example, lend themselves to greater within-topic differentiation of the complexity of the material; therefore, individual differences can be accommodated more easily in heterogeneous groups. And, of course, age or grade level and the subject matter area interact with one another in making decisions about grouping students for special services. Within-class differentiation in literature, for example, is easier to accomplish at the elementary or middle school levels, but an advanced literature class is a more specialized option at the high school level.

Figure 2.4 provides a graphic representation of the continuum of special services. Options such as special schools at the high school level, the number of Advanced Placement courses offered, and enrollment in college courses are a function of school and district size and geographic location. The continuum of special services can also be expanded as more offerings become available through increased availability of electronic media and distance learning.

Although the enrichment clusters and the SEM-based modifications of the regular curriculum provide services to meet individual and group needs, *a program for total talent development still requires a range of ancillary services that challenge young people who are capable of working at the highest levels of their special interests and abilities.* The continuum of special services might be viewed as the talent development counterpart to the kinds of special services that schools have always made available to students with remedial or compensatory educational needs.

These services, which cannot ordinarily be provided in enrichment clusters or the regular curriculum, are familiar to most educators and have been in place in some schools for many years. Some of these services are represented by the extracurricular program; in other cases they may be part of special class options or existing internship or work-study programs. A continuum of special services that focuses on talent development typically includes:

- Individual or small group counseling.
- Direct assistance in facilitating advanced-level work.
- Mentorships with faculty members or community persons.

The Continuum of Special Services

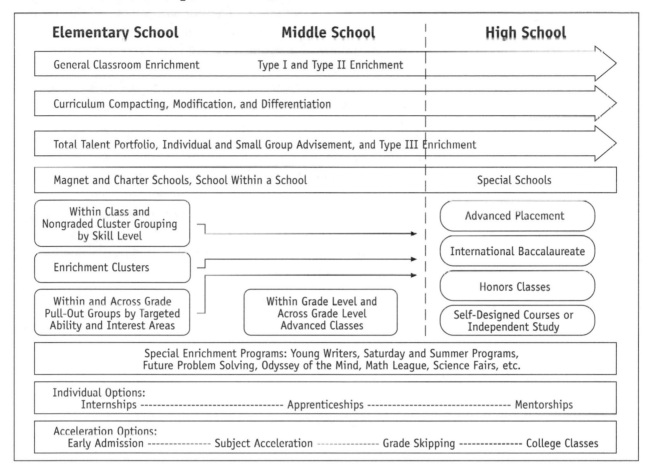

Figure 2.4

- Within and across-grade cluster groups for students with extremely advanced performance in a particular area.
- Connections between students and out-of-school persons, resources, and agencies.

Direct assistance also involves setting up and promoting student, faculty, and parental involvement in special programs such as Future Problem Solving, Odyssey of the Mind, the Model United Nations program, National History Day Competition, and state and national essay, creative writing, arts, mathematics, and science competitions. Another type of direct assistance consists of arranging out-of-school involvement for individual students in summer programs, on-campus courses, special schools, theatrical groups, scientific expeditions, and apprenticeships at places where advanced level learning opportunities are available.

There are three keys to developing a comprehensive continuum of special services:

1. Identifying the types of programs and opportunities available for students of varying age levels within certain geographic areas.
2. Obtaining information about how schools can access these programs and opportunities.
3. Enlisting school personnel and parent volunteers who are willing to devote time to organizing and managing special service options.

Many of the programs and opportunities available for young people can be located by contacting professional organizations and societies. *The Encyclopedia of Associations* (Yakes and Akey, annual), which is available in most university and large public libraries, lists thousands of organizations by both topic and geographic area, and almost all professional organizations and special interest groups can now easily be located through the World Wide Web.

Some organizations have databases that list special opportunities for students by category and age or grade levels. The Council for Exceptional Children, for example, conducts computer searches for special summer program opportunities for a modest fee.[3] The Educational Opportunity Guide published by the Duke University Talent Program lists hundreds of opportunities for students to explore an area of interest.

Organizing Special Services

The overall responsibility for organizing a broad-based continuum of special services is usually assumed by the schoolwide enrichment teaching specialist working in cooperation with the schoolwide enrichment team. At the middle and secondary school levels, these teams are frequently organized within departments—special services that represent the individual interests of department members or the department as a whole. Examples could include the following:

- A social studies teacher with a particular interest in world peace encouraged his students to prepare essays and submit them to a contest sponsored by the United States Institute for Peace.
- An entire mathematics department served as coaches for a Math League team within their school.
- An industrial arts teacher, working in cooperation with a local craftsman, assisted a group of interested students in the construction of furniture for display at a state fair.
- A group of parent volunteers at an elementary school organized and conducted a series of after-school enrichment courses that focused on a wide range of student interests. Some of these courses were so popular that they later were used as the basis for forming enrichment clusters.

The continuum of special services is a marvelous way to use inexpensive and often neglected resources that contribute to talent development. It is also a good vehicle for using cultural institutions and private sector resources as well as promoting more community involvement in the schools. A well-planned program of special services may take several years to develop, but as the program expands to include a full range of offerings, all students can benefit from the diversity of resources encompassed within this component of the SEM. The self-selection of special services also helps students work with other young people and adults who share common interests. This factor alone is a powerful force in promoting group acceptance, developing self-concept, and providing situations in which students develop respect for one another. In this regard, the continuum of special services shares many of the characteristics of the enrichment clusters.

ABOUT GROUPING AND TRACKING

Grouping is a complex and often polarizing issue that has become highly politicized. The debate that surrounds this issue is a distraction from providing appropriate and meaningful learning activities for all students. Accordingly, it is important to confront this topic now and clarify its role with respect to the School Enrichment Model.

Grouping is an intensely debated, controversial practice. The pendulum between homogeneous and heterogeneous grouping has swung back and forth since the beginning of public education. Before presenting recommendations about grouping within the context of the SEM, we discuss some of the concerns that make grouping such a contentious issue.

Grouping versus Tracking

It is crucial to make a very clear distinction between grouping and tracking. We view tracking as the general and usually permanent assignment of students to classes that are taught at a certain level and that are usually taught using a whole-group instructional model. Tracking is most prevalent at the secondary school level, and there are several features about tracking that have made it a detrimental procedure, especially for students who end up in low tracks. A concentration of low-achieving students in one classroom almost always results in a curriculum that emphasizes remediation, isolated and repetitive practice of skills such as phonics and computation at the expense of problem solving and comprehension, and low expectations for all students in the group (Oakes 1985; Slavin 1987; Slavin 1990).

Critics of tracking point out that students frequently are locked into all low-track or "general" track classes. Unlike college or vocational tracks, these classes have a dead-end orientation rather than an orientation toward post-secondary education or entrance into the skilled labor market. This lack of purposefulness frequently results in low student motivation and self-esteem, underachievement, behavior problems, absenteeism, and school dropouts. Low-track classes are usually taught in such a way that they become ends in

> A well-planned program of special services may take several years to develop, but as the program expands, . . . all students can benefit from the diversity of resources encompassed within this component of the SEM.

... prevent grouping from becoming tracking by initiating a systematic practice called *group jumping*.

themselves, rather than places where students are being prepared to move into higher track classes. Economically disadvantaged students are disproportionately represented in low-track classes, and this practice further reinforces their sense of failure and feelings about the limited value of a formal education.

In contrast, at the elementary level, within-class instructional groups are common practice, and they serve an important purpose in accommodating different levels of achievement within the classroom. It is essential, however, to have a built-in review process so that students who are ready to progress to a more advanced group do not get locked into a lower group for reasons of mere convenience. Without such a review process, instructional groups can serve as de facto tracks; as such, they play a role in the cumulative development of underachievement.

Our first recommendation, therefore, is purposefully intended to prevent grouping from becoming tracking by initiating a systematic practice called *group jumping*. We recommend regularly scheduled formal and informal assessments should be used—regardless of the types of grouping arrangements a school uses—so students can progress to achievement-level groups that offer maximum challenges. Students and parents should be informed about the group jumping policy (in writing), and information about group placement should be routinely provided.

The Politics of Grouping

The argument over grouping has been long and passionate, and every faction rattles off its cache of research studies while simultaneously pointing out the shortcomings of research presented by the opposition. And like all of the armies that ever took up weapons, each group is convinced that rightness is on *their* side. Adversaries even lay claim to the same study by adding their own surplus interpretation or procedure for reanalyzing the data. The only thing certain about the research on ability grouping and its relation to achievement is that there are well-documented arguments on both sides of the issue (Kulik 1992; Oakes 1985; Rogers 1991, Slavin 1987, 1990).

Gifted and special education programs may be conceived of as one form of ability grouping, but they also involve many other changes in curriculum, class size, resources, and goals that make them fundamentally different from comprehensive ability grouping plans. Slavin (1987) has pointed out:

> . . Studies of special programs for the gifted tend to find achievement benefits for the gifted students...and others, would give the impression that ability grouping is beneficial for high achievers and detrimental for low achievers. *However, it is likely that characteristics of special accelerated programs for the gifted account for the effects of gifted programs, not the fact of separate grouping per se.* . . . (Slavin 1987, 307, italics added)

Slavin presents a clear message: If positive growth is the result of curriculum adaptations, class size, resources, and goals, why then cannot we apply the same explanation to cases in which growth is not shown? More important, shouldn't we be using the know-how of educational practices that emerges from studies of favorable achievement to explore ways of promoting better performance in lower achieving students? This is exactly the rationale that underlies the SEM. But the grouping issue, rather than a focus on what must be done to create favorable acts of learning, has taken center stage, and it is offered as a quick-fix approach to improving our schools. Slavin (with Gutiérrez), pursuing the same distinctions pointed out above, offers an alternative to traditional forms of ability grouping.

> In the nongraded plan, students are flexibly grouped for major subjects (especially reading and math) across class and age lines, so that the resulting groups are truly homogeneous on the skills being taught. Further, by creating multiage groups from among all students in contiguous grade levels, it is possible for teachers to create entire reading or math classes at one or, at most, two levels, so that they need not devote much class time to follow-up. (Gutiérrez and Slavin 1992, 339)

The research summarized by Gutiérrez and Slavin (1992) clearly indicates that multiage grouping based on the skills being taught has proven to be an effective practice. But we also believe that even within a homogeneous, skill level group, provisions must also be made for curriculum compacting and cluster grouping that are based on other considerations (e.g., interests, learning styles) as well as achievement levels. We also believe that group jumping should be the goal of all group assignments. Like the Boy Scout and Girl Scout merit badge program, the goal should be to demonstrate competency in a skill area, after which the individual moves on to a more advanced level of involvement.

Nongraded Instructional Grouping and Within Classroom Cluster Grouping

In the SEM, grouping is viewed as a much more flexible (i.e., less permanent) arrangement of students than the frequently unalterable group arrangements that characterize tracking. And although we will present recommendations for various types of instructional and cluster groups, note that there are many other factors about grouping that should be taken into consideration *in addition* to achievement level, and sometimes *in place of* achievement level. These factors include motivation, general interests (e.g., drama) and specific interests within a general area (e.g., writing plays, acting, directing), complementary skills (e.g., an artist who might illustrate the short stories of students in a creative writing group), career aspirations, and even friendships that might help promote self-concept, self-efficacy, or group harmony. In the real world, which serves as the rationale for many of the procedures that guide the SEM, the most important reason people come together is because they are pursuing a common goal. And in most cases, the effectiveness of the group is a function of the different assets that are brought to bear on a mutual purpose. The major criteria for group effectiveness are commonality of purpose, reciprocal respect and harmony, group and individual progress toward goals, and individual enjoyment and satisfaction. It is these criteria that helped to create the rationale for the enrichment clusters as well as the enrichment learning and teaching strategies that will be described in detail in chapter 5.

Another factor that should be taken into consideration is the age level of students and the material being taught. Many elementary-level students begin to fall behind and have difficulty catching up when they are placed in lower-level groups. And while nongraded instructional groups and cluster groups within the classroom may be necessary to accommodate varying achievement levels in basic skills, variations in teaching style can also be used to deal with diversity in students' knowledge and skills. In studies of Asian teachers, Stigler and Stevenson (1991) point out how Asian teachers thrive in the face of diversity and indicate that some teaching practices actually depend on diversity for their effectiveness.

Stigler and Stevenson credit the highly skilled professionalism of Asian teachers for their remarkable success and the widespread excellence of their lessons. They also point out that the techniques used by Asian teachers are not foreign or exotic. Although one of the goals of the SEM is to provide professional training that allows teachers to expand their repertoire of teaching practices, the range of diversity in American schools and our educational traditions will continue to make grouping an issue in school improvement.

Although curriculum compacting and other modification techniques are important procedures within the SEM for meeting individual differences in achievement levels, we also recommend that instructional groups be formed *within* the classroom and across grade levels. There is both research support (Gutiérrez and Slavin 1992; Kulik 1992; Rogers 1991) and a commonsense rationale for forming advanced instructional groups for students who are achieving several years above grade level.

Two criteria, however, should guide the formation of advanced instructional groups. First, a course description rather than a group label should be used, and the course should be defined by the level of instruction and the amount of material to be covered. This approach avoids the stigma of calling it an honors or gifted group. Defining advanced classes by the level and amount of material ensures that certain predetermined standards will be met, that we will avoid watering down the course, and that success in the course is dependent on certain expectations. A detailed description of the amount of material, the rate of coverage, reading and writing assignments, homework expectations, and evaluation criteria should be provided.

> There is both research support . . . and a commonsense rationale for forming advanced instructional groups for students who are achieving several years above grade level.

The second criterion for advanced instructional groups is that standardized test scores should not be a factor in determining admittance. If, after examining the course description and understanding the expectations of the teacher, a student expresses an interest in enrolling, that student should be given an opportunity, regardless of test scores and previous grades. High motivation on the part of a student, coupled with supplementary assistance from a teacher or other adult, may very well enable a lower achieving student to maintain the level of standards that define the course. A key issue related to this second criterion is that students may volunteer to take a course. Consider the procedure used with Advanced Placement (AP) courses. The content, standards, and examinations are set, but taking the AP exam is not required. In addition to its attractiveness to some students (and the teachers who offer AP courses), the benefits of such courses are more in the nature of incentives and bonuses rather than penalties. Students get credit for passing an AP course, and there is an additional bonus if they pass the official AP exam at a level that earns them advanced standing in participating colleges.

A good example of how carefully defined standards for rigorously demanding, high level classes can have an impact on at-risk students can be found in the multiracial San Diego High School. A program based on the International Baccalaureate[4] curriculum was developed at this inner-city school that serves a mainly low socioeconomic minority population. Students can select from among nine academic requirements that include traditional courses; an interdisciplinary course in the philosophy of knowledge; participation in a creative, aesthetic, or social service activity; and an extended essay based on independent research. Students' performance is evaluated through written and oral external examinations that are used worldwide, and oral presentations, lab books, portfolios, and research papers are also evaluated externally. Following the inception of the International Baccalaureate Program, the academic performance of all students at San Diego High School improved dramatically, and three years later, 85 percent of the graduating class went on to college. The school became a "hot" recruiting place for many Ivy League colleges seeking to increase their minority student enrollments.

If we are serious about improving the standards of American education and providing greater access to advanced courses for students who traditionally have been locked into lower tracks, it will also be necessary to concentrate on basic skills achievement at lower grade levels. But we also need to have alternative routes to advanced courses for those students who have the motivation to enroll but who lack some of the skills necessary for high level instruction. Transitional preparatory classes and individual or small group tutoring are ways of helping motivated students prepare for more advanced classes. These approaches, however, should not fall into the remedial trap, that is, revert to the lowest common denominator of a subject matter area. If, for example, students are preparing for an advanced literature class, the focus should be on literature rather than more practice on grammar.

Managing Within Classroom Cluster Groups

Although the use of cluster grouping within classes is a major improvement over tracking or large group instruction, in practice this approach is usually less effective than it could be because students are often placed in clusters on the basis of a single criterion. In most classrooms that use cluster grouping, all high-achieving math students or all low-achieving reading students are typically members of the same group. The students within this small group are usually given the same instruction and assignments, despite the fact that high-achieving or low-achieving students can differ from one another with respect to their strengths and weaknesses within the various strands or sub-disciplines in a given subject area.

For example, two students who score in the 95th percentile on the math subtest of a norm-referenced achievement test score may be markedly different in their achievement with respect to fractions, decimals, problem solving and/or measurement skills. One student in the high achieving group may need more help on fractions but less assistance with problem solving. But by using an average score to reflect individual achievement in a subject area, and grouping students according to this number, we continue to "wash out" the differences between students and within the subject area. When this happens, the potential benefits of small group teaching as a means of maximizing individual student performance are decreased because individual differences between the students and within each of the ability groups are not addressed. As a result, teachers may not see increased achievement for students who were placed in such groups when compared to students who were taught similar objectives through large group instruction. In other words, the use of small groups for instruction will not, in and of itself, guarantee student achievement (Kulik and Kulik 1987; Slavin 1987; Walberg 1984).

The quality of small group instruction depends on what goes on within the cluster groups. More specifically, the achievement of students in these groups depends upon the ability of the teacher to group students flexibly and then adapt the learning objectives, teaching strategies, modeling activities, practice materials, and pacing to match the students' needs. Flexible cluster grouping allows students to participate in group instruction when the unit pretesting reveals wide differences among students with regard to mastery of learning objectives for a given unit of study. Once groups of students are formed for instruction, characteristics of individuals comprising the cluster dictate the learning objectives, the type of modeling, the type and amount of practice materials, and the pacing.

Although cluster grouping and concomitant instructional changes represent "common sense" with respect to teaching practices, cluster grouping should not dominate classroom instruction. Instead, a balance between whole class and cluster grouping is determined by the teacher according to the purpose of instruction and the degree to which students differ with respect to various curricular objectives. Large group activities such as storytelling, discussions, debriefings, class meetings, audio visual aids, visitations, lectures, and demonstrations are used to motivate students, to introduce or extend a curriculum unit, or to teach content or skills that are new for all students. Individual or small group activities are used for intensive study or exploration of specific topics within the unit that reflect strong personal interest or when wide differences exist among students with respect to mastery of learning objectives in a given unit of study.

When teachers implement small group instruction, classroom management issues inevitably arise. "What will I do with the other students in the room?" "How will I know they are meaningfully engaged while I am working with the small groups?" In the 1950s, the answer to these questions was to assign seatwork to the students who were not meeting in a small group. In too many cases, worksheets were used as busywork to fill students' time. This seatwork involved ineffective and uninteresting drill and repetition that bore little resemblance to the way the skills were actually used and applied in real-world situations.

One possible solution is offered by the practice of using flexible skill groups in the regular classroom (Hoover, Sayler, and Feldhusen 1993). In these instances, teachers help students in each small group work cooperatively to practice and apply the skill or objective that was the focus of the teacher-led group instruction. By working cooperatively, students are not reduced to practicing the kind of repetitive drill that the old seatwork approach produced. These cooperative practice groups meet and work with the teacher on a rotating basis; specifically, teachers meet with 2-4 groups a day to evaluate student progress, provide instruction and/or new scaffolding to support their learning, and assess the appropriateness of grouping arrangements and reassign (e.g., "group jump") students accordingly. This application of cooperative learning principles ensures that all students in a small group are supporting and helping one another *and* that they are all striving to achieve a common objective that is appropriate for *all* group members.

Still other students can be allowed to use interest centers, learning centers, classroom libraries, and software and technology to pursue individual interests or to extend and enrich a curriculum unit. Students provided with these enrichment options demonstrate mastery of curriculum objectives in the assessment of student knowledge that preceded instruction. Class meetings are used to explain enrichment options and to teach the skills necessary for students to work independently. Student logs can be used to provide the teacher with information about what each student does each day, and contracts can be written by students and teachers, using compromise and consensus, to ensure that each student has a relevant and realistic plan for his or her enrichment time.

> This application of cooperative learning principles ensures that all students in a small group are supporting and helping one another and that they are all striving to achieve a common objective that is appropriate for all group members.

Concluding Thoughts on Grouping

It is easy to point out the social consequences of grouping, the grouping practices followed in other nations, and the level of professionalism required

> ... the issue is what is done *within* groups, regardless of how they are organized, to help all students maximize their potentials and view learning as both a valuable and enjoyable experience.

for teachers to accommodate the diversity that is always present when two or more students come together. Our schools are a reflection of the society at large and the educational traditions that this society has created. Schools do, indeed, play a role in shaping society; however, they have thus far been an abysmal failure at influencing larger societal issues such as housing, health care, and equal job opportunities. These larger societal issues also are forms of grouping that must be addressed *at the same time* that we struggle with the most equitable forms of grouping that should take place in our schools. Schools cannot shoulder the entire burden of shaping and improving our multicultural society. Until these larger issues are addressed, and until dramatic changes take place in the funding of education, the levels of preparation of our teachers, and developing a national commitment to improve standards for all students, grouping will continue to be a practice for accommodating the broad range of diversity that characterizes our school population. We believe that grouping per se is not the issue. Rather, the issue is what is done *within* groups, regardless of how they are organized, to help all students maximize their potentials and view learning as both a valuable and enjoyable experience. It is for this reason that the SEM *focuses on the act of learning rather than the types of administrative arrangements that have been offered as school reform paradigms*. By concentrating on what and how we teach, grouping becomes incidental to the overall process of school improvement.

ENDNOTES

1. The major studies confirming this distressing fact are too numerous to list. Research-based reports identifying the status of US students have been released by The College Board, the Twentieth Century Fund, the National Science Foundation, the Educational Commission of the States, the National Commission on Excellence in Education, and the International Association for Educational Achievement.

2. It is interesting to note that massive increases in the amount of time devoted to repetition and drill (euphemistically called "time-on-task") have not significantly increased the general achievement of disadvantaged students. And no one ever seems to question the transition to three (or sometimes even two) class meetings per week when students matriculate from high school to college, where there is an implicit assumption that the material is more difficult and demanding.

3. For information about this service, contact the Council for Exceptional Children, 1920 Association Drive, Reston, VA 22091.

4. Information about the International Baccalaureate program can be obtained by writing to: International Baccalaureate North America, 200 Madison Avenue, New York, NY 10016.

Using the
Total Talent
Portfolio

▶   ▶   ▶   ▶   ▶   ▶   ▶   ▶   ▶   ▶

Every learner has strengths or potential strengths. The Schoolwide Enrichment Model capitalizes on these strengths by developing a portfolio of student assets in the areas of abilities, interests, and learning styles. The SEM pays equal attention to interests and learning styles as well as to the cognitive abilities that have been used traditionally for educational decision making. Assets related to these three clusters of learner characteristics are documented in individual student portfolios; this information is used to make decisions about various types of student involvement in the full range of regular curriculum and enrichment opportunities that are available in schools using the SEM.

Although information obtained from formal assessment is a part of student portfolios, additional information gained through informal, performance-based assessment is equally valuable in maximizing the use of the portfolio. The best ways to capitalize on student performance are to:

1. Provide opportunities for participation in a broad range of activities within and across interest areas.
2. Observe and document performance, satisfaction, and enthusiasm.
3. Make decisions about subsequent activities that will capitalize on positive reactions to previous experiences.

Student portfolios are used to document strength assessment activities. Regularly scheduled meetings with staff members, parents, and students are used to make decisions about appropriate follow-up, needed resources, and the development of future performance assessment situations. Whereas the traditional diagnostic-prescriptive learning model focuses on remediating student weaknesses, this approach accentuates the positive, because it uses positive reactions to learning experiences as vehicles for attacking deficiencies in basic skill learning.

For example, a child who has developed a spirited interest in dolphins, but who also experiences difficulties in reading and basic language skills, is far more likely to read background material and improve written and oral language skills when he or she works on a research project based on this abiding interest in dolphins. All cognitive behavior is enhanced as a function of the degree of interest present in an act of learning, wherever that cognitive behavior may be on the continuum from basic skill learning to higher levels of thinking and creative productivity. For this very reason, the SEM uses performance-based assessment within the context of student interests as well as in basic skill learning.

> The Total Talent Portfolio is a vehicle for gathering and recording information systematically about students' abilities, interests, and learning styles.

WHAT IS THE TOTAL TALENT PORTFOLIO?

The Total Talent Portfolio is a vehicle for gathering and recording information systematically about students' abilities, interests, and learning styles. The major dimensions of the portfolio and the specific items that guide data gathering within each dimension are presented in Figure 3.1.

The Total Talent Portfolio centers on a key issue: creating learning experiences that encourage the development of strong interests. How did the student in the example develop the interest in dolphins that served as a launching pad for subsequent activity? This interest might have been discovered through formal assessment such as responses to items on an instrument called the *Interest-A-Lyzer* (discussed later in this chapter), or it might have resulted from purposefully planned interest development activities.

But identifying interests through formal or performance-based activities is only a first step. Other strategies in the model deal with specific steps for nurturing interests, examining the ways in which the student might like to pursue interests, and providing the teacher guidance and resources necessary to escalate the level of student productivity. Two unique features about the Total Talent Portfolio that distinguish it from other compilations of student records are discussed next.

Status and Action Information

The portfolio consists of both status information and action information. Status information is anything we know or can record about a student prior to the instructional process that tells us something about learner characteristics. Examples of status information are test scores, course grades, teacher ratings of various learning behaviors, and formal and informal assessments of interests and learning styles.

Action information consists of annotated recordings of *events* that take place within the instructional process. Action information, by definition,

The Total Talent Portfolio

ABILITIES	INTERESTS	STYLE PREFERENCES				
Maximum Performance Indicators	*Interest Areas*	*Instructional Styles Preferences*	*Learning Environment Preferences*	*Thinking Styles Preferences*	*Expression Styles Preferences*	
Tests • Standardized • Teacher-Made Course Grades Teacher Ratings **Product Evaluation** • Written • Oral • Visual • Musical • Constructed (Note differences between assigned and self-selected products) Level of Participation in Learning Activities Degree of Interaction with Others Ref: General Tests and Measurements Literature	Fine Arts Crafts Literary Historical Mathematical/ Logical Physical Sciences Life Sciences Political/Judicial Athletic/ Recreation Marketing/ Business Drama/Dance Musical Performance Musical Composition Managerial/ Business Photography Film/Video Computers Other (specify) Ref: Renzulli 1977b	Recitation & Drill Programmed and Computer Assisted Instruction Peer Tutoring Lecture Lecture/ Discussion Discussion Guided Independent Study* Learning/Interest Center Simulation, Role-Playing, Dramatization, Guided Fantasy Learning Games Replicative Reports or Projects* Investigative Reports or Projects* Unguided Independent Study* Internship* Apprenticeship* *With or without a mentor Ref: Renzulli & Smith 1978	**Inter/ Intrapersonal** • Self-Oriented • Peer-Oriented • Adult-Oriented • Combined **Physical** • Sound • Heat • Light • Design • Mobility • Time of Day • Food Intake • Seating Ref: Amabile 1983; Dunn, Dunn, & Price 1978; Gardner 1983	Analytic (School Smart) Synthetic/Creative (Creative, Inventive) Practical/ Contextual (Street Smart) Legislative Executive Judicial Ref: Sternberg, 1984, 1988, 1990	Written Oral Manipulative Discussion Display Dramatization Artistic Graphic Commercial Service Ref: Kettle, Renzulli, & Rizza 1998; Renzulli & Reis 1985	

Figure 3.1

cannot be recorded beforehand because it is designed to document the ways in which students react to various learning experiences as well as other experiences that take place outside the formal learning environment. Documentation procedures such as the *Action Information Message* (see Figure 3.2) and staff development techniques related to the use of this form are designed to capture episodes in which remarkable interests, unusual insights, or other manifestations of learning are displayed. By seizing the moment to record

Action Information Message

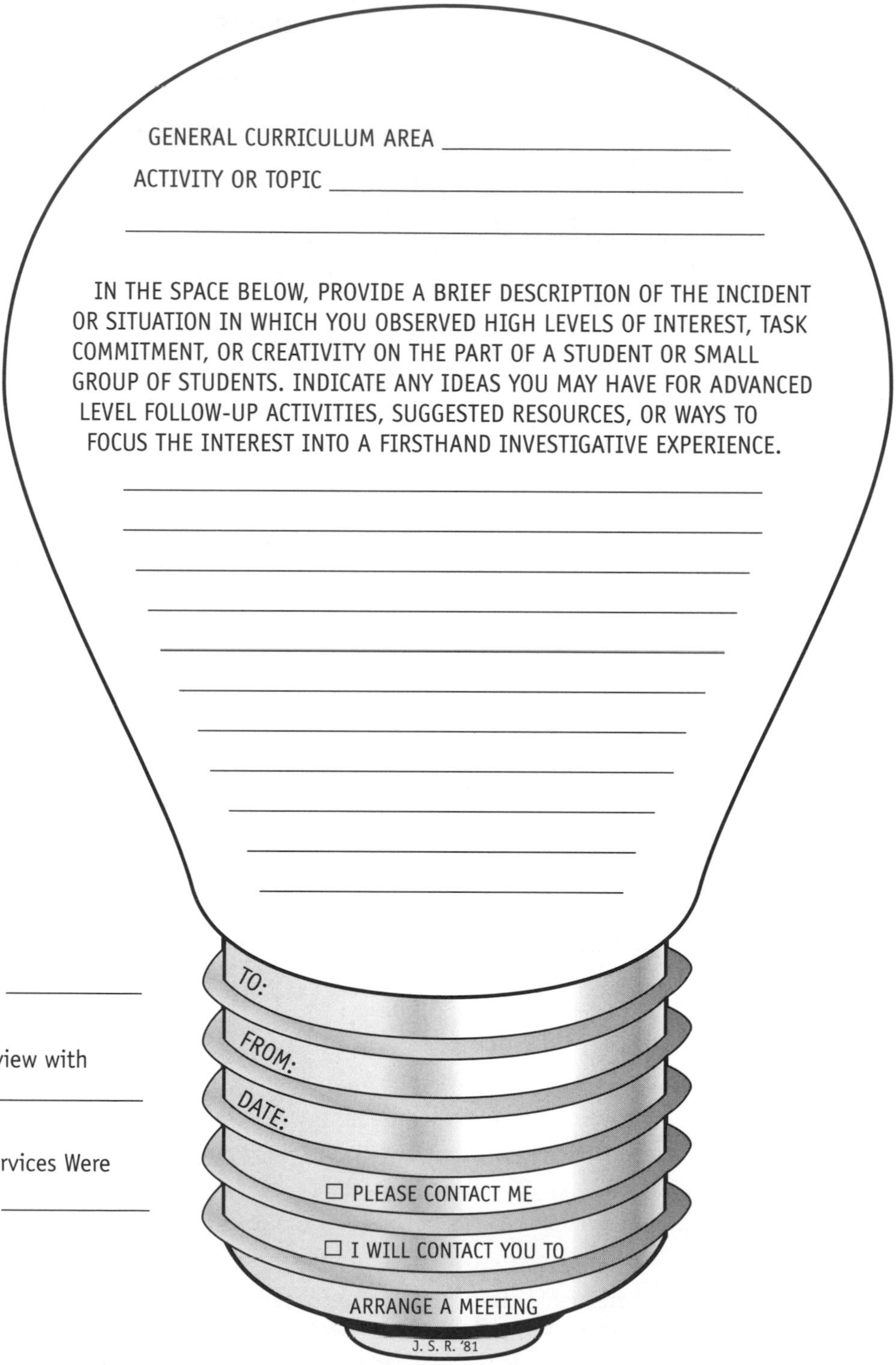

GENERAL CURRICULUM AREA _____

ACTIVITY OR TOPIC _____

_____

IN THE SPACE BELOW, PROVIDE A BRIEF DESCRIPTION OF THE INCIDENT
OR SITUATION IN WHICH YOU OBSERVED HIGH LEVELS OF INTEREST, TASK
COMMITMENT, OR CREATIVITY ON THE PART OF A STUDENT OR SMALL
GROUP OF STUDENTS. INDICATE ANY IDEAS YOU MAY HAVE FOR ADVANCED
LEVEL FOLLOW-UP ACTIVITIES, SUGGESTED RESOURCES, OR WAYS TO
FOCUS THE INTEREST INTO A FIRSTHAND INVESTIGATIVE EXPERIENCE.

TO:

FROM:

DATE:

☐ PLEASE CONTACT ME

☐ I WILL CONTACT YOU TO

ARRANGE A MEETING

J. S. R. '81

Date received _____

Date of Interview with
Child _____

Date When Services Were
Implemented _____

Figure 3.2

this information, teachers and students have a vehicle for documenting what might be starting points to high levels of follow-up activity.

Action information also consists of annotated work samples of completed assignments and other performance-based observations and assessments. These annotations can be both informal notes and more structured analyses of student work.

Focus on Strengths

The second unique feature of the Total Talent Portfolio is its focus on strengths and high-end learning behaviors. An educational tradition has caused us to use student records mainly for spotting deficiencies. Our adherence to the medical (i.e., diagnostic-prescriptive) model has almost always been pointed in the negative direction: "Find out what's wrong with them and fix them up!" Total talent assessment emphasizes the identification of the most positive aspects of each student 's learning behaviors. Documentation based on the categories in Figure 3.1 should be carried out by inserting any and all information in the portfolio that calls attention to strong interests, preferred styles of learning, and high levels of motivation, creativity and leadership as well as the academic strengths that can lead to more advanced learning activities.

Portfolios of any type are only as valuable as the use to which they are put. Portfolios as prime examples of performance-based assessment are receiving a great deal of attention in the professional literature; they are being considered as supplements to or replacements for traditional evaluation procedures such as standardized tests. Although the information gathered in a Total Talent Portfolio can be used for program evaluation purposes, *the primary use of the portfolio within the context of the SEM is to make educational programming decisions for individual students or for small groups of students who share common abilities, interests, or learning styles.*

> Portfolios of any type are only as valuable as the use to which they are put.

Portfolio Engineering

Through a process that might best be described as *portfolio engineering*, examples of positive performance are accumulated on a continuing basis, and regularly scheduled reviews are used to make decisions about subsequent talent development activities. These decisions may relate to guidance regarding the selection of enrichment clusters, within-class special projects, curriculum compacting, group jumping, or individual learning opportunities that are a part of the continuum of special services discussed earlier.

Portfolio engineering also involves conducting conferences among groups of teachers and specialists, meeting with parents, and conveying information about student strengths to subsequent-year teachers, college admission officers, and prospective employers. The theme of the Total Talent Portfolio might best be summarized in the form of two questions: What are the very *best* things we know and can record about a student? and What are the very best things we can *do* to capitalize on this information? The first question is addressed in the following three sections that deal with student abilities, interests, and learning styles. The second question is addressed in the remaining chapters of the book.

GATHERING AND RECORDING INFORMATION ABOUT ABILITIES

Abilities, or maximum performance indicators, as traditionally defined in the psychometric literature, deal with competencies that represent the highest level of performance a student has attained in a particular area of aptitude or scholastic achievement. This dimension of school performance has traditionally been evaluated by tests or course grades. The first column of Figure 3.1 includes these conventional assessments, but it also includes a number of additional procedures by which maximum performance can be examined. These procedures may not be as reliable and objective as traditional tests, but they do have the advantage of letting us know how students perform on more complex tasks and on tasks that require the application of knowledge to assigned or self-selected learning activities.

The merits of formal testing versus alternative forms of assessment have been debated extensively in the literature, and it is not our purpose here to reexamine this debate or to argue for one approach or the other. We believe that any and all sources of information are valuable if they improve our understanding of potential for future performance and if they provide direction for enhancing future performance. We do argue, however, that alternative forms of assessment are equal in value to formal tests, and that a Total Talent Portfolio that does not include alternate assessment information will seriously limit the purposes of this component of the SEM.

Standardized Tests and Teacher-Made Tests

The concept of ability implies the measurement of competencies in terms of maximum performance. The traditional use of the term "ability," at least in educational settings, has almost always been linked with standardized test scores and expressed in a normative or comparative fashion with the scores of other students in the same age or grade group. Arguments about the value of standardized tests have existed since the time these instruments came onto the educational scene, and the tests themselves are a reality in our schools. In those cases where the tests meet the criteria of reliability, validity, objectivity, and audience appropriateness, they can provide us with useful information if used properly within the context of the SEM. At the risk of dwelling on a cliché, the tests are not as much of a problem as the uses to which they are put.

Although standardized test scores are gathered and recorded in the Total Talent Portfolio, these scores are only one source of information about students' abilities. The most important use of standardized test scores is to identify which general area or areas are a student's greatest strengths. To do this, we need only look at *one student's* scores, and we should avoid comparative information such as percentiles or other norms based on national or even local comparisons. Instead, we focus on this question: In which curricular areas or aptitudes does this student show his or her greatest strengths?

Teacher-made assessments usually are designed to assess the degree of mastery of a specific unit that has been taught and to evaluate competence in an entire course or a segment thereof. Objective teacher-made tests (e.g., multiple-choice, matching, short answer) provide information about knowledge acquisition, the mastery of basic skills, and, in some cases, problem-solving strategies. This information is valuable for determining general levels of proficiency, but the most valuable kind of teacher-made assessments, so far as the purposes of the Total Talent Portfolio are concerned, are those that elicit open-ended or extended responses.

Responses of this type enable teachers to gain insight into complex student abilities such as constructing convincing arguments, using expressive written or oral language, generating relevant hypotheses, applying creative solutions to complex problems, and demonstrating deep levels of understanding. Open-ended responses also provide excellent opportunities for students to demonstrate artistic and scientific creativity and to display advanced abilities such as analysis, generalization, and evaluation. Whenever teacher-made tests result in a student's exemplary manifestations of these more complex learning abilities, the tests should be copied, annotated, and entered into the student's portfolio.

The majority of teacher-made assessments generally fall into the short-answer, recognition, or recall category. For this reason, there is a need to provide teachers with guidance in constructing and evaluating questions that elicit more complex responses. Fortunately, a good deal of new technology is available for this purpose, mainly as a result of advances that have been made in the area of performance-based assessment.

Grades

The grades students have received in previously completed courses can also provide information about particular strength areas. When grades reflect both performance on teacher-made assessments and other accomplishments in less structured situations, they provide a more comprehensive picture of student abilities than can be derived from test scores alone. The advantages and disadvantages of course grades are well documented in the literature on tests and measurements, and all teachers have had experiences related to the grading process and the usefulness of grades. The value of course grades in the Total Talent Portfolio is similar to standardized and teacher-made assessments: They all provide a quick overview of general strengths that may be capitalized upon when making decisions about possible modifications in the regular curriculum, enrichment cluster placement, or access to special opportunities that are available in the continuum of special services.

For example, Mark, a sixth-grade student with consistently poor grades and a lack of interest in all subjects except science, was placed in a science enrichment cluster. This placement may seem obvious, but prior to the initiation of a SEM program, the only supplementary services made available to him related to his deficiencies. Special science opportunities were actually denied to Mark because he did not "measure up" in other curricular areas. The enrichment program was also the catalyst for curricular modifications. Decisions made in meetings of Mark's middle school teachers provided him opportunities to substitute nonfiction and science fiction reading selections for other required reading in language arts, and creative writing assignments were replaced with writing that focused on scientific interests. The social studies teacher also allowed him to replace regular assignments with reports about scientific persons and events in the countries they were studying, and the enrichment specialist arranged for Mark to assist the computer specialist by repairing equipment.

Teacher Ratings

One of the instruments that has been a long-standing part of the SEM is a series of rating scales used to identify behavioral characteristics reflecting superior learning potentials. *The Scales for Rating the Behavioral Characteristics of Superior Students* (SCRBSS—Renzulli, Smith, White, Callahan, and Hartman 1977) have been used widely for special program assessment; however, their use in the Total Talent Portfolio is not intended to label students. Rather, the purpose of the scales, like all other items in the portfolio, is to contribute information that will result in a comprehensive picture of a student's strengths. The SCRBSS consists of the following ten scales, each of which is named for the specific ability area it is designed to evaluate: Learning, Motivation, Creativity, Leadership, Art, Music, Dramatics, Communication (Precision), Communication (Expressiveness), and Planning. Each scale is composed of a series of items derived from the research literature dealing with specific manifestations of superior abilities within the ten areas.

When using the SCRBSS, it is important to analyze students' ratings on each of the selected scales separately. The ten dimensions of the instrument represent relatively different sets of behavioral characteristics, and, therefore, *no attempt should be made to add the subscores together to form a total score.* Because of variations in student populations, the range of learning options that may be available in a particular school, and the availability of other types of data, it is impossible to recommend a predetermined set of superior scores for the scales. The best norm or frame of reference for SCRBSS is the individual student.

Like all information in the Total Talent Portfolio, SCRBSS ratings should be used in conjunction with other information as part of a comprehensive system for identifying student strengths. Every effort should be made to capitalize on individual strengths revealed by the ratings by devising learning experiences that develop these capacities. For example, a student who achieves high ratings on the Motivation Scale will probably profit from experiences that provide opportunities for self-initiated pursuits and an independent study approach to learning. A student with high scores on the Leadership Characteristics Scale should be given opportunities to organize activities and to assist the teacher and his classmates in developing plans of action for carrying out projects. Thus, a careful analysis of scale ratings can assist teachers in their efforts to develop more individualized learning experiences for individual and small groups who share common strengths.

GATHERING AND RECORDING INFORMATION ABOUT STUDENT INTERESTS

The second dimension of the Total Talent Portfolio is student interests. If there is a keystone in the overall structure of the SEM, it is students' interests. *All cognitive behavior is enhanced as a function of the degree of interest that is present in an act of learning, wherever that cognitive behavior may be on the continuum from basic skill learning to higher levels of conceptualization and creative productivity.*

The relationship between interest and learning was undoubtedly recognized by the first humans on earth, but it became a topic of scientific inquiry in the nineteenth century when philosophers recognized the close relationship between interest and learning (Herbart 1965a, 1965b; James 1890). Dewey (1913) and Thorndike (1935) called attention to the important role that interests play in all forms and levels of learning. They also recognized the importance of the interestingness of tasks and objects[1] as well as the personal characteristics of the learner. Piaget (1981) argued that all intellectual functioning depends on the energizing role that is played by affective processes such as interests, and he used the term "energetic" to describe this dimension of human information processing. Numerous empirical studies have also demonstrated that individual interests have profound influences on learning (Krapp 1989; Renninger 1989, 1990; Schiefele 1989), and developmental theorists have also acknowledged the importance of interests. "It is primarily in those areas in which one takes a deep personal interest and has staked a salient aspect of one's identity that the more individualized and 'creative' components of one's personality are engaged and expressed" (Albert and Runco 1986). Gruber (1986) argued that the main force in the self-construction of the extraordinary is the person's own activities and interests. Research studies that have examined the long-range effects of participation in enrichment-based programs have indicated that the single best indicator of college majors and expressions of career choice on the parts of young adults have been intensive involvement in projects based on early interests (Hébert 1993). Studies have also shown that students who participated in a SEM program for five years or longer, and exhibited higher levels of creative productivity than their peers, displayed early, consistent and more intense interests (Reis and Renzulli 1994).

The *Interest-A-Lyzer*

Building educational experiences around student interests is probably one of the single most effective ways to guarantee that enrichment practices will be introduced into a school. In numerous evaluation studies of SEM programs, student comments about most favored practices almost always dealt with greater freedom for selecting at least a part of the work they pursued. A planned strategy for helping students examine their present and potential interests is based on an instrument called the *Interest-A-Lyzer*.

Sample items from the *Interest-A-Lyzer:*

- Imagine that your class has decided to create its own Video Production Company. Each person has been asked to sign up for his or her first, second, or third choice for one of the listed jobs such as actor/actress, director, prop person, scenery designer, etc.
- Computers and telephone technology allow us to communicate with people all over the world. Imagine that your school has installed an Internet or telephone system that will allow you to communicate with anyone in the world. With whom would you correspond?
- Imagine that you have the opportunity to travel to a new and exciting city. You can select three places to visit (art gallery, symphony orchestra, courtroom, zoo, stock market, historical sites). Select three places to visit.

This instrument has been used with students in grades 4–9, and it has also been adapted for use with younger children (McGreevy 1982), secondary students (Hébert, Sorenson, and Renzulli 1997) and adults (Renzulli 1977b). The items consist of a variety of real and hypothetical situations to which students are asked to respond in terms of the choices they would make (or have made) were they involved in these situations. The main purpose of the *Interest-A-Lyzer* is to open up communication both within the student and between students and teachers. It also is designed to facilitate discussion between groups of students with similar interests who are attempting to identify areas in which they might like to pursue advanced level studies.

Field tests of the *Interest-A-Lyzer* have shown that this instrument can serve as the basis for lively group discussions or in-depth counseling sessions with individual students. Field tests have shown, also, that the self-analysis of interests is an ongoing process that should not be rushed, and that certain steps should be taken to avoid peer pressure that may lead to group conformity or stereotyped responses. An attempt has been made to overcome some of these problems by developing a careful set of directions for the instrument; however, teachers should allow students maximum freedom of choice in deciding how and with whom they would like to discuss their responses.

Another problem that came to our attention during field tests of the *Interest-A-Lyzer* was that young children often have only limited exposure to certain topics. One item for example, deals with a hypothetical situation in which students are asked to indicate their preferences for working on various feature sections of a newspaper. Since many students involved in the field test were unfamiliar with the diversity of feature sections, a brainstorming activity was planned in which students were asked to identify and cut out many different parts of newspapers. The clippings were displayed in the form of a bulletin board collage, and group discussions were used to call attention to the nature and function of each section. This activity helped students to respond to the questionnaire item in a more meaningful way. It is recommended that persons using this instrument consider each item in relation to the age and maturity of students with whom they are working, and that activities such as the one described here be organized whenever there is any doubt as to students' familiarity with the content of the respective items. Teachers may also want to modify or add their own items to the instrument, especially when dealing with very young children or students from culturally diverse populations.

> The *Interest-A-Lyzer* is not the type of instrument that yields a numerical score; rather, it is designed in a way that allows for *pattern analysis*.

The *Interest-A-Lyzer* is not the type of instrument that yields a numerical score; rather, it is designed in a way that allows for *pattern analysis*. The major patterns or factors that might emerge from the instrument are as follows:

1. Fine Arts and Crafts
2. Scientific and Technical
3. Creative Writing and Journalism
4. Legal, Political, and Judicial
5. Mathematical
6. Managerial
7. Historical
8. Athletic and Outdoor-Related Activities
9. Performing Arts
10. Business
11. Consumer Action and Environment-Related Activities

Remember that (1) these factors represent general fields or families of interest and (2) numerous ways exist in which an individual may be interested in any particular field. Thus, identifying general patterns is only the first step in interest analysis. General interests must be refined and focused so that students eventually identify specific problems within a general field or a combination of fields. Additional preferences that we should look for in discussions based on the *Interest-A-Lyzer* are as follows:

- Activities that require precision and accuracy (e.g., editing, scientific experiments, observation, musical conducting)
- Preferences for meeting and dealing with people (e.g., teaching, organizing a clean-up-the-environment campaign)

- Activities that show preferences for helping people (e.g., serving as a volunteer at a daycare center or kindergarten classroom; becoming a doctor, dentist, or veterinarian)
- Preferences for activities that involve color, materials, artistic products that have eye appeal and any and all types of design (e.g., costumes, clothing play sets, landscape, jewelry, metal sculpture)
- Preferences for working with machines, tools, or precision equipment (e.g., photography, building scenery, refinishing furniture)
- Activities that involve creative expression through music, writing, drawing, or movement (e.g., cartooning, writing plays, composing, choreography)
- Preferences for leadership, making money, or "running things" (e.g., play director, business manager, officer in an organization)
- A concern for legal, moral, or philosophical issues (e.g., circulating a petition to start an animal shelter, campaigning for equal participation of girls in sports activities)
- Activities that show a preference for working with computational and numerical problems (e.g., using calculators, computers, Internet resources, inventing mathematical games or puzzles, working on brain teasers)
- Activities that show a preference for outdoor work (e.g., growing things, camping, studying wildlife)

Many interrelationships and areas of overlap exist in the above examples; a great deal of the art of good teaching is to sort out interests with the greatest potential for further and, we hope, more intensive follow-up. Information and conclusions that result from the analysis of student interests should be noted on the *Interest-A-Lyzer* or similar documents and then placed in the Total Talent Portfolio.

STYLE PREFERENCES
Individualization and the Role of Learning Styles

One of the major assumptions underlying the SEM is that total respect for the individual learner must also take into consideration how the child would like to pursue a particular activity, as well as the rate of learning and the child's preference for a particular topic or area of study. This is not to say that complete freedom of choice can or should exist for all educational activities. On the contrary, there are certain basic skill areas that are taught more appropriately by one approach than another. The number of such cases, however, is more limited than current practices would suggest, and additional steps toward individualization for learning style seem warranted.

Research studies are currently available that support a concept of learning that educators have known about and talked about for years. The concept is that students usually learn more easily and enjoyably when they are taught in a manner consistent with their preferred style(s) of learning. Preferences may vary within the individual according to content area and interest in certain topics; however, if some effort is not made to identify and accommodate these preferences, a valuable opportunity to improve both student achievement and enjoyment for learning will be wasted. As Torrance (1965) has pointed out, ". . . alert teachers have always been aware of the fact that when they change their method of teaching, certain children who had appeared to be slow learners or even non-learners become outstanding achievers" (p. 253).

A large number of studies have concluded that matching students with various learning environments affects cognitive outcomes and student satisfaction with different types of educational processes (Brophy and Good 1974; Hunt 1971; Kagan 1966; Smith 1976). Overall, the findings from these investigations suggest that an effort to match teaching strategies to students' learning style preferences can be beneficial. Learning style matching approaches were found not only to give students an opportunity to become involved in planning their educational experiences, but also to enhance students' attitudes toward the subject matter under consideration, and, in some cases, to increase scores on end-of-unit examinations. These positive findings, combined with the growing concern about the importance of learning styles, lead us to suggest that a comprehensive model must pay serious attention to the assessment and analysis of styles as well as abilities and interests. This concern is even more relevant today because of greater efforts to organize learning experiences that pay greater attention to multicultural differences among the school population.

Accordingly, the third dimension of the Total Talent Portfolio is a series of indicators of student preferences for learning. They consist of instructional styles preferences, learning environment preferences, thinking styles preferences, and preferences for various types of product styles and formats. These indicators provide information about what individuals are likely to do in a variety of learning situations. Whereas maximum performance indicators and interests are usually specific to a particular aptitude or content domain, preferences for performance cut across content domains, interpersonal relations, and various ways in which schools are organized for learning. Preferences represent the characteristic ways in which students adapt and organize the assets they bring to various learning situations. For example, the student mentioned earlier who was interested in dolphins may prefer to pursue this interest through a group project or aquarium internship rather than through a lecture/discussion or simulation format. Although we recognize that it is impossible to accommodate all of these preferences within the context of standard classroom operation, we believe that an understanding of the factors in general, and familiarity with at least some of their manifestations in students, will greatly enhance those opportunities when teachers can introduce enrichment experiences into the schedule. And even within more flexible school structures such as the enrichment clusters and the continuum of special services, it may not be possible to accommodate the full range of individual attributes represented in the four style preference categories of Figure 3.1. Nevertheless, using as much of this information as possible, whenever possible, should be a major goal of all learning situations. It is only through the use of these types of information that schools can break through the barrier of depersonalization that makes these institutions uninviting places and learning unimportant for so many of our students.

Instructional Styles Preferences

The third column of Figure 3.1 lists a broad range of instructional techniques that are familiar to most teachers. In some cases, these instructional techniques or styles can also be found in the literature under the title of Learning Styles. Although several definitions of instructional styles can be found in the educational and psychological literature (Smith 1976), the definition we recommend focuses on (1) the specific and identifiable techniques for organizing learning for individuals or for groups of varying size and (2) the degree of structure inherent in any instructional technique. Our definition and related descriptions of instructional style alternatives have been adopted in an attempt to remove some of the mystery that surrounds the notion of learning styles. By focusing on instructional practices familiar to most teachers, we overcome the drawback of working with a "psychological middleman" that requires teachers to second-guess how certain psychological concepts (e.g., abstract-random learner) might be used in a learning situation. While alternative conceptions have value with respect to stimulating follow-up research that could eventually affect educational practice, our concern is for a theoretically sound, yet practical, approach that has direct and immediate implications for classroom practice.

Examination of the third column of Figure 3.1 reveals that the several instructional styles listed exist on a continuum, beginning with highly structured approaches to learning and progressing to less structured learning situations. Entire books have been devoted to the study of various instructional techniques, and it is beyond the scope of this book to present a comprehensive analysis of this literature. However, for the purpose of providing a common frame of reference for the discussion that follows, we will present a brief description of the progression from structured to unstructured techniques.

Recitation and Drill

This traditional and widely used approach to instruction involves a teacher asking questions and calling on students to respond with the appropriate information. In contrast to discussion, where students are called upon to think about the relationships among facts, recitation typically entails questions that can be answered by statements of fact. The responses that students provide for these questions are evaluated in terms of the correctness of facts. Recitation is usually preceded by assignment of a topic and rote study on the parts of students.

Programmed and Computer Assisted Instruction

This type of instruction is based on students working alone on material that has been sequenced to teach a particular concept. The material characteristically consists of short statements that terminate with a question or a blank to be filled in. The statements are presented electronically or in a textbook or workbook. Other features of programmed instruction include a provision for immediate feedback, students' determination of their own rates of progress, highly organized content, and low rate of student error. A good deal of computer software has been developed in recent years, and it tends to take one of three forms: tutorial, in which the computer presents new information; drill and practice, in which the computer is used for remediation; and simulations, which involve the learner in relatively complex problem solving.

Peer Tutoring

This technique involves the use of students as teachers of other students. The tutoring situation can be highly structured (e.g., the teacher assigns a tutor to a particular child and defines the content to be covered), or it can be relatively unstructured (e.g., students select their own tutors and cover material that they determine). While peer tutoring can involve upper grade students tutoring younger children, the practice is usually limited to cooperative arrangements within a classroom.

Lecture

Lecture refers to a verbal presentation in which the teacher or another individual perceived as an expert in a particular area communicates the ideas and concepts to be acquired. The lecture method is usually marked by a lack of discussion or interchange between teacher and students; the teacher "talks to" students. The lecturer organizes and presents the material in the sequence and style he or she prefers.

Discussion

Discussion is characterized by two-way interaction between teacher and students or among students. As opposed to the straight lecture method, group discussion involves a greater degree of active participation on the parts of students. Ideally, discussion as a technique requires students to think about the relationships among facts and concepts, to weigh the significance of facts and concepts, and to engage in critical analysis of them. Varying degrees of teacher domination are found, ranging from instances in which the teacher plays a nondirective, mediating role to ones in which the teacher asks most of the questions and provides the agenda and procedures to be followed.

Teaching Games and Simulations

Teaching games are activities that are fun for students to participate in and, at the same time, involve content that the teacher wants students to learn. Teaching games do not need to be realistic to be effective. They can involve the entire class or be geared to individual students or small groups of students. Simulations, on the other hand, are constructed around real-world situations that are used to teach content and skills through role-playing. Generally, a specific concept, problem, or social process is outlined and students are asked to role-play within this context. The student-player must make decisions on the spot. These decisions, in turn, affect the next move of other players. The function of the teacher in this context is generally to coordinate the proposed actions. Realism is a primary concern in the development of simulations. Indeed, the more a simulation reflects "real-world" circumstances, the more successful the learning experience will be. The growing concern in recent years to introduce more realism into the curriculum has resulted in greater popularity for this technique and an accompanying increase in the availability of simulation materials. One company that publishes a broad variety of simulations is Interact (see the Resource Guide). Interactive computer software has also added new opportunities for problem solving through the use of simulations.

Independent Study

> Independent study can be highly structured . . . or less structured, allowing students to pursue topics or areas of their own choice.

Independent study can be based on independent choice of a topic, independence from the classroom at large, or both. Independent study can be highly structured (as in cases where a course guide, assignments, and proficiency tests are prescribed), or less structured, allowing students to pursue topics or areas of their own choice. Less structured independent study is characterized by freedom from constant supervision, although there is interaction with others when needed. Typically, the student chooses an area of study, develops his or her own approach to gathering information, and produces some kind of outcome, such as an oral presentation or a research paper. If students cover a regular course or unit through independent study, they are usually held accountable to the same evaluation criteria as students who take the course through traditional procedures. Using a combination of guided and unguided independent study is an excellent way to allow individuals or small groups to cover material at a faster pace than the pace of a classroom in general. Self-directedness, effective time management skills, and the ability to work cooperatively with others are characteristic of persons who prefer this style of learning.

Projects

The project method, which is also described in the literature as the group investigation model, shares several characteristics with unguided independent study. This method will be dealt with at greater length in our discussion of Type III Enrichment in chapter 5. The project method is characterized by individual pursuits and/or by groups of students working together. In some cases the project may fulfill the requirements of an assignment, and students frequently extend their work beyond the original requirements to create a product with real-world application. In other cases the project may originate with the students. In all cases the project results in a final product or service that can be shared with other students. Students work with varying degrees of direction from the teacher or other adults, but, typically, the major responsibility for project management rests with students.

Internships, Apprenticeships, and Mentorships

Learning experiences in this category usually involve placing individuals or small groups of students in workplace situations under the direction of adults with high degrees of expertise in a particular profession or area of study. This approach to learning dates back to ancient times and was the forerunner of formal schools. The degree of structure within these situations varies according to the amount of control exercised by adults with whom young people work; however, use of internships, apprenticeships, and mentorships has been found to be a highly successful method for students who do not adjust well to formal classroom situations and for students who have already developed high levels of interest, motivation, and achievement in a particular area.

Learning Environment Preferences

Environmental preferences have not been investigated to the same extent as preferences for instructional style; however, a small body of research and a large measure of common sense suggest that the social and physical aspects of the environment affect various kinds of school performance. Amabile (1983) reviewed research dealing with social and environmental factors that influence creativity in school-age learners. The social contexts within which people operate reflect their preferences for closeness and interaction with others. When one is given freedom of choice, the extent to which she or he pursues group affiliation is almost always an indicator of social style preferences. Some students thrive in small or large peer group situations, others prefer to work with a single partner, and still others prefer to work alone or with an adult. Environmental preferences, like the instructional preferences discussed earlier, may vary as a function of the material being taught, the nature of the task to be accomplished, and the social relationships that exist within any given group of students. Most modern classrooms provide variations in the learning environment, but these variations are usually offered to students on a one-choice-at-a-time basis. In other words, a teacher may alternate among organizational arrangements such as individual seatwork, cooperative learning groups, and sustained silent reading; however, students are usually not given a choice outside the organizational arrangement selected by the teacher. Although a predominant organizational arrangement may be necessary for purposes of efficiency and classroom control, we recommend that some attention be given to modification or "waivers" when it is clear that some students will benefit from a variation in the learning environment.

Dunn and Dunn (1978, 1992, 1993) investigated factors that affect learners in four general categories. The first categories consist of environmental influences such as sound, light, temperature, and the physical design of the learning environment. The second category consists of emotional factors such as motivation, persistence, responsibility, and the degree of structure in learning situations. The third category focuses on the sociological needs of learners and is based on preferences for learning group arrangements (e.g., self, pair, small group, large group, with or without adults). The fourth category comprises factors related to the physical environment such as perceptual modality preferences (e.g., auditory, visual, tactile, and kinesthetic), food intake, time of day, and the amount of mobility that is permitted in the learning environment. A 100-item instrument entitled the *Learning Style Inventory* (Dunn, Dunn, and Price 1975), provides factor scores and profiles for each of the four categories described earlier, and the authors have provided numerous practical suggestions for designing educational environments that take maximum advantage of individual learning styles.

A series of instruments designed by Henderson and Conrath (1991) uses a computerized assessment format to provide individual student profiles for modality preferences (visual, auditory, bodily-kinesthetic), group preferences (individual, group), expression preferences (oral, written), and preferences for linear sequential activities or random intuitive activities. A guide to implementation activities (Henderson, Hartnett, and Wair 1982) provides suggestions for accommodating different learning styles in a variety of classroom situations.

BENEFITS OF THE TOTAL TALENT PORTFOLIO

The main purpose of the portfolio is to provide as comprehensive a picture as possible about each student's *strengths* in the areas of abilities, interests, and styles. The easiest way to use the portfolio is to prepare a folder for each student, and include in the folder a copy of Figure 3.1. Circling items that reflect strength areas on this figure provides a comprehensive picture of strengths that can be capitalized on in various learning situations. Circled items should be backed-up by including in the folder examples of student work that are illustrative of the circled items. More detailed profiles can be prepared by simply pasting each of the six columns in Figure 3.1 on the left-hand side of blank pages and using the remainder of each page to record anecdotal notes, observations, and references to work samples included in the portfolio. Note that the categories listed in each column are only guides for recording certain types of information. Additional types of proficiency information may be included as a result of particular learning opportunities that may exist within certain schools or classrooms, or because of certain behavioral strengths displayed by students that fall outside of the categories and items specified in the columns of Figure 3.1. This figure, or any form derived from it, is designed to call attention to documented student characteristics, to provide an overview of all information in the portfolio, and to serve as the basis for discussions geared toward making programming decisions. Student work, selected by teachers and students, should be placed in the portfolio, and examples of particular strengths within a work sample should be marked and annotated with attached notes or marginal comments by the teacher and student.

Portfolios should be reviewed by teams of teachers at least four times a year, and portfolios should also serve as focal points for meetings with parents. The cover sheet of the portfolio should include summary notations about particular accomplishments within each of the school structures upon which the SEM is targeted. The portfolio should travel with a students from year to year and should serve as the basis for briefing subsequent year teachers about individual student strengths and accomplishments.

In order for the Total Talent Portfolio to achieve maximum effectiveness, it is necessary to avoid three pitfalls that have characterized other systems for gathering and recording information about student performance. These pitfalls are:

1. The escalation of needless paperwork.
2. The tendency to look at discrete items in student records.
3. The focus on deficiencies that characterizes so much of school record keeping.

Any process for recording information about students can easily turn into another "paperwork nightmare" for teachers. When this happens, the original intent of vehicles such as the portfolio becomes lost in yet another round of record keeping overkill and resistance on the part of teachers to use the information in positive ways. We can avoid this pitfall by not converting the portfolio into another set of boxes, checklists, numerical ratings, or percentile scales. Even when the portfolio does include information derived from instruments that yield psychometric scores, we should not take this information too seriously. Most psychometric reporting is based on normative scales that are designed to compare groups of students within categories (e.g., age, grade, gender, socioeconomic level). *The Total Talent Portfolio is intended to look at individual students in a noncomparative way.* We do not want to know how a student stacks up against other students. Rather, we want to know how particular abilities, interests, and styles stack up within the student him or herself, and we want to know this in a very general way. "Liza's best academic area is math" is a statement that allows us to make educational decisions that capitalize on a strength. We do not need complex, comparative statistics to make these decisions for us.

The second pitfall, focusing on discrete items, can best be avoided by noting the interactions among several items in the portfolio that result in a comprehensive picture of student performance and potential. "Liza's best academic area is math, she seems to like science and computers best, she likes to work in small groups, and she likes to draw," is a rich source of information that extends far beyond any individual element of the statement. A teacher may not be able to accommodate all of these strengths, interests, and preferences all of the time, or even most of the time. But if they are not accommodated at least part of the time, an exceptional opportunity is lost to capitalize on those things that make Liza a unique person and a unique learner. The payoff that results when we make adjustments that accommodate each student's uniqueness is not only in terms of better performance but also in higher motivation and greater enjoyment of learning.

A focus on deficiencies is the most serious pitfall of student record keeping systems. The Total Talent Portfolio differs from traditional permanent record folders in both the use and the psychology of the portfolio as well as the information contained in it. Most permanent records are used for class placement in schools where ability grouping is practiced and for placement in skill level groups within-classrooms. They also are notorious for calling attention to learning deficiencies and to personal, social, or family problems. In most instances when a permanent record folder is pulled during the school year, it is almost always in connection with a present or impending problem. *We do not want this psychology of deficit and rehabilitation to be cast over the Total Talent Portfolio; therefore, we recommend that it not become a part of the traditional permanent record folder.* Nor do we recommend that it become a replacement for existing records. Our focus on positive attributes should remain unmixed from information about problems and deficits because the power of negative information about students always seems to predominate, and, therefore, circumscribe the positive focus that the portfolio is designed to accentuate. *A ground rule when reviewing and discussing portfolios is, therefore, that their only use should be for making decisions about specific and positive actions that will further a student's strength area(s).*

No one is naive enough to believe that in the foreseeable future schools will magically convert from a curricular decision-making process that is externally driven and group-oriented to one that is tailored to the broad range of characteristics documented in the Total Talent Portfolio. The complexity of the educational system, and the many "masters" teachers are required to serve, make it difficult to accommodate the broad array of abilities, interests, and styles that characterize individual learners. But the widespread and well-documented dissatisfaction with schools in general suggests that the opportunity is ripe for experimentation and the small steps toward organizing learning environments that are more responsive to the uniquenesses of individual students. Systemic educational reform should begin in the classroom, where learners, teachers, and curriculum interact, rather than in yet another set of regulations or list of standards and outcomes. The Total Talent Portfolio is a tool that can help focus attention on the interactions that represent the act of learning.

ENDNOTE

1. The interestingness of a task or object is viewed as a property of the task or object rather than a property of the person. Interestingness does, however, have the power to promote personal interests in the learner.

> The Total Talent Portfolio is a tool that can help focus attention on the interactions that represent the act of learning.

Curriculum Modification and Differentiation

▶ ▶ ▶ ▶ ▶ ▶ ▶ ▶ ▶ ▶

A major service delivery component of the Schoolwide Enrichment Model consists of a series of procedures and recommendations for curriculum modification and differentiation so that the abilities and interests of all students can be served. The category discussed in this chapter consists of a step-by-step procedure for modifying existing curriculum. This procedure, entitled Curriculum Compacting, can be used to help ensure a better match between the achievement levels of individual learners and the curriculum. It can be used with traditional curriculum in any subject area and grade level, and it can also be used to make modifications in teacher-developed curricular activities.

> Curriculum Compacting can be used to help ensure a better match between the achievement levels of individual learners and the curriculum.

RATIONALE FOR CURRICULUM COMPACTING

Before initiating the curriculum compacting process, it is important to be able to explain and provide a rationale for using this instructional practice. Teachers and administrators who need supporting information about the rationale for compacting can use the following reasons to demonstrate why this procedure should be implemented in most classrooms.

1. Students already know much of their texts' content before learning it.
2. Textbooks have been "dumbed down."
3. The quality of textbooks has failed to improve significantly.
4. The needs of high-ability students and students with special interests are not often met in classrooms.
5. Curricular modification frees time for more challenging learning experiences.

In this chapter, we will present an overview of curriculum compacting, describe the compacting process, and briefly highlight other forms of within-classroom differentiation of the curriculum. A complete rationale for curriculum modification can be found in Reis, Burns, and Renzulli (1992).

AN OVERVIEW OF CURRICULUM COMPACTING

One solution to the lack of challenge in textbooks and curriculum is to write new textbooks. However, the writing, publishing, and adoption of new textbooks takes many years. Until such time as new (and hopefully improved) textbooks are available, curriculum compacting can be used to modify existing curriculum to create a better match between the abilities of students and their learning experiences.

> Curriculum compacting is a system designed to adapt the regular curriculum to meet the needs of students by either eliminating work that has been previously mastered or streamlining work that can be mastered at a pace commensurate with the student's motivation and ability.

Curriculum compacting is a system designed to adapt the regular curriculum to meet the needs of students by either eliminating work that has been previously mastered or streamlining work that can be mastered at a pace commensurate with the student's motivation and ability. In addition to creating a more challenging learning environment, compacting helps teachers guarantee proficiency in the basic curriculum and provide time for more appropriate enrichment or acceleration activities. The time gained by compacting is referred to as *compacted time*.

Many good classroom teachers already compact the curriculum as part of their daily tasks. Following is an example of compacting in its simplest form.

A teacher might have one student who requires one or more review worksheets to understand a particular skill. Another student who has mastered the skill would receive more challenging work while the other student completes his or her review worksheets. The first student is allowed to master the skill at his or her own pace while the second student does not spend more time reviewing a skill he or she has already mastered.

The Compacting Process

The compacting process consists of three phases:

1. Defining goals and outcomes.
2. Identifying candidates for compacting.
3. Providing acceleration and enrichment options.

Each of the three phases of curriculum compacting is discussed briefly in the next section.

Phase I: Defining Goals and Outcomes

The goals and outcomes of a given unit or segment of instruction need to be specified and defined at the outset. This information is readily available in most subjects because specific goals and outcomes usually can be found in teachers' manuals, curriculum guides, scope-and-sequence charts, and some of the curricular frameworks that have emerged in connection with the growing emphasis on content standards.

Teachers should examine these objectives to determine which represent the acquisition of new content or thinking skills as opposed to reviews or practice of material that has previously been taught. The scope and sequence charts prepared by publishers or a simple comparison of the table of contents of a basal series provides a quick overview of new versus repeated material.

A major goal of this phase of the compacting process is to help teachers make individual programming decisions; a larger professional development goal is to help teachers be better analysts of the material they are teaching and better consumers of textbooks and prescribed curricular material.

Phase II: Identifying Candidates for Compacting

The second phase of curriculum compacting is to identify students who have already mastered the objectives or outcomes of a unit or segment of instruction that is about to be taught. The first step of this phase consists of estimating which students have the potential to master new material at a faster-than-normal pace. Knowing one's students is, of course, the best way to begin the assessment process. Scores on previous tests, completed assignments, and classroom participation are the best ways of identifying highly likely candidates for compacting. Standardized achievement tests can serve as a good general screen for this step because they allow teachers to list the names of all students who are scoring one or more years above grade level in particular subject areas.

Step two in the identification of candidates is to find or develop appropriate tests or assessment techniques that can be used to evaluate student performance on specific learning outcomes or content standards. Unit pretests can be administered for this purpose. An analysis of pretest results enables the teacher to document the student's proficiency in specific skills, and to select instructional activities or practice material necessary to bring the student up to a high level on any skill that may need some additional reinforcement.

The process is modified slightly for compacting content areas that are not as easily assessed as basic skills and for students who have not mastered the material but are judged to be candidates for more rapid coverage. First, students should have a thorough understanding of the goals and procedures of compacting, including the nature of the replacement process. A given segment of material should be discussed with the student (e.g., a unit that includes a series of chapters in a social studies text), and the procedures for verifying mastery at a high level should be specified. These procedures might consist of answering questions based on the chapters, writing an essay, or taking the standard end-of-unit test. The amount of time for completion of the unit should be specified, and procedures such as periodic progress reports or log entries for teacher review should be selected. And, of course, an examination of potential acceleration and/or enrichment replacement activities should be a part of this discussion.

An alternative is to assess or pretest all students in a class when a new unit or topic is introduced. Although this may seem like more work for the teacher, it provides the opportunity for all students to demonstrate their strengths or previous mastery in a given area. Using a matrix of learning objectives, teachers can fill in test results and establish small, flexible, and temporary groups for skill instruction and replacement activities.

Phase III: Providing Acceleration and Enrichment Options

The final phase of the compacting process can be one of the most exciting aspects of teaching because it is based on cooperative decision making and creativity on the parts of both teachers and students. Efforts can be made to gather enrichment materials from classroom teachers, librarians, media specialists, and content area or gifted education specialists. These materials may include self-directed learning activities, instructional materials that focus on particular thinking skills, and a variety of individual and group project-oriented activities that are designed to promote hands-on research and investigative skills.

Compacting saves time. This time provides opportunities for stimulating learning experiences that include:

- Small group, special topic seminars that might be directed by students or community resource persons
- Community-based apprenticeships or opportunities to work with a mentor
- Peer tutoring situations
- Involvement in community service activities
- Opportunities to rotate through a series of self-selected mini-courses

Decisions about which replacement activities to use are always guided by factors such as time, space, and the availability of resource persons and materials. Although practical concerns must be considered, the ultimate criteria for replacement activities should be the degree to which they increase academic challenge and the extent to which they meet individual needs. Great care should be taken to select activities and experiences that represent individual strengths and interests rather than the assignment of more-of-the-same worksheets or randomly selected kits, games, and puzzles.

This aspect of the compacting process should also be viewed as a creative opportunity for an entire faculty to work cooperatively to organize and institute a broad array of enrichment experiences. A favorite mini-course that a faculty member has always wanted to teach, or serving as a mentor to one or two students who are extremely invested in a teacher's beloved topic are just two examples of the ways that replacement activities can add excitement to the teachers' part in this process as well as the obvious benefits for students.

We also have observed another interesting occurrence that has resulted from the availability of curriculum compacting. When some previously bright but underachieving students realized that they could both economize on regularly assigned material and earn time to pursue self-selected interests, their motivation to complete regular assignments increased. As one student put it, "Everyone understands a good deal!"

The best way to get an overview of the curriculum compacting process is to examine an actual example of how the management form that guides this process is used. An example of this form, entitled The Compactor, is presented in Figure 4.1. The form is both an organizational and record-keeping tool. Teachers should fill out one form per student, or one form for a group of students with similar curricular strengths. Completed Compactors should be kept in students' academic files, and updated on a regular basis. The form can also be used for small groups of students who are working at approximately the same level (e.g., a reading or math group). The Compactor is divided into three sections:

- The first column should include information on learning objectives and student strengths in those areas. Teachers should list the objectives for a particular unit of study, followed by data on students' proficiency in those objectives, including test scores, behavioral profiles, and past academic records.

- In the second column, teachers should detail the pretest vehicles they select, along with test results. The pretest instruments can be formal measures, such as pencil and paper tests, or informal measures, such as performance assessments based on observations of class participation and written assignments. Specificity is extremely important. Recording an overall score of 85 percent on ten objectives, for example, sheds little light on what portion of the material can be compacted, since students might show limited mastery of some objectives and high levels of mastery on others.

- The third column is used to record information about acceleration or enrichment options. In determining these options, teachers must be fully aware of students' individual interests and learning styles. We have used two instruments to help us make decisions about replacement activities that place major emphasis on student preferences: The *Interest-A-Lyzer* and the *Learning Styles Inventory* (Renzulli and Smith 1978) provide profiles of general categories of student interests, and the types of learning activities that students would like to use in pursuing these interests.

Eileen: A Sample Compactor Form

Eileen is a fifth grader in a self-contained heterogeneous classroom. Her school, which is very small, is located in a lower socioeconomic urban school district. While Eileen's reading and language scores range between two and

Individual Educational Programming Guide

THE COMPACTOR

Prepared by Joseph S. Renzulli and Linda M. Smith

NAME _____ AGE _____ TEACHER(S) _____

SCHOOL _____ GRADE _____ PARENT(S) _____

Individual Conference Dates and Persons Participating in Planning of IEP

_____ _____ _____

Curriculum areas to be considered for compacting. Provide a brief description of basic material to be covered during this marking period and the assessment information or evidence that suggests the need for compacting.	*Procedures for compacting basic material.* Describe activities that will be used to guarantee proficiency in basic curricular areas.	*Acceleration and/or enrichment activities.* Describe activities that will be used to provide advanced level learning experiences in each area of the regular curriculum.
NAME IT.	**PROVE IT.**	**CHANGE IT.**
What material needs to be covered?	Exactly what material is to be excluded?	What enrichment and/or acceleration activities will be included?
What evidence shows a need for compacting?	How will you prove mastery?	• Independent Study • Acceleration • Mini-Courses • Honors Courses • College Courses • Mentorships
		Small group investigations Work study

☐ Check here if additional information is recorded on the reverse side.

Figure 4.1

five years above grade level, most of her 29 classmates are reading one to two years below grade level. This presented Eileen's teacher with a common problem: What was the best way to instruct Eileen? He agreed to compact her curriculum. Taking the easiest approach possible, he administered all of the appropriate unit tests for the grade level in the Basal Language Arts program, and excused Eileen from completing the activities and worksheets in the units where she showed proficiency (80 percent and above). When Eileen missed one or two questions, the teacher checked for trends in those items and provided instruction and practice materials to ensure concept mastery.

Eileen usually participated in language arts lessons one or two days a week. The balance of the time she spent with alternative projects, some of which she selected. This strategy spared Eileen up to six or eight hours a week with language arts skills that were simply beneath her level. She joined the class instruction only when her pretests indicated she had not fully acquired the skills or to take part in a discussion that her teacher thought she would enjoy. In the time saved through compacting, Eileen engaged in a number of enrichment activities. First, she spent as many as five hours a week in a resource room for high ability students. This time was usually scheduled during her language arts class, benefiting both Eileen and her teacher, since he did not have to search for all of the enrichment options himself. The best part of the process for Eileen was she did not have to make up regular classroom assignments because she was not missing essential work.

Eileen also visited a regional science center with other students who had expressed a high interest in and aptitude for science. Science was a second strength area for Eileen, and based on the results of her *Interest-A-Lyzer*, famous women was a special interest. Working closely with her teacher, Eileen choose seven biographies of noted women, most of whom had made contributions in scientific areas. All of the books were extremely challenging and locally available. Three were on an adult level, but Eileen had no trouble reading them. Eileen's Compactor, which covered an entire semester, was updated in January. Her teacher remarked that compacting her curriculum had actually saved him time—time he would have spent correcting papers needlessly assigned! The value of compacting for Eileen also convinced him that he should continue the process. The Compactor was also used as a vehicle for explaining to Eileen's parents how specific modifications were being made to accommodate her advanced language arts achievement level and her interest in science. A copy of the Compactor was also passed on to Eileen's sixth grade teacher, and a conference between the fifth and sixth grade teachers and the resource teacher helped ensure continuity in dealing with Eileen's special needs.

THE MULTIPLE MENU MODEL: A GUIDE TO IN-DEPTH LEARNING AND TEACHING

The second category of procedures covered in this chapter consists of three curriculum models that can be used to create instructional units. They differ from traditional approaches because they place greater emphasis on (1) content and process, (2) students as firsthand inquirers, and (3) the interconnectedness of knowledge. The Multiple Menu Model (Renzulli 1988) is a guide that teachers and curriculum writers can use to develop in-depth curriculum units for classroom use. It is based on the work of theorists in curriculum and instruction, including Ausubel (1968), Bandura (1977), Bloom (1954), Bruner (1960, 1966), Gagné and Briggs (1979), Kaplan (1986), Passow (1982), Phenix (1964), and Ward (1961). It consists of a series of six interrelated components (see Figure 4.2), called menus because each contains a range of options from which curriculum developers can choose as they create units of study.

Multiple Menu Model for Developing Differentiated Curriculum

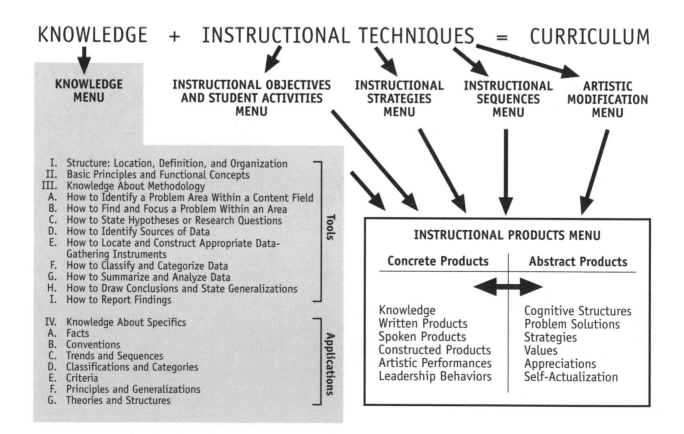

Figure 4.2

(Renzulli 1988)

The six components include: the Knowledge Menu, the Instructional Objectives and Student Activities Menu, the Instructional Strategies Menu, the Instructional Sequences Menu, the Artistic Modification Menu, and the Instructional Products Menu, which is composed of two interrelated menus, Concrete Products and Abstract Products Menu. The first menu, the Knowledge Menu, is the most elaborate and concerns the field of selected study (e.g., mythology, astronomy, choreography, geometry). The second through the fifth menus deal with pedagogy or instructional techniques. The last menu, Instructional Products, is related to the types of products that may result from student interactions with knowledge about a domain or interdisciplinary concepts and how that knowledge is constructed by firsthand inquirers. Although it was originally developed as a way of differentiating curriculum for high ability students, the guide can easily be used by teachers who want to encourage firsthand inquiry and creativity among all students.

The Knowledge Menu

This menu is underpinned by two particularly important assumptions: (1) the belief that it is futile, if not impossible, to teach everything important in a discipline, and (2) the necessity of inquiry.

Rather than focusing on the conclusions of a discipline, the Multiple Menu Model focuses on inquiry itself, asking curriculum developers to select the most important concepts to teach learners. Accordingly, the first menu, The Knowledge Menu, requires curriculum developers to examine a discipline from four perspectives: its purpose and placement within the larger context of knowledge, its underlying concepts and principles, its most representative topics and contributions to the universe of knowledge and wisdom, and its methodology. This first of these perspectives follows.

Locating the Discipline

Teachers using curriculum units based on the Multiple Menu Model must first locate for students the targeted discipline in the larger domain of knowledge (e.g., the novel is a field within the domain of literature). Teachers and students construct a knowledge tree to illustrate how the selected area of knowledge fits within the larger domain. Next, they examine the characteristics of the discipline and subdisciplines to learn the reasons why people study a particular area of knowledge, and what they hope to contribute to human understanding. This first dimension of the Knowledge Menu helps students examine, for example, What is sociology? What do sociologists study and why? How is sociology similar to and different from other disciplines, (e.g., psychology and anthropology)? What, then, is social psychology or social anthropology, and how does each fit into the larger picture and purpose of the social sciences? These questions about the structure of disciplines help students understand not only where the discipline is located but also the discipline's connectedness with other disciplines.

Selecting Concepts and Ideas

Subsequently, the teacher identifies and selects basic principles and concepts to teach—the second perspective of the knowledge menu. Representative concepts and ideas consist of themes, patterns, main features, sequences or organizing principles, and structures that define an area of study. With respect to science, for example, organizing principles and structures include, not exclusively: change, stability, systems, interactions, energy, chemical composition, volume, light, and color. With respect to the novel, representative elements that cut across all literary contributions include plot, setting, character, and theme. Large concepts exist within each of these elements, as well. For example, the buffoon and tragic hero are archetypal characters who appear in literary contributions throughout time. It is precisely because these concepts and ideas exist across time that they can be used as the bases for interdisciplinary units. Accordingly, curriculum developers must select representative concepts that will most clearly define the discipline being taught.

Selecting Representative Topics

Third, teachers select curricular topics to illustrate the basic principles and representative concepts. In some ways, the selection process is similar to the process that teachers have used in the past; namely, the material must take into consideration the age, maturity, previous study, and experiential background of the students. Beyond age, grade, maturity level, and experience, however, the Multiple Menu Model selection process is different. Unlike traditional instruction, which asks teachers to cover an entire text by the end of the year or semester, the Multiple Menu Model asks teachers to winnow down all the possible pieces to those few that truly represent the field's principles and concepts. A three-phase approach to the selection of content is recommended. This approach takes into consideration the interaction between intensive coverage and extensive coverage as well as group learning and individual learning situations. The following example points out how the procedure has been used in a literature course.

PHASE I (INTENSIVE/GROUP). In Phase I a representative concept in literature, such as the genera of tragic heroes, was dealt with through intensive examination of three prototypical examples (e.g., *The Merchant of Venice, Joan of Arc*, and *The Autobiography of Malcolm X*). Selections of more than a single exemplar of the concept allow for both in-depth analysis and opportunities to compare and contrast authors' styles; historical perspectives; ethnic, gender, and cultural differences; and a host of other comparative factors that single selections would prohibit. Preteaching/learning analysis dealt with an overview of the concept and why it was being studied. Since one of the main purposes is to learn *how* to study tragic heroes, *who* should be studied (i.e., which tragic hero) is less important, as long as the hero is representative of the genera. An emphasis on how rather than who also legitimizes a role for students. The payoff as far as transfer is concerned is to follow the in-depth coverage with a postlearning analysis that focuses on factors that define the representative concept of tragic heroes (e.g., characteristic themes, patterns, etc.). The goal of the postlearning analysis is to help consolidate cognitive structures[1] and patterns of analysis developed through in-depth study of a small number of literary selections so that they are readily available for use in future situations.

PHASE II (EXTENSIVE/GROUP). Phase II consists of the perusal of large numbers of literary contributions dealing with tragic heroes to which similar cognitive structures and patterns of analysis can be applied. In our sample situation, students working in small interest groups compiled categorical lists and summaries of tragic heroes within their respective areas of special interest. For example, groups focused on tragic heroes in sports, politics, science, civil rights, religion, the women's movement, arts and entertainment, or other area(s) in which special interests were expressed. Identifying tragic heroes within categories and preparing brief summaries of them developed research and writing skills as well as communication skills for group discussions and oral presentations that were a part of the planned activities. A key feature of this phase of the work was that students were not expected to read entire books about the persons on their lists. Summaries of nonfictional persons were prepared from descriptions found in textbooks or encyclopedias, and fictional tragic heroes were summarized from material found in *Master Plots* or *Cliffs Notes*. Although perusal of large numbers is recommended, coverage should be purposefully superficial, *but geared toward stimulating follow-up on the parts of interested individuals or small groups.*

PHASE III (INTENSIVE/INDIVIDUAL OR /SMALL GROUP). Phase III consists of in-depth follow-up of selected readings based on the personal preferences of students that emerge from Phase II. Phase III in our example was pursued in a variety of ways. Activities included formal study modeled after the procedures used in the Great Books or Junior Great Books study groups, informal discussions about selected tragic heroes by interested groups of students, or simply the more sophisticated appreciation that could now be derived from reading for pleasure or viewing a play or film based on the life or exploits of a tragic heroine. Some of this follow-up took place immediately, and in other cases it was deferred until a similar process was followed with other genera. And, of course, it can take place on a personal level at any time in the future. Once students learned how to analyze particular genera, and after they explored categorical representatives of a genus, they were empowered to apply these skills to future assignments or reading for pleasure.

The three-phase process described here requires that teachers understand the pivotal ideas, representative topics, unifying themes, and internal structures that define a field of knowledge or that horizontally cut across a number of disciplines. This is not an easy task for teachers who traditionally have relied on textbooks for curricular decision making. There are, however,

> The three-phase process . . . requires that teachers understand the pivotal ideas, representative topics, unifying themes, and internal structures that define a field of knowledge . . .

excellent resources available to assist in this process. Books such as the *Dictionary of the History of Ideas* (Wiener 1973) contain essays that cover every major discipline, but the emphasis of the essays is on interdisciplinary, cross-cultural relations. The essays are cross-referenced to direct the reader to other articles in which the same or similar ideas occur in other domains. Similar resources for teachers can be found in books such as the *Syntopicon* (Adler and Hutchins 1952), which is an organizational structure for the great ideas of the Western world.

New curricular materials are also available to assist teachers in the development of in-depth learning units. The recent concern about excellence for all students has prompted the development of new content area standards, including mathematics, science, and social studies standards. The development of these standards has, in turn, prompted the assessment of curricular materials. Some of these curriculum review initiatives are using criteria aligned with the central concepts of the Multiple Menu Model. Unlike traditional review criteria that focused on readability levels and the sheer amount of factual material included within the text, the criteria for this new review were concerned, for example, with the significance of the scientific concepts covered and the amount of practice provided in the processes of scientific inquiry.

A Final Consideration: Appeal to the Imagination

Within the context of in-depth teaching and learning, there is still one additional consideration that should be addressed. Phenix (1964) termed this concept the appeal to the imagination, and he argues very persuasively for the selection of topics that will lift students to new planes of experience and meaning. First, he points out that the means for stimulating the imagination differ according to the individual, his or her level of maturity, and the cultural context in which the individual is located. Second, the teacher must model the imaginative qualities of mind we are trying to develop in students and be able to enter sympathetically into the lives of students. Finally, imaginative teaching requires faith in the possibility of awakening imagination in any and every student, regardless of the kinds of constraints that may be placed on the learning process.

There are, undoubtedly, different perspectives about how to select content that will appeal to the imagination. Topics with such a focus could easily fall prey to material that deals with seductive details or esoteric and sensational topics. Seductive details are not inherently inappropriate as topics for in-depth study. Indeed, they often serve the important function of stimulating initial interests and creating what Whitehead (1929) called the romance stage with a topic or field of study. But if seductive details and sensational topics become ends rather than means for promoting advanced understanding, then we have traded appeal to the imagination for romanticism and showmanship.

How, then, should we go about selecting curriculum material that appeals to the imagination but that is not based purely on sensationalism? The answer rests, in part, on selecting topics that represent powerful and controversial manifestations of basic ideas and concepts. Thus, for example, the concepts of loyalty versus betrayal might be examined and compared from political, literary, military, or family perspectives, but always in ways that bring intensity, debate, and personal involvement to the concepts. An adversarial approach to ideas and concepts (e.g., loyalty versus betrayal) also guarantees that the essential element of *confrontations with knowledge* will be present in selected curricular topics. In a certain sense, it would be feasible to write the history of creative productivity as a chronicle of men and women who confronted existing ideas and concepts in an adversarial fashion, and who used existing information only as counterpoints to what eventually became their own unique contributions to the growth of knowledge. It was these confrontations that sparked their imaginations, and it is for this reason that an appeal to the imagination should be a major curricular focus for the coverage of in-depth topics.

> Combining content and process leads to a goal that is larger than the sum of the respective parts.

Examining the Methodology of the Discipline

Throughout a unit of study, teachers explain, illustrate, and involve students in the process of research as defined by the methodology dimension of the Knowledge Menu (e.g., identify a problem area in the study of tragic heroes, focus the problem, state a hypothesis, locate resources, classify and organize data, summarize data, draw conclusions, report findings). The cluster of diverse procedures that surround the acquisition of knowledge—that dimension of learning commonly referred to as process or thinking skills—should themselves be viewed as a form of content. It is these more enduring skills that form the cognitive structures and problem-solving strategies that have the greatest transfer value. When we view process as content, we avoid the artificial dichotomy and the endless arguments about whether content or process should be the primary goal of learning. Combining content and process leads to a goal that is larger than the sum of the respective parts. Simply stated, this goal is the acquisition of a scheme for acquiring, managing, and producing information in an organized and systematic fashion.

Armed with the tools learned in the knowledge menu and a more mature understanding of the methodology of the field, students are no longer passive recipients of information and are able to begin the process of generating knowledge within the field. With respect to the tragic heroes unit that has been developed, students may want to interview contemporary authors regarding which characteristics they believe define the tragic heroes of today.

The Instructional Techniques Menus

The second, third, fourth, and fifth menus from the model concern pedagogy or instruction. Specifically, these menus provide curriculum developers with a range of options related to how they will present learning activities to students based on the principles and concepts they have selected. The

Instructional Objectives and Student Activities Menu focuses on the thinking and feeling processes (e.g., application, analysis, synthesis) that are used by learners as they construct knowledge about a discipline. It is important that curriculum writers design learning activities that incorporate a balanced variety of these thinking and feeling processes. The balance provides learners with practice in the spectrum of encoding and recoding activities associated with learning new information, concepts, and principles. The next menu, the Instructional Strategies Menu, provides a range of specific teaching methods (e.g., discussion, dramatization, independent study) that teachers can use to present new material. A variety of carefully selected instructional strategies from this menu provides students with multiple ways to be engaged with knowledge and to employ the full range of their intellectual abilities and learning styles. Teachers and curriculum writers are provided with a relatively fixed order of events for teaching information through the next component, The Instructional Sequences Menu. For example, teachers open most lessons by gaining the attention of their students, linking the present lesson with previously covered material, and pointing out other applications for what has been introduced. Accordingly, the Instructional Sequences Menu is a rubric that can accommodate any instructional or pedagogical strategy. Finally, the Artistic Modification Menu invites teachers to personalize lessons by sharing an anecdote, observation, hobby, or personal belief about an event, topic, or concept. As such, it can be used with any instructional strategy and during any point in the instructional sequence. Personalizing lessons in this fashion generates interest and excitement among students.

The Instructional Products Menu

The Instructional Products Menu is concerned with the outcomes of learning experiences presented by the teacher through the curricular material and pedagogy; in this case, however, outcomes are viewed in much more complex learning behaviors than the lists of basic skills typically found in the literature on standards and outcomes. Two kinds of outcomes emerge: concrete products and abstract products. The concrete products are physical constructions that result from learner interaction with the knowledge, principles, and concepts. These physical constructions include, for example, speeches, essays, dramatizations, and experiments. Abstract products include behaviors (such as leadership activities related to an issue), increased self-confidence, and the acquisition of new methodologies (such as interviewing skills). Note that the two kinds of products are mutually reinforcing. As students produce new kinds of concrete products, they will also demonstrate new abstract products, such as methodological skills and self-assurance. As self-confidence and leadership opportunities increase, it is likely that additional physical products will emerge as well.

Textbook Analysis and Surgical Removal of Unchallenging and Redundant Content

Does a place exist within the Multiple Menu Model and in-depth teaching for the use of traditional textbooks? The answer to this question is an emphatic yes, provided textbooks are closely examined by teachers prior to their use with curricular units. This scrutiny might best be called "textbook analysis and surgical removal." The procedures for carrying out the textbook analysis and surgical removal are based on the argument that less is better when it comes to content selection, but it is necessary to make wise decisions when determining which material will be covered in greater depth. A prerequisite is that teacher groups, working in collaboration with curriculum specialists, must have a solid understanding of (1) the goals and content of a particular unit of study and (2) the reasons why they are covering given segments of material.

The first step in the process might best be described as "textbook triage." Each unit of instruction is examined to determine (1) which material is needless repetition of previously covered skills and concepts, (2) which material is necessary for review, and (3) which material is important enough to cover in either a survey or an in-depth manner. These decisions obviously require an understanding of the goals and content of the curricular materials being used and some know-how about the use of criteria for making curricular modification decisions. There is a growing body of literature dealing with this process (see, for example, Conn 1988; Osborne, Jones, and Stein 1985) that parallels the skills necessary for carrying out effective curriculum compacting. It is recommended that the following five factors be considered by teachers when they make decisions about the suitability of textbooks as resources for units of study constructed around the Multiple Menu Model.

1. Content. Examine the table of contents.
   - Is the content accurate?
   - Is it representative of themes, concepts, principles, and/or structures in the discipline?
   - Are sufficient examples/selections provided to explain and elaborate upon the concept under consideration?
   - Does the content highlight the interrelationships among other curricular areas?

2. Organization. Examine the chapters and table of contents.
   - Do the chapters and units address a single concept or theme?
   - Are ideas integrated across lessons and chapters?
   - Is there a forward-moving framework controlling the presentation of content (e.g., simple listing, thematic framework, temporal sequence, problem/solution format)?
   - Is the framework appropriate for the discipline?

3. Questions. Review the chapter and unit questions.
   • Are the questions related to the chapter and unit content?
   • Are they balanced with respect to the levels of thinking and feeling processes (e.g., knowledge, comprehension, application, analysis, synthesis, evaluation)?

4. Resources. Examine the reading or resource suggestions in both the teacher and student editions.
   • Are the resources correlated with the chapter content?
   • Are they sufficient in number and diverse in nature for the perusal of related works?
   • Do they offer sufficient connections to other disciplines?
   • Do they encourage or facilitate independent investigations?

5. Adaptability.
   Students:
   • Does the content consider the age, maturity level, experiential background, and knowledge base of the student?
   • Can the content be adapted to a range of student ability levels?
   • Does the content provide for varied student interests and learning preferences?
   • Does the content appeal to the students' imagination?
   • Can the material be used by groups and individuals?
   Teachers:
   • Does the content encourage teacher initiative and adaptation?
   • Does the content appeal to the teacher's imagination?

> . . . this model enables learners to become firsthand inquirers and creators of information, a far more intensive, productive engagement in the school setting than what students experience as consumers of information.

What makes the Multiple Menu Model unique is its deep connections with the how-to of disciplines. Other models provide teachers with the skills to enrich curriculum by increasing the amount of material related to a subject, the rate at which it is covered, or by varying the products that emerge from learner interaction with the material in a discipline. *The Multiple Menu Model takes the teacher and student to the very heart of a discipline to examine its location in the domain of information and to understand the methodology employed by those who produce knowledge in the field.* Accordingly, this model enables learners to become firsthand inquirers and creators of information, a far more intensive, productive engagement in the school setting than what students experience as consumers of information.

What teachers teach is at the very heart of professional competency. The textbook analysis and surgical removal process offers teachers an opportunity to come together as a group of professionals around specific tasks within and across grade levels and subject areas. Effective group work using this process will undoubtedly contribute to individual teacher growth as far as content mastery is concerned, and this approach has the added benefit of promoting the types of consultation and sharing of knowledge and experience that characterize other professions. In order for this process to occur, however, school leaders need to make available the time and resources for this essential school improvement activity, and teachers must be willing to devote some of their nonteaching professional time to the process. We also believe that creative contributions to curricular modification should be included in the professional reward structure that is a part of the SEM staff development model presented in Appendix C.

INTERDISCIPLINARY MODELS
Kaplan's Grid

Kaplan (1986) developed a model to guide the construction of curricular units called The Grid (see Figure 4.3). Although it was written as a model to differentiate instruction for high ability students, it can be used as a model to develop talent among all children. Specifically, The Grid helps curriculum writers make decisions about an overarching theme, the essential elements of curriculum, and the format for the creation of learning experiences.

Kaplan suggests that curriculum writers begin developing units by identi-

Curriculum Development Model—The Grid

Content	Processes	Product	Affective
The subject matter selected for the curriculum reflects knowledge that is mandatory for all students to learn, knowledge that is commensurate with the level of conceptualization and level of knowledge particular to the needs and interests of the students.	The skills and competencies students are expected to master include, but are not limited to, fundamental, rudimentary, or basic skills; productive (logic, creative problem-solving, and critical-thinking) skills; research skills or the skills of accessing, interpreting, summarizing, and reporting information; and personalized skills.	The communication or transmission of the knowledge and skills students have assimilated requires experiences (1) in a variety of media, including the latest forms of technology and (2) with materials for appropriate and accurate production of the developed work.	The attitudes, appreciation, and values introduced to students are an integral feature of, rather than an adjunct to, the curriculum. An understanding of the student as an individual and contributor, who values learning and productivity, and awareness of the roles and responsibility for leadership are some of the affective learnings to be included in the curriculum.

Sandra N. Kaplan

Figure 4.3

SkyLight Professional Development

fying themes or concepts, such as power, humor, extinction, the unexpected, or journeys. Like the concept of the tragic hero described earlier, these themes are principles that cut across time and disciplines. It is precisely for this reason that they can be the center of interdisciplinary units. Kaplan suggests that four questions guide the selection of concepts:

1. Is the theme related to a discipline?
2. Is it a significant area of study?
3. Is the theme neither age nor time dependent?
4. Does the theme allow for a variety of teacher and student options for study?

The theme becomes a way to organize and connect individual learning units, thereby providing meaningful connections among the disciplines studied in school.

Once curriculum writers have identified the theme with which they will work for a specified period of time, Kaplan suggests they focus on selecting the content, processes, and products for the unit. Content refers to the knowledge or subject matter that is to be taught, and Kaplan believes that the selection of content is the most difficult aspect of curriculum development. She provides specific rules for selecting content. Content should: (1) be related to the theme under consideration, (2) be multidisciplinary (allow for extensions to other disciplines), (3) be consonant with the needs of the learner, and (4) provide a time orientation wherein past, present, and future are related. Processes refer to skills or competencies related to the subject matter (e.g., note taking, interpreting, analyzing) that students will be required to learn. Kaplan recommends that teachers refer to a variety of taxonomies during this phase of the curriculum writing process and that targeted competencies be part of a larger scope and sequence of process skills that students are required to learn. Products refer to the forms of communication students need to learn in order to transmit the knowledge they have assimilated (e.g., essays, debates, dramatizations, computer software applications). The value of the product is twofold, according to Kaplan. First, it is verification that learning has taken place, and second, it is a tool that can be used again and again.

The Interdisciplinary Concept Model

Hayes-Jacobs (1989) also developed an interdisciplinary approach to developing curriculum units and, like Kaplan, suggested curriculum writers begin by selecting a theme. Hayes-Jacobs suggests that this first phase be completed collaboratively by teachers and students. Once the topic is selected, she recommends that the theme be explored from all disciplinary angles. To facilitate this exploration, she provides a graphic device: a six-spoked wheel (see Figure 4.4). Brainstorming is used by students and teachers to generate the discipline-specific questions, topics and issues related to the theme.

Interdisciplinary Concept Model: A Unit on Flight

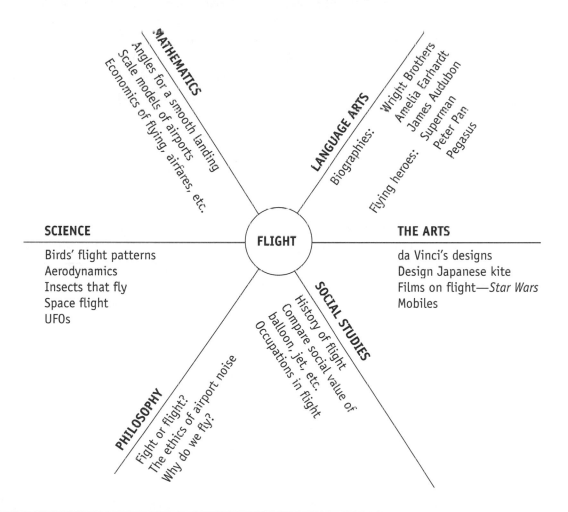

MATHEMATICS
Angles for a smooth landing
Scale models of airports
Economics of flying, airfares, etc.

LANGUAGE ARTS
Biographies: Wright Brothers
Amelia Earhardt
James Audubon
Flying heroes: Superman
Peter Pan
Pegasus

FLIGHT

SCIENCE
Birds' flight patterns
Aerodynamics
Insects that fly
Space flight
UFOs

THE ARTS
da Vinci's designs
Design Japanese kite
Films on flight—*Star Wars*
Mobiles

SOCIAL STUDIES
History of flight
Compare social value of balloon, jet, etc.
Occupations in flight

PHILOSOPHY
Fight or flight?
The ethics of airport noise
Why do we fly?

Figure 4.4

Hayes-Jacobs suggests that Bloom's (1954) taxonomy guide the next phase of curriculum development: writing activities to explore the questions. To ensure that a balance exists among the learning activities related to the theme, Hayes Jacobs recommends that each activity be charted under the proper heading of Bloom's taxonomy: knowledge, comprehension, application, analysis, synthesis, or evaluation. At a glance, the content-process matrix of activities provides the curriculum writer with the overall design of the learning experiences. The final phase includes assessment, and Hayes-Jacobs recommends that specific behavioral objectives are critical to the successful measurement of performance assessments.

Kaplan's and Hayes-Jacobs' models are similar; specifically, they both require the identification of a linking theme or concept to provide students with the big picture approach to knowledge. Additionally, both provide curriculum writers with methods to select content and process skills. Finally, curricular units designed by using Kaplan's or Hayes-Jacobs' model help ensure talent development among learners for two reasons. First, their thematic approach provides students with a rich foundation from which to make meaningful connections across domains of knowledge. When learners are provided with a larger number of meaningful ways to connect and interact with knowledge, interests are more likely to emerge and to be nurtured. Second, curriculum generated from either model can be individualized to accommodate for student learning styles, interests, and ability levels. Adjusting the abstractness of knowledge and levels of process skills, as well as product types to individual learners, ensures a match between learners and the curriculum. When optimal conditions for learning are provided, talent development is more likely to occur.

Differences between the models are related to the methodologies for the selection of interdisciplinary topics, the guidelines for selecting content, and the taxonomies recommended for selecting process skills. Kaplan leaves the selection of themes to curriculum writers and provides key questions to guide the selection process; Hayes-Jacobs believes theme selection should be a collaborative effort between students and teachers. Similarly, Kaplan provides teachers with guidelines to formulate content; Hayes-Jacobs provides an open-ended six-spoke wheel graphic organizer to assist students and teachers in developing specific content. Finally, Kaplan suggests that several taxonomies be used to articulate the process skills in the curricular unit and integrate them within the larger scope and sequence; Hayes-Jacobs suggests using one taxonomy, Bloom's, to ensure the proper balance of process skills.

We can summarize this chapter, then, by reiterating that we want textbooks to improve, and we believe that the strategies for textbook use and modification described here can serve as a driving force for reconsideration on the parts of textbook publishers. The consumer-driven marketplace will become more responsive to the issue of textbook quality if educators become more sophisticated about the levels of present texts and if they take specific steps to augment or replace existing texts. If, on the other hand, we sit idly by and do nothing, textbooks will continue to be the dominant force in the school curriculum. Making changes in the ways we use texts, and in the substitution of in-depth material for mundane textbook content will require three conditions on the parts of teachers and policy makers. First, teachers will need to pursue the kinds of professional growth that will empower them to analyze textbook content and to gain deeper understandings of the material they are teaching. For example, teachers cannot prepare and teach an in-depth unit on the genera of tragic heroes unless they acquire an in-depth understanding of this topic. Second, school and departmental faculties will have to organize themselves into special purpose teams that focus on increased knowledge and know-how about both content and process, and about improved pedagogy, as well. A discussion about the types of professional improvement process and the role and function of special purpose teams is discussed in the chapter on staff development (chapter 6). Finally, policy makers and school leaders need to provide the time and staff development resources necessary for curricular modification and, perhaps most important, for the sincere endorsement of the process.

ENDNOTE

1. Cognitive structures are the ways individuals see the physical and social worlds; the ways in which they organize and interrelate facts, concepts, beliefs, and expectations; and the ways they form patterns of interactions between whole/part relationships. A cognitive structure might best be thought of as a mental formula, plan of attack, or set of blueprints that a person has stored in his or her brain for use in addressing a familiar or closely related problem.

> . . . policy makers and school leaders need to provide the time and staff development resources necessary for curricular modification and . . . for the sincere endorsement of the process.

Enrichment Learning and Teaching

▶ ▶ ▶ ▶ ▶ ▶ ▶ ▶ ▶ ▶

CHAPTER 5

WHAT ARE ENRICHMENT LEARNING AND TEACHING?

Enrichment learning and teaching are practices based on the ideas of a small number of philosophers, theorists, and researchers. The work of these theorists, coupled with our own research and program development activities, has given rise to the concept that we call "enrichment learning and teaching." The best way to define this concept is in terms of the following four principles.

> Learning is more meaningful and enjoyable when content . . . and process . . . are learned within the context of a real and present problem.

1. Each learner is unique, and, therefore, all learning experiences must be examined in ways that take into account the abilities, interests, and learning styles of the individual.
2. Learning is more effective when students enjoy what they are doing. For that reason, learning experiences should be constructed and assessed with as much concern for enjoyment as for other goals.
3. Learning is more meaningful and enjoyable when content (i.e., knowledge) and process (i.e., thinking skills, methods of inquiry) are learned within the context of a real and present problem. Therefore, students should be given opportunities to choose problems, comment on the relevance of the problem for individual students at the time the problem is being addressed, and be the recipients of strategies that will assist them in personalizing problems they might choose to study.
4. Some formal instruction may be used in enrichment learning and teaching, but a major goal of this approach to learning is to enhance knowledge and thinking skill acquisition gained through *teacher*

instruction with applications of knowledge and skills that result from *students' con*struction of meaningfulness.

The ultimate goal of learning that is guided by these principles is to replace dependence and passive learning with independence and engaged learning. Although all but the most conservative educators will agree with these principles, much controversy exists about how these (or similar) principles may be applied in everyday school situations. A danger also exists that these principles might be viewed as yet another idealized list of glittering generalities that cannot easily be manifested in schools already overwhelmed by the deductive model of learning. Developing a school program based on these principles is not an easy task. Over the years, however, we have achieved a fair amount of success by gaining faculty, administrative, and parental consensus on a small number of easy-to-understand concepts and related services, and by providing resources and training related to each concept and service delivery procedure. The first two service delivery components (i.e., The Total Talent Portfolio and Curricular Modification) have been discussed previously.

> The ultimate goal of learning that is guided by these principles is to replace dependence and passive learning with independence and engaged learning.

This chapter rounds out the overall Schoolwide Enrichment Model by describing a model that serves as the core of enrichment learning and teaching. This model, entitled the Enrichment Triad Model (Renzulli 1977a), was originally developed in the early 1970s as an alternative to didactic models for talent development. In the ensuing years, numerous research studies (Renzulli and Reis 1994) and field tests in schools with widely varying demographics provided opportunities for the development of large amounts of practical know-how that are readily available for schools that would like to implement the SEM.

HOW CAN TEACHERS LEARN ENRICHMENT TEACHING?

This question is frequently asked, probably as a result of the ways in which we have prescribed and organized the work of teachers. Teaching in a natural way actually requires very little training. However, it does require that teachers understand the importance of serving as a facilitator rather than an instructor. This method of teaching has been described in detail in the chapter dealing with Type III Enrichment in the *Schoolwide Enrichment Model* (Renzulli and Reis 1997, 211–277). This method also requires that teachers know what to do in a situation that purposefully avoids lesson plans, unit plans, and other types of prescribed instructional approaches. Space does not permit a full explanation of this method of teaching, but some questions will illustrate how a group gets started in an enrichment cluster. Six key questions include the following.

1. What do people with an interest in this area (e.g., local history) do?
2. What products do they create and/or what services do they provide?
3. What methods do they use to carry out their work?

4. What resources and materials are needed to produce high-quality products and services?
5. How, and with whom, do they communicate the results of their work?
6. What steps do we need to take to have an impact on intended audiences?

The teacher's role as a facilitator, for example, included helping the poetry subgroup identify places where they might submit their work for publication. With the help of a librarian, the teacher located a book entitled *Directory of Poetry Publishers.* This book, which contains hundreds of outlets for poets' work, is the type of resource that makes the difference between a teacher who teaches poetry in a traditional fashion and a facilitator who develops talent in young poets.

The most difficult part of being a good enrichment cluster facilitator is to stop teaching and to replace traditional instruction with the kinds of "guide-on-the-side" responsibilities used by mentors and coaches. Persons who fulfill these roles instruct only when there is a direct need to accomplish a task that is part of product development. Many teachers who have served as yearbook advisors, drama club directors, 4-H Club advisors, athletic coaches, and facilitators of other extracurricular activities already have the techniques necessary for facilitating a successful enrichment cluster.

Extracurricular activities have the following basic characteristics.

1. Students and teachers select the area in which they participate.
2. Students produce a product or service that is intended to have an impact on a particular audience.
3. Students use the authentic methods of professionals to produce a product or service.

They may operate at a more junior level than adult professionals, but their goal is exactly the same—to produce as high a quality of product or service as possible within their level of experience and the availability of resources.

The teacher's role in an enrichment cluster is to assist in the procurement of methodological resources and to help students understand how to use the resources. The only time that direct instruction should take place is when the instruction is necessary to help produce and improve the product or service. Thus, for example, students doing a community survey in a social science cluster might receive direct instruction on procedures for developing an authentic questionnaire, rating scale, or survey instrument.

THE ENRICHMENT TRIAD MODEL

In order for enrichment learning and teaching to be applied systematically to the learning process in the regular classroom, it must be organized in a way that makes sense to teachers and students. An organizational pattern called the Enrichment Triad Model (Renzulli 1977a) is used for this purpose. The three types of enrichment in the model are depicted in Figure 5.1.

Type I enrichment consists of general exploratory experiences designed to expose students to topics and areas of study not ordinarily covered in the regular curriculum. Type II enrichment consists of group training in thinking and feeling processes; learning-how-to-learn skills; research and reference skills; and written, oral, and visual communication skills. Type III enrichment consists of firsthand investigations of real problems. Before discussing the role and function of each type of enrichment, it is necessary to discuss three considerations that relate to the model in general.

Learning in a Natural Way

The Enrichment Triad Model is based on the ways in which people learn in a natural environment rather than the artificially structured environment that characterizes most classrooms. Just as scientists look to nature when they attempt to solve particular types of problems, the process of learning is examined as it unfolds in the nonschool world. This process is elegant in its simplicity. External stimulation, internal curiosity, necessity, or combinations of these three starting points cause people to develop an interest in a topic,

The Enrichment Triad Model

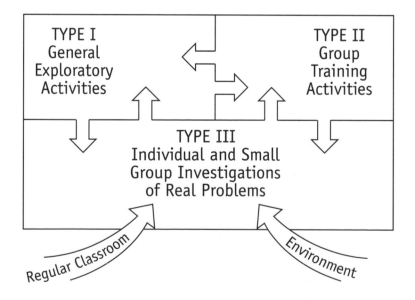

Figure 5.1

SkyLight Professional Development

problem, or area of study. Humans are, by nature, curious, problem-solving beings, but in order for them to act upon a problem or interest with some degree of commitment and enthusiasm, the interest must be a sincere one and one in which they see a personal reason for taking action. Once the problem or interest is personalized, a need is created to gather information, resources, and strategies for acting upon the problem.

Problem solving in nature almost always results in a product or service that has a functional, artistic, or humanitarian value. The learning that takes place in real-problem situations is *collateral learning* that results from attacking the problem in order to produce a product or service.

Consider a group of pioneers (or engineers or Boy or Girl Scouts) who want to build a bridge across a creek or river. They do not stand at the river bank and say, "Let's learn about geometry." Rather, they examine the scope of the problem, what they already know, and what they need to know and do to build the bridge. In the process, they may learn about geometry, strength of materials, planning and sequencing, cooperation, structural design, spatial relationships, aesthetics, mechanics, and a host of other things necessary to get the job done.

It was precisely this kind of natural problem-solving situation that gave rise to the Enrichment Triad Model. The only difference between the natural learning that takes place in real-life situations and the use of the Triad Model within the more structured world of the school is that we view products as vehicles through which a wide variety of more enduring and transferable processes can be developed. The products are essential because they give realness, purpose, and satisfaction and enjoyment to the present endeavor. The processes developed within the context of real-problem learning are also essential because schools must be concerned with preparation for the future and with the continuity of development in young people over long periods of time. Learning that focuses on the interaction between product and process results in the kinds of learning experiences that enhance both the present and the future.

The Importance of Interaction

A second general consideration about the Enrichment Triad Model is that the *interaction* between and among the three types of enrichment is as important as any type of enrichment or the collective sum of all three types. In other words, the arrows in Figure 5.1 are as important as the individual cells because they give the model dynamic properties that cannot be achieved if the three types of enrichment are pursued independently. A Type I experience, for example, may have value in and of itself, but it achieves maximum payoff if it leads to Type II or III experiences.

In this regard, it is a good idea to view Types I and II enrichment as identification situations that may lead to Type III experiences, which are the most advanced type of enrichment in the model. As Figure 5.1 indicates, the regular curriculum and the environment in general (i.e., nonschool experiences) can also serve as pathways of entry into Type III activities. An identification situation is simply an experience that allows students and teachers an opportunity to (1) participate in an activity, (2) analyze their interest in and reaction to the topic covered in the activity and the processes through which the activity was pursued, and (3) make a purposeful decision about their interest in the topic and the diverse ways further involvement may be carried out. Type I and Type II are general forms of enrichment that are usually pursued with larger groups of students, and they are often a prescribed part of enrichment offerings. Methods of presentation span the continuum from deductive to inductive methods of learning. Type III enrichment, on the other hand, is pursued only on a voluntary and self-selected basis, and the methodology is mainly inductive.

The interactive nature of the three types of enrichment also includes what are sometimes called the backward arrows in Figure 5.1 (e.g., the arrows leading back from Type III to Type I, etc.). In many cases, the advanced work (i.e., Type III) of students can be used as Type I and II experiences for other students. Thus, for example, a group of students who carried out a comprehensive study on lunchroom waste presented their work to other groups for both awareness and instructional purposes, and for purposes of stimulating potential new interests on the parts of other students. In this regard, the model is designed to renew itself and to bring students inside the pedagogy of the school enterprise rather than view learning from a spectator's perspective.

Personal Knowledge

The Enrichment Trial Model was designed to help students gain personal knowledge about their own abilities, interests, and learning styles. If, as Socrates said, "The unexamined life is not worth living," then we should also consider a corollary to this axiom about life in school: "The unexamined lesson is not worth learning." While it would be desirable to apply this corollary to all school experiences, the types of enrichment advocated in the Triad Model are excellent vehicles for examining preferences, tastes, and inclinations that will help students gain a greater understanding of themselves.

This corollary is operationalized in the model by recommending debriefings and post-learning analyses (sometimes called meta-learning) about both *what* has been learned, and *how* a particular segment of learning has been pursued. A scenario related to helping students understand learning and teaching style preferences, for example, might begin with the following teacher comment at the beginning of an instructional unit: "We are going to study the economic law of supply and demand by engaging in a *simulation* in which each of you will have control over the buying and selling of major food product groups." The teacher should explain what a simulation is, why it has been selected for use in connection with this topic, and how it compares with other instructional styles through which the topic might be taught. These advanced organizers call attention to the pedagogy of the learning situation as well as to the content and processes to be learned.

Following significant exposure to a particular instructional style, a careful post-learning analysis should be conducted that focuses on the unique properties of the purposefully selected instructional technique. Students should be encouraged to discuss and record in personal journals their reactions to the instructional technique in terms of both efficiency in learning and the amount of pleasure they derive from the technique. The goal of the post-learning analysis is to help students understand more about themselves by understanding more about their preferences in a particular situation. Thus, the collective experiences in learning styles should provide (1) exposure to many styles, (2) an understanding of which styles are the most personally applicable to particular subjects, and (3) experience in how to blend styles in order to maximize both the effectiveness and satisfaction of learning. The ultimate goal of teaching students about learning styles should be to develop in each student both a repertoire of styles and the strategies that are necessary to modify styles to better fit tasks they will encounter in future learning or career tasks. In much the same way that a golf player examines distance, wind conditions, and obstacles before selecting the appropriate golf club, so also should we teach students to examine learning situations with an eye toward selecting and applying the most appropriate styles.

In a certain sense, the type of training and analysis of styles suggested here might be viewed as a specific form of flexibility training typically associated with the pedagogy used in creative thinking. Although there are undoubtedly a variety of ways in which such training might be organized, the approach recommended in the Enrichment Triad Model focuses on a retrospective analysis of both *what* was learned (i.e., content) and how it was learned (i.e., process). Continued examination of these two aspects of learning helps students develop more concentrated future interests, and it also helps them gain an appreciation for their own learning style preferences on the scale of structured to unstructured learning.

In the sections that follow, we present each component of the Triad Model. As you review these sections, keep in mind the interactions between and among the three types of enrichment, and the ways in which this interaction can be heightened through debriefing and post-learning analysis. Remember also that the Triad Model is part of the service delivery component that is targeted on three school structures: the regular curriculum, the enrichment clusters, and the continuum of special services. In many ways, enrichment learning and teaching can be thought of as a transparent overlay that can be applied to these three school structures.

TYPE I ENRICHMENT: GENERAL EXPLORATORY EXPERIENCES

How do we motivate students to such an extent that they will act on their interests in creative and productive ways? The major purpose of Type I enrichment is to include within the overall school program selected experiences that are purposefully developed to be highly motivational. This type of enrichment consists of experiences and activities designed to expose students to a wide variety of disciplines, topics, ideas, concepts, issues, and events that are not ordinarily covered in the general curriculum. Typical Type I methods of delivery are bringing in a guest speaker, creating an interest center, showing slides, or hosting a debate.

Type I enrichment experiences can be based on regular curricular topics or innovative outgrowths of prescribed topics, but in order to qualify as a bona fide Type I experience, any and all planned activities in this category must *stimulate new or present interests that may lead to more intensive follow-up on the parts of individual students or small groups of students.* An activity can be called a Type I experience only if it meets the following three conditions.

1. Students are aware that the activity is an *invitation* to various kinds and levels of follow-up.
2. There is a systematic debriefing of the experience in order to learn who might want to explore further involvement and the ways the follow-up might be pursued.
3. There are various opportunities, resources, and encouragement for diverse kinds of follow-up.

An experience is clearly *not* a Type I if every student is required to follow up on an activity in the same or similar way. Required follow-up is a regular curricular practice, and although prescribed follow-up certainly has a genuine role in general education, it almost always fails to capitalize on differences in students' interest and learning styles.

There are three key issues related to Type I experiences.

1. Type I experiences should be selected and planned so that there is a high probability that they will be exciting and appealing to students.
2. A majority of Type I activities should be presented to all students in a classroom, grade level, or cross-grade group.
3. Although Type I experiences are, by definition, planned and presented, they need to retain flexibility.

In this section, we briefly discuss each of these three key issues. To make Type I experiences exciting to students, visiting speakers, for example, should be selected for both their expertise in a particular area *and* their ability to energize and capture the imagination of students. Persons presenting Type I experiences should be provided with enough orientation about the model to understand the objectives described previously and the need to help students explore the realms and ranges of opportunity for further involvement that are available within various age and grade considerations. Without such an orientation, these kinds of experiences may be viewed as merely informative; thus, even an exciting experience will not have the "feed forward" context that should characterize Type I enrichment activities.

Second, it is important to incorporate Type I activities into the regular classroom because these activities need to be seen as rooted in classroom instruction. For example, it may be worthwhile to introduce all middle grade students to a topic such as computer-assisted design (CAD) through a demonstration or presentation by a specialist on this topic. Following the activity and an assessment of the levels of interest of all students in the group, an advanced Type I might be planned for highly interested students that pursues the material in greater depth or that involves a field trip to a company or laboratory that uses CAD technology. In this case, there is an interest-based rationale for a special grouping or field trip that is different from offering field trips only to high ability students. A general or introductory Type I should, of course, include all students at given grade levels.

In terms of the flexibility of Type I activities, teachers should remember that a good menu of Type I experiences should be diversified across many topics and curricular categories. Such diversification improves the probability of influencing broader ranges of student interest, and, accordingly, increasing the number of students that will select an area in which they may like to pursue follow-up activities. Second, even prescribed Type I topics should be planned in a way that encourages maximum student involvement in an activity. Enrichment learning and teaching is more than just presenting unusual topics. Problem-solving activities—and activities that require discussion, debate, and confrontations with topics and issues—prompt the kinds of affective reactions that help students to personalize a topic and to make a commitment to more intensive follow-up.

The Type I dimension of the Enrichment Triad Model can be an extremely exciting aspect of overall schooling because it creates a legitimate slot within the school for bringing the vast world of knowledge and ideas that are above and beyond the regular curriculum to students' attention. It is also an excellent vehicle for teams of teachers, students, and parents to plan and work together on a relatively easy-to-implement component of the model. Type I enrichment is an excellent vehicle for getting started in an enrichment cluster.

TYPE II ENRICHMENT: GROUP TRAINING ACTIVITIES

If there is one area of school improvement about which virtually all educators agree, that area is the need to blend into the curriculum more training in the development of higher order thinking skills. In this section, we discuss a systematic approach for organizing a process skills component within the overall Schoolwide Enrichment Model.

SkyLight Professional Development

Type II enrichment consists of instructional methods and materials that are purposefully designed to develop a broad range of process skills in the following five general categories:

1. cognitive training
2. affective training
3. learning-how-to-learn training
4. research and reference procedures
5. written, oral, and visual communication procedures

When we refer to these strategies, we use the term *process skills*. Examples of specific skills within each of these five general categories (and related subcategories) can be found in a taxonomy that is included in Appendix B.

Type II enrichment also serves a motivational purpose similar to that discussed in connection with Type I activities. Next, we focus on two general considerations that should be taken into account in developing a schoolwide plan for Type II enrichment. These considerations are (1) levels and audiences for Type II activities, and (2) the objectives and strategies for implementing this component of the Enrichment Triad Model.

Levels and Audiences

Within each category of Type II enrichment, the targeted skills exist along a continuum ranging from very basic manifestations of a given skill to higher and more complex applications of any given process. Thus, for example, skills such as conditional reasoning or recording data from original sources can be taught to students at any grade, but the level and complexity of the specific activities will vary according to students' developmental levels. Primary grade students, for instance, can learn observational and data-gathering skills by counting and recording the number of times that different kinds of birds come to a bird feeder during a given period of time. These data might be presented by using simple tallies or pictograms. Older students can develop the same skills at higher levels by, for example, observing and recording pulse and blood pressure measures while controlling for factors such as age, height/ weight ratios, and specified periods of exercise. And the advanced mathematics and computer skills of older students might enable them to engage in more sophisticated statistical analyses of their data.

Teachers' knowledge of students' developmental levels, together with students' previous experiences in using a particular thinking skill, are important considerations when selecting materials and activities for Type II training. One of the ongoing activities of teachers and curriculum specialists using the SEM is to be continually searching for and examining enrichment materials that might enhance regular curriculum topics, or that might serve as useful resources for enrichment clusters or special service situations. Professional journals, publishers' catalogs and Web sites, and displays of materials at conferences are good sources of new materials.

There are three different methods for presenting Type II enrichment. The first method consists of planned, systematic activities that can be organized in advance for any unit of instruction within the general curriculum. These are the kinds of Type II activities that are planned in advance and are part of an ongoing framework to develop a comprehensive scope and sequence of process-oriented activities that parallel regular curriculum topics. The main criterion for selecting Type II activities in this category is that the activity bears a direct or indirect relationship to the subject matter being taught. For example, an activity entitled *Gold Rush: A Simulation of Life and Adventure in a Frontier Mining Camp* (Flindt 1978), can be used in connection with a social studies unit on westward expansion in US history. This activity is designed to develop decision making and creative writing skills within the context of the historical period covered in the unit. Activities in this category are ordinarily used with all students in a particular classroom, although advanced-level follow-up or related Type II training should take student interests and learning styles into account.

The second method for presenting Type II enrichment consists of activities that cannot be planned in advance because they grow out of students' reactions to school or nonschool experiences. In other words, this dimension is characterized by responsiveness to student interests rather than preplanning. For example, a group of students who developed an interest in investigative reporting were provided with advanced training in questioning and interviewing techniques, verifying information sources, and other skills related to this area of specialization. The interest resulted from a Type I presentation by a local journalist; however, the interest could also have been an outcome of a unit on journalism in the language arts curriculum, or a reaction to an important local or national news event. Enrichment in this dimension can also fulfill the motivational goal of the model by stimulating interests that may lead to more intensive follow-up in the form of Type III enrichment.

Type II enrichment in this category can also be used to provide direction for students in a particular enrichment cluster. Because a cluster is composed of students and teachers who have already declared interests in particular areas of study, Type II training that provides methodological skills within the area will help the group generate problems to which the methods can be applied. For example, a group of students who expressed strong interests in environmental issues was provided with a mini-course that taught them how to analyze the chemical properties of soil and water. A brainstorming and problem-focusing session resulted in making contact with a state agency, meeting with water pollution specialists, and eventually conducting a very professional study on acid rain in their geographic area. This is a good example of how learning the methodology first provided the impetus for the extended work of the cluster that followed.

The third method for presenting Type II enrichment consists of activities that are used within the context of already initiated Type III investigations. Activities used in this way represent the best application of inductive learning. Simply stated, an individual or group learns a process skill because they need the skill to solve a real and present problem.

Objectives and Strategies for Type II Training

The Type II component of the Enrichment Triad Model provides students with training opportunities to improve a wide variety of process skills not normally taught within the grade-level curriculum. Teachers or other adults who provide Type II training do so for diverse purposes, in multiple settings, with varied teaching strategies and resources, and for a wide range of students. Seven major objectives for students participating in Type II training are as follows.

1. Improve student ability to use higher order cognitive skills to organize, analyze, and synthesize new information.
2. Improve student leadership and interpersonal skills.
3. Improve student ability to gather, organize, and analyze raw data from appropriate primary and secondary sources.
4. Improve student ability to use a wide range of sophisticated reference materials and techniques when searching for answers to their personal research questions.
5. Demonstrate a more organized and systematic approach to research, experimentation, and investigation.
6. Improve the quality and appropriateness of the products that students create in conjunction with real-world problem solving.
7. Use the methods and techniques of various adult professionals to find problems, gather and organize data, and develop products.

In general, Type II training provides students with various learning opportunities designed to improve their independent learning skills as well as the quality of their personal assignments, projects, and research. Type II enrichment also includes a broad range of affective training activities designed to improve interpersonal and intrapersonal skills and to promote greater degrees of cooperation and mutual respect among students. By placing this instruction within the framework of the regular curriculum or the enrichment clusters, teachers can offer these valuable training activities without the risk of having the training viewed as an end in and of itself.

The Type II Taxonomy and Resource List

Since the need for Type II training with a specific skill varies from student to student, from grade to grade, and from one subject area to another, there is no finite list of skills that should be taught as part of the Type II component. The developers of the Schoolwide Enrichment Model have, instead, used the objectives listed previously as category labels to collect and organize a set of over 400 process skills within a document called the Type II Taxonomy (Renzulli and Reis 1997). This Taxonomy can be used by teachers to gain a holistic perspective on the Type II component and its comprehensive nature. The Taxonomy can also be used as a "menu" to help teachers select the most appropriate Type II skills and materials for their students.

In some districts, a committee of faculty members has used this list to create a scope and sequence document that specifies which Type II skills will be taught through large group instruction in the regular classroom or within enrichment clusters or other multiage groupings. The scope and sequence document also ensures that their SEM program is offering a comprehensive set of training opportunities within all grade levels and to all students in the school. The seventeen skill categories within the Type II Taxonomy have also been used to create databases of selected commercial materials for the teaching of process skills. Some of these databases may be found on the SEM Web site (http://www.gifted.uconn.edu). Although many teachers may prefer to create their own Type II lessons and units, many of these commercial materials can be used for supplementary activities or as resources for teachers who are unfamiliar with Type II instructional techniques.

The Who, When, Where, and How Decisions

Type II training can be offered as a result of observed student need, as a follow-up to a Type I exploration, as a result of expressed student interest, or within the parameters of a student's individual Type III investigation. It is extremely important to ensure that a specific Type II skill is offered at the appropriate time, in the appropriate setting, with the appropriate teaching strategies, and for the appropriate students. Teachers or faculties should use their knowledge of students and curriculum to make the best decisions possible about which students will receive specific kinds of Type II training, and which settings and teaching strategies will be most advantageous.

Some classroom teachers who have modified their textbook-based curriculum and are designing their own curriculum units (Conn 1988; Osborne, Jones, and Stein 1985; Renzulli 1988) may integrate or infuse Type II training within these units as a way of teaching related process skills (e.g., teaching students how to conduct oral history interviews during a unit on the Vietnam War). At other times, classroom teachers may prefer to develop a stand-alone unit that focuses exclusively on a single Type II skill to ensure that novice learners receive explicit instruction in how to acquire and use this skill process (e.g., teaching a unit on creative problem solving). Still other Type II skills can be embedded within students' investigations or research projects and taught only when they are needed for specific and immediate purposes (e.g., a student wants to learn how to recognize the trees in the woods behind the school because she is creating a nature trail).

In addition to varying the nature of the instructional strategy used to teach Type II skills, teachers should also vary the audience of students who will receive this training. Some Type II lessons can and should be taught to all students in a class or grade level, some skills can be taught in a small group setting to only those students who have not already acquired the skill, and other skills might be taught to only those students interested in learning them. Teachers who sponsor or facilitate enrichment clusters may also find their students need or request Type II training as a result of their common interest in a subject area or local problem. A cluster of students interested in journalism might receive training in editing, proofreading, layout, or advertising techniques. An enrichment cluster concerned with environmental problems might receive Type II training in how to draft a petition, how to lobby effectively, how to write an editorial, or how to write a letter to key government officials.

The resources for teaching these Type II skills can also vary. Although many classroom teachers will assume responsibility for teaching specific Type II skills to all students or small groups of students within their class, enrichment specialists can also schedule a variety of mini-courses for interested students. This approach facilitates multiclass and multiage groupings and allows teachers to progress to advanced levels because of heightened student interests. Community resources (doctors, gardeners, lawyers, dietitians, etc.) and content area teachers or specialists from the faculty or among the student population can also be recruited to offer Type II training to interested groups of students. In addition, learning centers, computer software, pamphlets, videos, and how-to books can be used by individual students who prefer self-instruction for selected Type II skills. Care should be taken, however, to ensure that Type II training is offered on an as-needed basis as often as possible. Teachers must be aware that some students have already acquired many of the Type II skills through modeling or informal learning opportunities; other students require a great deal of time, explicit teaching, and coaching in order to master new skills; and still others will not be ready to learn a given Type II skill until they see the immediate relevance for the skill's use.

Whether Type II skills are infused in the content curriculum, taught explicitly, or embedded in a student's interest exploration or problem-solving endeavors, all students who participate in Type II training should have numerous extension opportunities to transfer and apply their learned skills to new academic content, to their own research questions, or to their product development efforts. Although process skill training has been a staple of gifted education programs for many years, our research has shown that this kind of training can be used with all students. While it may be true that not all students will use their newly acquired skills for personal research, experimentation, or investigation, all students can apply these skills to new and challenging academic content. When successful, Type II training helps students improve their academic achievement by showing them how to acquire and assimilate new content more rapidly and effectively, and these skills also have important transfer value to subsequent learning and the world of work.

TYPE III ENRICHMENT: INDIVIDUAL AND SMALL GROUP INVESTIGATIONS OF REAL PROBLEMS

Type III enrichment consists of investigative activities and the development of creative products in which students assume roles as firsthand investigators, writers, artists, or other types of practicing professionals. Although students pursue these kinds of involvement at a more junior level than adult professionals, the overriding purpose of Type III enrichment is to create situations in which young people are thinking, feeling, and doing what practicing professionals do in the delivery of products and services. Type III enrichment experiences should be viewed as vehicles in which students can apply their interests, knowledge, thinking skills, creative ideas, and task commitment to self-selected problems or areas of study. In addition to this general goal, there are four objectives of Type III enrichment.

1. Acquire advanced-level understanding of the knowledge and methodology used within particular disciplines, artistic areas of expression, and interdisciplinary studies.
2. Develop authentic products or services that are primarily directed toward bringing about a desired impact on one or more specified audiences.
3. Develop self-directed learning skills in the areas of planning, problem finding and focusing, organizational skills, resource utilization, time management, cooperativeness, decision making, and self-evaluation.
4. Develop task commitment, self-confidence, feelings of creative accomplishment, and the ability to interact effectively with other students and adults who share common goals and interests.

Type III enrichment is the vehicle within the total school experience through which everything from basic skills to advanced content and processes comes together in the form of student-developed products and services. In much the same way that all of the separate but interrelated parts of an automobile come together at an assembly plant, so, also, do we consider this form of enrichment as the assembly plant of mind. This kind of learning represents a synthesis and an application of content, process, and personal involvement. The student's role is transformed from one of lesson learner to firsthand inquirer, and the role of the teacher changes from an instructor and disseminator of knowledge to a combination of coach, resource procurer, mentor, and, sometimes, a partner or colleague. Although products play an important role in creating Type III enrichment situations, a major concern is the development and application of a wide range of cognitive, affective, and motivational processes.

Since this type of enrichment is defined in terms of the pursuit of real problems, it is necessary to define this term at the outset. The term "real problem," like many other concepts in education, gets tossed around so freely that after a while it becomes little more than a cliché. Research on the meaning of a real problem (Renzulli 1983) did not produce a neat and trim definition, but an examination of various connotations of the term yielded four characteristics that serve as the basis for our discussion. First, a real problem must have a personal frame of reference for the individual or group pursuing the problem. In other words, it must involve an emotional or internal commitment in addition to a cognitive or scholarly interest. Thus, for example, stating that global warming or urban crime are real problems does not make them real for an individual or group unless they decide to do something to address the problem. These concerns may affect all people, but until a commitment is made to act upon them, they are more properly classified as "societal issues." Similarly, telling a person or group that "you have a problem" does not make it real unless the problem is internalized and acted upon in some way.

A second characteristic of real problems is that they do not have existing or unique solutions for persons addressing the problem. If there is an agreed-upon, correct solution or set of strategies for solving the problem, then it is more appropriately classified as a training exercise. As indicated earlier, it is not our intent to diminish the value of training exercises. Indeed, many of the activities that make up the Type II dimension of the Triad Model are exercises designed to develop thinking skills and research methods. They fail, however, to qualify as real problems because they are externally assigned, and there is a predetermined skill or problem-solving strategy that we hope learners will acquire. Even simulations that are based on approximations of real-world events are considered to be training exercises if their main purpose is to teach content or thinking skills.

The third characteristic of a real problem is best described in terms of why people pursue these kinds of problems. The main reason is that they want to bring about some form of change in actions, attitudes, or beliefs on the parts of a targeted audience, or they want to contribute something new to the sciences, arts, or humanities. The word "new" is used here in a local rather than global way; therefore, we do not necessarily expect young people to make contributions that are new "for all humankind." But even replications of studies that have been done many times before are new in a relative sense if they are based on data that have not been gathered previously. Thus, for example, if a group of young people gathered data about television watching habits across grade levels in their school or community, these data and the resulting analysis would be new in the sense that they never existed before.

The final characteristic of real problems is that they are directed toward a real audience. Real audiences are defined as persons who voluntarily attend to information, events, services, or objects. A good way to understand the difference between a real and contrived audience is to reflect for a moment on what students might do with the results of a local oral history project. Although they might want to practice presenting the material before their classmates, an authentic audience would more properly consist of members of a local historical society or persons who choose to read about the study in a local newspaper, magazine, or shopping guide. The practicing professional, upon whose work Type III enrichment is modeled, almost always begins his or her work with an audience in mind. Audiences may change as the work evolves, but they serve as targets that give purpose and direction to the work.

Essential Elements of Type III Enrichment

In this section, we discuss how the characteristics of real problems, coupled with our earlier examination of inductive learning, can be used to guide teachers and students in the Type III process. The discussion that follows is organized around five essential elements of Type III enrichment.

A Personal Frame of Reference

The first essential element is that problems being pursued through this type of learning experience must be based on individual or group interests. Teachers and other adults can certainly provide guidance and some creative steering toward the formulation of a problem, but they must avoid at all costs crossing the line from suggestion to prescription. If a problem is forced upon students, we endanger the personal frame of reference discussed earlier, and the kind of affective commitments that result in a willingness to engage in creative and demanding work. In most cases, the division of labor that takes place in group Type III situations causes a broader range of talents to be developed and promotes the kinds of real-world cooperation and mutual respect that we are attempting to achieve in the SEM. In addition to allowing for various types of involvement, problems that require a diversity of specialties also create opportunities for more personalization on the parts of individuals in the group. When each person feels that she or he owns a part of the problem, the first characteristic of a real problem is met.

> Audiences may change as the work evolves, but they serve as targets that give purpose and direction to the work.

A Focus on Advanced-Level Knowledge

The second essential element of Type III Enrichment is that it should draw upon authentic, advanced-level knowledge. If we want students to approximate the roles of practicing professionals, then it is important to examine the characteristics of persons who have displayed high levels of expertise in their respective domains of knowledge. During the past two decades, cognitive psychologists have devoted much research to the topic of experts and expertise and the role of knowledge in attaining expert performance. Studies ranging from the characteristics of chess masters to the acquisition of routine tasks in unskilled or semi-skilled jobs (e.g., taxi driving) have uncovered a number of generalizations across the various domains that have been studied. Glaser (1990) has summarized some of the key characteristics of experts' performance, and these characteristics can be used to provide guidance for this dimension of the Enrichment Triad Model.

Experts mainly excel in their own domain, and they spend much more time than novices analyzing information within their respective fields of study. Experts also perceive large, meaningful patterns in their domain, and they understand how knowledge is organized in their domain. They tend to represent problems at deeper levels by creating conceptual categories rather than categories based on surface or superficial features, they are goal-oriented, and they access knowledge mainly for its applicability to present problems. Finally, experts develop self-regulatory skills such as judging problem difficulty, apportioning their time, asking questions, reviewing their knowledge, and predicting outcomes.

High levels of expertise in a topic or domain obviously emerge from extensive experience gained over long periods of time. If we contrast this characteristic of expert performance with the traditional forty-two minute period alloted for instruction in most schools—combined with superficial coverage of topics—it is clear that we must extend the amount of time that students are allowed to work on problems that have a personal frame of reference. Time allocations for individual or small group Type III investigations, whether in enrichment clusters, regular classes, or other organizational arrangements, should be unbounded and expandable, as long as motivation remains high and progress toward goals is clearly evident.

The amount and complexity of knowledge available to students pursuing advanced studies and investigations must also be expanded. Guidelines for identifying both advanced-level content and methodology are available through content standards developed by various professional associations, such as the National Council of Teachers of Mathematics and the National Council of Teachers of English. Finally, there has been a significant movement within teacher education programs to emphasize subject area competency as well as pedagogy. The amount of advanced-level knowledge that teachers possess will be a major determinant of the level of the courses they teach.

A Focus on Methodology

The third essential element of Type III enrichment is the use of authentic methodology. This characteristic is essential because one of the goals of Type III enrichment is to help students extend their work beyond the usual kinds of reporting that often results when teachers and students view research as merely looking up information. Some reporting of previous information is a necessary part of most investigations. Indeed, the pursuit of new knowledge should always begin with a review of what is already known about a given topic. The end result of a Type III investigation, however, should be a creative contribution that goes beyond the existing information typically found in encyclopedias and other all-about-books.

Every field of organized knowledge can be defined, in part, by its methodology, and the methodology of most fields can be found in certain kinds of guidebooks or manuals. These "how-to" books are the key to escalating studies beyond the traditional report writing approach that often passes for research.

Every field of knowledge can also be partly defined by the kinds of data that represent the raw material of the field. New contributions are made in a field when investigators apply well-defined methods to the process of making sense out of random bits and pieces of information. Although some investigations require levels of sophistication and equipment that are far beyond the reach of younger investigators, almost every field of knowledge has entry level and junior level data-gathering opportunities.

We have seen scientifically respectable questionnaire studies on food and television preferences carried out by primary grade students. A group of middle grade students gathered and analyzed water samples as part of a large regional study on the extent and effects of acid rain. This work was done with such care that the students' findings were requested for use by a state environmental agency. Another group of elementary students used professional techniques in every aspect of producing a weekly television show broadcast by a local cable television company. A fifth-grade student wrote a guidebook that was adopted by his city's government as the official historical walking tour of the city; a group of high school students engaged in a sophisticated community research and citizens' action project that resulted in the appropriation of $200,000 for a citywide system of bike paths. The success and high level of product development reflected in these examples can be traced to the proper use of authentic methods and techniques, even if these techniques were carried out at a somewhat junior level than those used by adult inquirers.

The teacher's role is to help students identify, locate, and obtain resource materials and/or persons to provide assistance in the appropriate use of investigative techniques. In some cases, it may be necessary to consult with librarians or professionals within various fields for advice about where and how to find methodological resources. Professional assistance may also be needed in translating complex concepts into material students can understand. Although methodological assistance is a major part of the teacher's responsibility in Type III enrichment, it is neither necessary nor realistic to expect teachers to have mastered a large number of investigative techniques. The most important skill is the ability to know where and how to help students obtain the right kind of material and the willingness to reach out beyond the usual school resources for specialized kinds of materials and resource persons.

A Sense of Audience

The fourth essential element of Type III enrichment is that products and services resulting from this kind of involvement are targeted to real audiences. The magic key that has unlocked the success of so many Type III projects is the sense of audience that students have developed in connection with their work. This sense of audience gives students a reason for wanting to improve the quality of their products and develop effective ways of communicating their results with interested others. A sense of audience is also a primary contributor to the creation of task commitment and the concern for excellence and quality that has characterized so many Type III investigations.

If the Type III dimension of our model is to have maximum value in the overall development of young people, major attention must be given to helping them find appropriate outlets and audiences for their most creative efforts. This concern is modeled after the modus operandi of creative and productive individuals. If we could sum up in a few words the raison d'etre of creative and productive people, it would certainly be *impact upon audience*. Type III enrichment provides natural opportunities for the kinds of personal satisfaction and self-expression that result from bringing an important piece of work to fruition. Writers hope to influence thoughts and emotions, scientists do research to find better ways to contribute new knowledge to their fields, and artists create products to enrich the lives of those who view their works. Teachers can help young people to acquire this orientation by encouraging them to develop a sense of audience from the earliest stages of a Type III investigation.

The teacher's role requires helping students take one small but often neglected first step in the overall process of product development. This important step is to consider *what* people in a particular field produce, and *how* they typically communicate their results with other interested persons. Once again, we can look to the activities of practicing professionals and the how-to books for guidance. In most cases, young artists and scholars will be restricted to local outlets and audiences, but there will be occasions when products of unusual excellence can be shared with larger audiences.

Although school and local audiences are obvious starting points in the search for outlet vehicles, teachers should always help students gain a perspective for more comprehensive outlet vehicles and audiences beyond local opportunities. Many organizations, for example, prepare newsletters and journals at the state and national levels, and they are usually receptive to high-quality contributions by students. Similarly, state and national magazines and Web sites oftentimes carry outstanding work by young people. The search for more widespread audiences should only be encouraged when student work is high quality and when it has achieved local recognition. Exploring external audiences helps students develop standards of quality, and it also provides them with real-world experiences about the rigors and challenges of reaching out to wider audiences. Exploring external audiences involves an element of risk-taking and the chance that work will not be accepted in the wider arenas of publications and dissemination. But by beginning a search for audiences at the local level, an element of success is likely to be achieved.

Authentic Evaluation

The fifth essential element of Type III enrichment is that work carried out using this approach to learning is evaluated in an authentic rather than artificial manner. The ultimate test of quality in the world outside the school is whether or not products or services achieve a desired impact on clients or selected audiences. *For this reason, Type III products should never be graded or scored.* This traditional school practice is antithetical to the ways in which work is evaluated in the real world. Students can be provided with categorical feedback using a guide such as the Student Product Assessment Form (Renzulli and Reis 1981), but even this instrument should only be used to help students refine and improve their work. Teachers and other adults should view their role in the feedback process as that of a "resident escalator." Sensitive and specific recommendations about how particular aspects of the work can be improved will help students move slowly but surely toward higher and higher levels of product excellence. Every effort should be made to pinpoint specific areas where suggested changes should be implemented. This approach helps avoid student discouragement and reconfirm a belief in the overall value of their endeavors.

> Teachers and other adults should view their role in the feedback process as that of a "resident escalator."

APPLYING THE TYPE III PROCESS TO ENRICHMENT CLUSTERS

The enrichment clusters are ideal places to implement Type III enrichment. By using information from the Total Talent Portfolio to form the clusters, we are assured of at least some commonality of interest on the parts of students in the various clusters. Mutual interests are a good starting point for accelerating motivation and promoting harmony, respect, and cooperation among group members. An orientation session should emphasize the objectives and essential elements of Type III enrichment and the characteristics of a real problem. Students grasp this approach to learning quickly if teachers are consistent in their transformed role as coach and mentor rather than conventional instructor.

The biggest single problem in implementing enrichment clusters is getting started. *Type III enrichment represents qualitatively different learning experiences, and it is important for teachers to realize that they themselves must engage in some activities which differ from the traditional activities that define the traditional teacher's role.* This point cannot be overemphasized. It is impossible to foster *differential* types of learning experiences through the use of ordinary teaching methods. If we want young people to think, feel, and act like practicing professionals (or firsthand inquirers), then teachers must also learn how to raise a few of the questions that professionals ask about the nature and function of their own work. In other words, teachers must go one step beyond the questions that are ordinarily raised in problem-solving situations. This step involves problem finding and problem focusing, which is how practicing professionals begin their work.

Almost everything that young people do in traditional classrooms casts them in the role of lesson learners. Even when working on so-called research reports, students nearly always perceive their main purpose as that of "finding out about. . . ." One need only ask youngsters why they are working on a particular report. Invariably, they reply: To find out *about* the eating habits of the gray squirrel; *about* the exports of Brazil; *about* the Battle of Gettysburg. There is nothing wrong with finding out about things—all student and adult inquirers do it—but practicing professionals do it for a purpose *beyond* merely finding out about something for its own sake. This purpose, which we might refer to as the application purpose, is what Type III enrichment is all about. Thus, the key to helping youngsters feel like firsthand inquirers rather than mere absorbers of knowledge is to explore with them some of the questions that professionals raise. The following six essential questions should be used at the outset of an enrichment cluster.

1. What do people with an interest in this area do?
2. What products do they create and/or what services do they provide?
3. What methods do they use to carry out their work?
4. What resources and materials are needed to produce high quality products and services?
5. How, and with whom, do they communicate the results of their work?
6. What steps need to be taken to have an impact on intended audiences?

Exploration of these questions can be pursued in a variety of ways. Type I experiences in the form of visiting speakers, discussions of career education materials, displays of typical products from the field(s) around which a cluster is organized, or videos of professionals at work can provide a picture of the products, services, and activities that characterize various fields of study. A library trip organized around a scavenger hunt format is a good way to help students broaden their perspective about the products and communication vehicles associated with various areas of inquiry.

Type II activities that provide direct or simulated experiences of typical pursuits in a particular field are also useful in helping young people answer the questions. How-to books are an especially valuable source for locating such activities. Thus, for example, a social science cluster can experience data gathering and analysis methods by using one of the sample activities on surveying, observing, or developing a research hypothesis that can be found in the book, *A Student's Guide to Conducting Social Science Research* (Bunker, Pearlson, and Schultz 1999). This entire book can be used at the introductory stages of a cluster to provide know-how and to generate ideas that will help students identify their own research interests. It is important, however, for students to be informed in advance that planned, deductive activities are preparatory for the self-selected, inductive work that should be the primary focus of an enrichment cluster. *Research Comes Alive! A Guidebook for Conducting Original Research with Middle and High School Students* (Schack and Starko 1998) and *Chi Squares Pie Charts and Me* (Baum, Gable, and List 1987) are two excellent resources for use with enrichment clusters.

A combined brainstorming and webbing technique such as the one pictured in Figure 5.2 can also be used to explore the types of products and communication vehicles that characterize given fields of study or topical interests. This activity can be done by individuals or small groups, after which the responses of the entire group can be entered on a wall chart. An activity such as this can be enhanced by asking students to interview local professionals, obtain career-related literature from professional societies and associations, and explore library products within selected fields and topics.

Brainstorming Web to Identify Products and Outlets

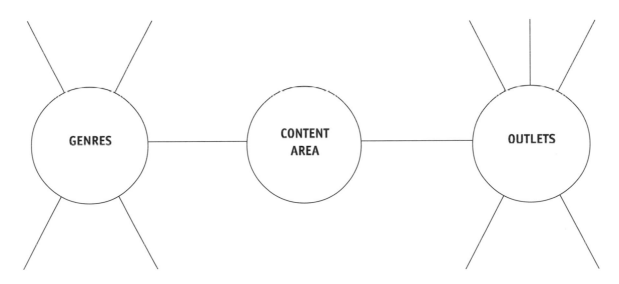

When used as a worksheet, this combined webbing/brainstorming activity follows an easy-to-use scenario. A group of students and teachers with a common interest in this general area came together to address six questions: What do people with an interest in this area do? What products do they create and/or what services do they provide? What methods do they use to carry out their work? How, and with whom, do they communicate the results of their work? A number of exploration activities (e.g., interviews, library searches, surveys) were used over a two-week period to address these questions. After dividing into subgroups by genre, they then addressed the last two questions: What resources and materials do we need to produce high-quality products and services? What steps do we need to take to have an impact on intended audiences? These last two questions help define the role of teachers (or other adults) in the cluster.

Figure 5.2

The teacher's role in the above situations is three-fold.

1. Teachers should organize and guide, but not dominate, the exploration process.
2. Teachers should assist in the location of methodological resource materials such as a book on puppet making or presenting data in graphic or tabular forms.
3. Teachers need to open doors for connecting student products with appropriate audiences.

When teachers assume these different kinds of responsibilities, students develop an entirely new attitude toward both their work and their teachers. There is one overriding goal to developing learning opportunities based on the concept of Type III enrichment. This goal is larger than the products students prepare or the methods they learn in pursuing their work. The largest goal is that students begin to think, feel, and act like creative and productive individuals. This component of the SEM is designed to develop an attitude that has reinforced the work of effective people since the beginning of time: I can do . . . I can be . . . I can create.

Organizational Components of the Schoolwide Enrichment Model

▷   ▷   ▷   ▷   ▷   ▷   ▷   ▷   ▷   ▷

This chapter discusses the following six organizational components of the Schoolwide Enrichment Model (SEM):

- The Schoolwide Enrichment Teaching Specialist
- The Schoolwide Enrichment Team
- The Professional Development Model
- The Schoolwide Enrichment Model Web Site
- Parent Orientation, Training, and Involvement
- A Democratic School Management Plan

These organizational components consist of practical strategies and resources that support the direct delivery of services to students. The components described in the following sections are based on several years of developmental work in programs that have used the SEM. The practicality of the components is reflected in the planning guides, lists of enrichment materials, sample letters, and teacher training materials that can be found in the companion volumes and databases that have been developed over the years to assist in the implementation of the SEM.

Resources of this type are always in the process of being updated, revised, and modified to reflect new developments in the model, changes that are taking place in general education, and creative contributions being made by persons using the model. Thus, for example, new concerns in American education for the inclusion of multicultural perspectives and environmental issues have resulted in extended searches for curricular materials on these topics. And the availability of electronic bulletin boards and interactive satellite

> Resources of this type are always in the process of being updated, revised, and modified to reflect new developments in the model, changes that are taking place in general education, and creative contributions being made by persons using the model.

broadcast capabilities for staff development have brought a new dimension to the professional development component of the model.

Some of the organizational components are at more mature stages of development than others; however, all of the components are real in the sense that they are actually being used in one form or another in schools that use the SEM. Educators use the SEM network through the SEM Web site; Confratute, an annual conference at the University of Connecticut; and active participation in workshops run by SEM specialists at local, state, and national conferences.

THE SCHOOLWIDE ENRICHMENT TEACHING SPECIALIST

> [the schoolwide enrichment teaching specialist encompasses] a broader application of many of the skills and responsibilities of gifted education specialists, some additional leadership responsibilities, and a commitment to apply gifted program know-how . . .

An essential ingredient for a successful enrichment program is a person within a school who is responsible for providing (1) direct services to students and (2) leadership in program development, staff development, and the infusion of enrichment know-how and materials into the school.

The role of the schoolwide enrichment teaching specialist evolved from the practical experience gained in schools that had expanded their traditional gifted programs into programs based on the SEM. Many of these specialists formerly served as teachers of the gifted and talented; their background and training were valuable assets in making the transition to an expanded, schoolwide model.

The schoolwide enrichment teaching specialist is not a separate or additional position in schools that employ teachers of the gifted. Rather, we view the position as encompassing a broader application of many of the skills and responsibilities of gifted education specialists, some additional leadership responsibilities, and a commitment to apply gifted program know-how to all of the school structures toward which the SEM is targeted.

The Three-Fifths Solution to Allocating an Enrichment Specialist's Time

Among the most frequently asked questions about the SEM are: What does the schoolwide enrichment teaching specialist do? With whom does he or she work? We have divided the work of these specialists into two categories: direct services to students and resource and leadership responsibilities.

Figure 6.1 is intended to convey the *approximate* proportions of time spent pursuing responsibilities in each category. Direct services to students are divided into two subcategories. One of these subcategories is face-to-face work with students in individual teaching, mentoring, and counseling situations. The other subcategory consists of arranging services that will be carried out in cooperation with, or under the direction of, other faculty members, community resource persons or agencies, or faculty members at nearby colleges and universities. These arrangements, which are part of the continuum of special services, also include local, state, and national programs such as the Intel (formerly Westinghouse) Science Talent Search, the Young American Newsmagazine for Kids, and the International Science and Engineering Fair.

Activities in the resource and leadership category include general enrichment program administration and coordination, dissemination of information about enrichment materials and methods, staff development and demonstration teaching, peer coaching, public relations and communication, and program monitoring and evaluation. This broad range of duties could easily be overwhelming for a single person; therefore, we have built into the model a support group in the form of a schoolwide enrichment team. The role and responsibilities of this team will be described in the section that follows. Although allocations of the enrichment specialist's time should be more or less guided by the proportions of time depicted in Figure 6.1, adjustments will need to be made in accordance with local school conditions and the degree of active participation on the parts of enrichment team members. Our experience has shown that in cases where enrichment specialists covered more than one school, the enrichment team was a crucial factor in providing the continuity necessary to ensure program success.

The Three-Fifths Solution

DIRECT SERVICES TO STUDENTS		RESOURCE AND LEADERSHIP RESPONSIBILITIES	
Face-to-Face Activities	**Services Provided Through Arrangements with Other Persons and Organizations**	Peer Coaching and Staff Development	Demonstration Teaching
• Individual and small group teaching and mentoring.	• Providing teachers with materials to use with a specific group or individual.	Working with Enrichment Teams	Reviewing Materials
• Direct coaching and supervision of Type III enrichment projects that are extensions of regular classes, enrichment clusters, or nonschool initiated interests.	• Coordinating mentorships with individual faculty or community resource persons and agencies.	Public Relations	Communications (Newsletters, Parent Meetings, etc.)
• Counseling and referring students about issues such as multipotentiality, underachievement, and other special needs.	• Organizing programs such as Odyssey of the Mind or the Artifact Box Program.	Program Evaluation, Mentoring	General Administrations
	• Arranging for students to attend summer programs in their talent areas.		

Figure 6.1

SkyLight Professional Development

Direct Services to Students

This section describes the rationale underlying the allocation of the specialist's time, and some important ground rules will be discussed. A number of practical and political realities must be taken into account when recommending support for any school position beyond those of existing classroom teachers and traditional administrative positions. Budgetary issues are always a major concern, and reluctance is growing to fund positions that focus on special services to relatively small proportions of school populations. Unless a supplementary position is defined in terms of services that have an impact on the entire student body, less likelihood exists that such positions will be initiated and supported on a continuing basis. And even when such positions are approved, it is essential for these persons to demonstrate their *usefulness* to the entire school program. We have thus defined the position of schoolwide teaching specialist in terms of both direct services to students and as a series of leadership responsibilities.

Another political reality is that schools are criticized for being administratively top heavy. Both teachers and the general public are skeptical about creating additional layers of administration, especially during times when tightened school budgets result in increased class size and the elimination of other personnel and services. By including the word *teaching* in the job description of the enrichment specialist, we emphasize the teaching responsibilities of persons in specialists' positions rather than duties they fulfill in the resource and leadership portion of their jobs.

There are, of course, other reasons why it is important for enrichment teaching specialists to maintain as much direct contact with students as possible. Developing talent in all students means that there will be times and circumstances when the performance, or the potential for performance, escalates to such a degree that the students require very concentrated and intense support. This support may be in the form of individual or small group instruction, guidance and counseling, apprenticeship or mentorship opportunities, or participation in out-of-school courses, cultural institutions, or business or professional workplaces and agencies.

Two ground rules should guide decisions about direct services provided by the enrichment teaching specialist. First, these services must be tied to *specific* areas in which high levels of talent potential have clearly been demonstrated. If, for example, a schoolwide enrichment teaching specialist teaches a cross-grade cluster group of advanced mathematics students for a few hours a week, a legitimate rationale exists for bringing this group together—the development of their advanced math talent. But if a group is brought together on a regular basis only because they have been preselected on the basis of general ability test scores, then we may be falling back into the traditional practice of designating one group of students as "the gifted" (or, in more recent terminology, "the truly gifted").

This practice has, by and large, resulted in what can only be described as *un*differentiated gifted programs. By undifferentiated, we simply mean that the programs have focused usually on preselected topics or units of instruction, the direct teaching of general process skills, a large measure of fun and games activities, and field trips and visiting speakers. Since these activities ordinarily are not tied directly to a specific area of talent development for a particular individual or small group, they should be made available to all students through the regular curriculum or the enrichment clusters. A field trip to a newspaper office, for example, is an excellent experience for students studying journalism as part of their language arts curriculum, or for an enrichment cluster that is actually producing a newspaper. But to take a group on such a trip merely because they have been designated as "the gifted" is to conjure up all the criticisms that have been leveled at special programs by persons from both within and outside the field of gifted education, as well as by the general public.

Our experience has shown that enrichment teaching specialists are more effective and accepted by all members of the school community when the direct service portion of their work concentrates on specific, high-level talent development activities that ordinarily cannot be accomplished in larger group situations (i.e., regular classrooms and enrichment clusters). Positive attitudes toward the enrichment teaching specialist have been observed in situations where she or he helped extend the work of classroom teachers. A third grade teacher, for example, asked the enrichment specialist to work individually with a student who had remarkable poetry writing ability. Curriculum compacting allowed the student to leave the regular classroom during reading and language arts periods. The two teachers worked out a mutually agreeable schedule that resulted in approximately one hour of individual assistance each week.

The second ground rule is that the work of enrichment teaching specialists must focus on talent development at the high end of students' work rather than remedial assistance or tutorial extensions of classroom assignments. Worst-case scenarios result when teachers view enrichment specialists as persons who fulfill the same role as teachers' aides or remedial specialists. Since enrichment and remedial specialists share common strategies when working with individuals or small groups, it is best to define the enrichment specialist's role in terms of the level of product rather than the instructional strategies. There is a subtle but important distinction between: "Will you please help this student who is having trouble with his term paper," and "This paper may be good enough to submit to the state essay contest, but it still needs major revisions and rewriting." We note in this second statement implications for the kinds of assistance that will lead to the development of a Type III product, and it is precisely this kind of assistance that should define the enrichment specialist's major responsibilities. An extension of work that may have originated in the regular classroom is certainly a legitimate domain for enrichment specialists; however, these extensions should be directed toward extraordinary levels of talent development.

These two ground rules will help clarify the role of schoolwide enrichment personnel as talent development specialists, and they set parameters for the kinds of direct contact specialists have with students. They should not be interpreted, however, as an indication that only enrichment specialists are responsible for talent development, or that the only purpose of the SEM is to concentrate resources on a select group of students. Many classroom teachers have guided the development of outstanding Type III products, both within regular classes and in the enrichment clusters. And, in numerous instances, the training and experience of *both* enrichment specialists and classroom teachers have been combined to produce maximal benefits for students. Talent development is everybody's job, and the enrichment teaching specialist, faculty, and other personnel have a collective responsibility for developing talent to the highest level possible in every student.

Resource and Leadership Responsibilities

The resource and leadership responsibilities of the enrichment specialist generally fall into the following four categories:

1. Gaining a familiarity with the vast amount of enrichment materials available, and collecting, reviewing, and disseminating information about these materials to administrators, faculty members, students, and parents.
2. Providing staff development and demonstration teaching sessions in the use of enrichment materials and general strategies for enrichment learning and teaching.
3. Preparing communication vehicles for parents and professionals, creating support through public relations activities, and maintaining contact with a network of schoolwide enrichment specialists.
4. Overseeing the organization, administration, and evaluation of the program and organizing the various subgroups and schoolwide enrichment teams that have responsibilities for implementing particular components of the model.

The Schoolwide Enrichment Model: A How-to Guide for Educational Excellence (Renzulli and Reis 1997, 39–71) includes a chapter on detailed information about implementing a SEM. This chapter includes guidance for organizing staff development sessions, providing orientation for parents and students, developing handbooks and other communication vehicles for teachers and parents, and preparing public relations and community awareness information. As is the case with all material developed in connection with the SEM, we encourage local adaptation according to the unique nature of individual programs, the availability of resources, and the specific ways in which the schoolwide enrichment teaching specialist allocates his or her time.

Enrichment specialists are the spark plugs that ignite most of the enrichment activities in a school, and they are the conceptual and practical adhesive that holds together the many dimensions of a SEM school. But the job is far too complex to be carried out effectively by one person, and, therefore, an organizational component has been built into the model that provides the enrichment specialist with a support system essential for the maximum delivery of services. This component is described in the section that follows.

CREATING A SCHOOLWIDE ENRICHMENT TEAM

One of the best ways to expand the full range of enrichment services to all students is by developing a schoolwide enrichment team. An enrichment team is not a policy making body or an advisory committee but, rather, a working group of faculty members and parents who have specific responsibilities for organizing the overall enrichment effort for an entire school. Enrichment team members serve as representatives of their grade level or department, and one of their responsibilities is to promote faculty involvement in schoolwide enrichment activities. Organizing an enrichment team develops a sense of faculty and community ownership in the SEM. We have found that when classroom teachers are encouraged to become actively involved in enrichment team activities, they eventually come to regard efforts to develop talent as a joint venture to be shared by all faculty members. Our experience has also shown that faculty members at large are frequently interested in planning and organizing enrichment activities, as well as in the direct delivery of services. Over the last several years we have worked with many school districts that have implemented outstanding enrichment programs. In almost every case, the first step after the SEM was adopted and administrative support assured was an orientation for all staff members about the components of the model and the establishment of an enrichment team.

Who Should Be on the Enrichment Team?

We have found the most effective way to organize an enrichment team is to recruit members from various segments of the school and community. We, therefore, suggest that the enrichment team include parents, community resource persons, administrators, classroom teachers who represent all grade levels, art, music, physical education and other special subject teachers, and the librarian or media specialist. At the secondary level, a general enrichment team includes representatives from each department; separate enrichment teams can be organized within departments as well. We have also found that it is extremely effective to include students on the enrichment team. One reluctant community resource person, for example, told us that he could have easily refused an adult's invitation to present a 45-minute workshop on his specialty area, but it was impossible for him to refuse the request when it was made by an excited fifth-grader!

An invitation to serve on the enrichment team should be extended to all faculty members. In one school system where all staff members were required to select two instructional objectives on which to be evaluated at the end of the school year, principals encouraged faculty members to select participation on the schoolwide enrichment team as an objective.

The number of team members can vary. We have seen effective teams with only three active members (in smaller schools) and teams of ten or twelve (in larger schools). It is also important to mention that in some school districts, negative, outspoken faculty members have been invited to serve on the enrichment team and, indeed, have been personally recruited by the principal and/or the enrichment specialist. In many cases, negative energy has been channeled into a more positive direction by simply including this kind of teacher on the team. We should caution, however, that as few as two negative persons can become a strong enough coalition to block positive action through the strength they gain from each other.

We recommend that the superintendent of schools write a "letter of appointment" to the individuals serving on the enrichment team, telling them how important their task is and commending them for volunteering. This practice exemplifies administrative support, and it also allows team members to know that the chief school officer is aware of their additional effort and involvement. We also recommend that, whenever possible, some type of budget be given to the team. Although the great majority of the enrichment experiences typically used in the SEM do not require supplementary funds, there may be occasions when a cost is involved. If the enrichment team has even a small budget with which to work, a great number of avenues may be opened up for the exploration of possible enrichment activities. Additionally, access to even limited funds helps legitimize the team in the eyes of the school community.

Finally, no one should ever be forced to serve on the enrichment team. We strongly advocate the inclusion of a building principal even if he or she attends meetings only on a periodic basis. But no one should serve on the team who truly does not want to be involved. We have found that once the benefits of the various types of enrichment experiences become obvious, more faculty members become interested in joining the team in subsequent years.

Who Should Serve as the Chairperson of the Enrichment Team?

If a schoolwide enrichment teaching specialist is available, it is advisable to have this person serve as chairperson of the team and to organize *regular* meetings. A resource teacher often has a more flexible schedule than classroom teachers. The chair should preside over a democratic decision-making process that leads to subdividing duties so that the responsibilities are shared among team members and the general faculty members whom they represent. The key to successful functioning of the enrichment team is specificity of tasks and a division of labor among team members.

A series of Action Forms (Renzulli and Reis 1997) have been developed to assist in this process. *Action Information* is an annotated record of events that take place within the instructional process. The idea is to take advantage of times when students react positively to different learning experiences that occur outside the formal learning environment. By documenting this information on the Action Information Message Form, teachers and students have a record of potential starting points for follow-up activities. Since team members can devote only relatively small portions of their time to this endeavor, it is essential that tasks be broken down into targeted activities that can be carried out with minimal expenditures of time. If a resource teacher or enrichment specialist is not present in the school, we recommend the election or appointment of a chairperson who is organized, efficient, and gets along with other faculty members. We strongly advise that this person have some release time for organizing the enrichment team's work in addition to his or her regularly scheduled planning time. Two or three hours a week that an administrator can arrange for the chairperson to use as planning time communicates a very important message to the chairperson and the entire faculty. Simply, that message is this: We value what you are doing, and we support your efforts to complete this task.

How Often Should the Team Meet and What Should It Accomplish?

For teams that are just beginning, we recommend regular weekly meetings for the first month or two of school. At these initial meetings, the logistical questions that face all enrichment teams should be discussed. These questions include, but are not limited to, the following:

1. When is the best time of the week to organize regular enrichment experiences?
2. Should most enrichment activities be conducted in regular classroom settings? In the enrichment clusters? In the continuum of special services?
3. How can we orient the faculty to realize that enrichment experiences are wide and varied and include more than speakers?
4. How can enrichment experiences be implemented to allow for equal representation across subject matter areas?
5. How many enrichment experiences should be organized for a given period of time?
6. How can we organize these activities with minimal disruption to the regular school day?
7. How can we involve as many faculty members as possible?
8. How can we recruit parents and community members and agencies?
9. How can we evaluate the effectiveness of enrichment activities?
10. How do we (the enrichment team) get started?

These and other logistical questions will require more organizational time for the enrichment team at the beginning of the year. We have found that the answers to these questions vary from school to school, depending upon the size of a school, availability of space for enrichment experiences, flexibility of the faculty, administrative attitudes toward the enrichment program, and the time that the enrichment team is able to spend working together.

THE PROFESSIONAL DEVELOPMENT MODEL

Although schools are supposed to be the major formal agencies for learning in our society, when it comes to the education of persons within the teaching profession, we consistently violate what is known about how people learn most effectively and the conditions under which they apply their knowledge to new situations. If, as John Goodlad tells us, today's schools bear a striking resemblance to schools at the turn of the century (Goodlad 1983, 1984), then we must reexamine the ways in which we prepare teachers in direct relation to the types of schools we are trying to create.

It has been argued that the old style inservice training, which focused almost exclusively on one-shot, skill-oriented workshops, is inadequate for bringing about real and lasting improvements in schools. But the history of professional development, and the enormity of the task of improved professionalism, require that proposals for change must be approached with caution and parsimony and an understanding of the process of change itself. The almost endless amount of time spent in poor quality training, the external restrictions that limit application of newly acquired methods, and the roles that teachers have played as recipients rather than decision makers about their own training, have produced a quiet skepticism about the entire issue of professional development. We will not attempt to rewrite the book on professional development because we do not believe there are any magical solutions to the complex problem of improving the professionalism of all school personnel. We will, however, offer some commonsense suggestions that have proven to be effective in bringing about school improvement within the context of the SEM.

The professional development model for the SEM is built around a three-phase process that includes (1) substantive examinations of theoretical, pedagogical, and curricular knowledge, (2) skill-oriented training that focuses on the know-how of implementing a particular teaching method or set of curricular materials, and (3) opportunities to apply knowledge and know-how in a relatively unrestricted and nonthreatening experimental setting. A graphic representation of this model is presented in Figure 6.2, and the sections that follow describe procedures for using the professional development model.

A group within the school should serve as a steering committee for making decisions about issues that will be the focus for professional development, and this group should gather suggestions from individuals and other teams that represent various subgroups of faculty, administration, and parents. A

Professional Development Triangle

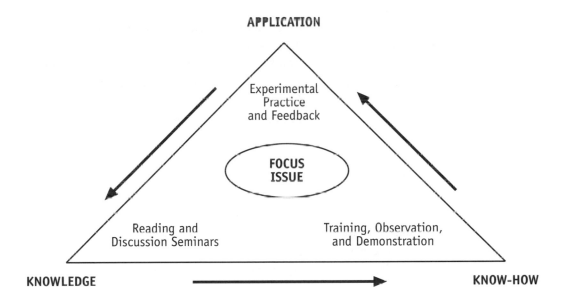

Figure 6.2

major criterion for determining which topics will become focus issues is how a particular topic relates to one of the components of the SEM. Thus, for example, the larger issue of curriculum modification and related theoretical and research information about curriculum compacting can serve as a focus issue for faculty discussion.

Knowledge Seminars

The knowledge component of the model is ordinarily the starting point of the staff development process, and it consists of selecting an idea, topic, curriculum issue, or teaching method that will be the *focus* of a particular school improvement initiative. This may be a macro-change initiative such as the exploration of the SEM, which, if adopted, can be followed by micro-change professional development activities. Following an introduction to the topic and the distribution of an economical set of background material for individual reading, small group seminars are conducted to discuss the full range of ramifications the topic generates. Persons organizing the seminar should also provide easy access to related research and theoretical literature about the topic, bibliographies of related material, and an open invitation for all persons to contribute background material of their own choosing. The seminars should have two inviolable ground rules. First and foremost, the seminar should be viewed as a community of professional scholars who are coming together to examine the theoretical and pedagogical merits of the focus issue. The main questions should be: "Will it (e.g., the method, curricular material, management procedure, grouping alternative, etc.) improve learning?" "Will it help make a difference in the lives of students?" "Will it help to make our school a better place?" By focusing on theoretical issues, we avoid getting mired down in the details of implementation and the admonitions of naysayers. The negativism that exists on the parts of many teachers is, in part, the result of not having opportunities to discuss important issues that lead to decision making. Our profession has had a tradition of bringing in the persons who will be charged with the responsibility for implementing a change only *after* theoretical issues have been considered by policy makers, and *after* decisions have been made about new initiatives. Little wonder that so many teachers and building administrators react negatively to proposed changes, and in some cases, even go so far as to undermine changes that they believe have been imposed upon them.

Another tradition in education is that teachers go to teacher workshops, administrators go to administrator workshops, and so on. This tradition has perpetuated the us-and-them syndrome and is clearly the best way to ensure poor communication and a lack of understanding of the problems and agendas of the respective groups. We believe that teachers, administrators, and supervisory personnel should be involved in all three phases of this professional development process. Research by Maeroff (1993) reports on the benefits of collaboration between administrators and teachers. Their teaming not only leads to shared convictions and a fresh willingness on the part of participants to accept part of the burden of leadership, but it also helps minimize the possibilities of miscommunication.

In order for the process to work effectively, a second important ground rule—that everyone's opinion must be valued and respected—must be followed. If administrative personnel, union representatives, or high status teachers pull rank, or if overt or subtle messages minimize the teachers' role in the group, then the process will be undermined from the outset. Similarly, if teachers put out negative messages about how administrators "don't truly understand the nuts and bolts of the real classroom," then the process will take on the same battle lines that have hindered past attempts at school improvement.

The knowledge seminars are, indeed, a part of the process for addressing practical problems and solutions, but the main purpose of this component of the professional development process is to provide a vehicle for the kinds of intellectual and creative thinking that are largely absent from so much of the work of practicing school personnel. We have experimented with these types of seminars with teachers and administrators involved in professional development related to the SEM, and two observations are immediately apparent. First, practitioners have consistently said that dealing with ideas and concepts about theoretical issues is a refreshing departure from the kinds of teacher training in which they are ordinarily involved. One teacher's comment typifies the reactions of many: "This is the first time since college that anyone expected me to actually use my *mind!*" Another teacher said, "They are always asking us to do something different, but we are never given an opportunity to deal with why we are doing it or what the research says about the benefits of doing it."

Second, far more teachers and administrators than we expected rose to the occasion of the intellectual challenges that were required for the discussion of theoretical and pedagogical issues. The degree of preparation and participation clearly indicates that we may have been underestimating teachers' interest in and ability to engage in the kinds of dialogue that tradition has generally restricted to policy makers and administrators, or to college courses that are often disconnected from school improvement activities. To be certain, the process did not take place easily and naturally in its early stages. Limited opportunities and experience in engaging in this kind of interaction are traditions that frequently turns teachers' meetings into gripe sessions and causes suspicion about the motivation for promoting this kind of professional involvement.

These traditions require time and hard work to overcome. When teachers view an examination of theoretical issues in the larger context of decision making, and as a prelude to possible follow-up of a more practical nature, the knowledge seminars take on a more important role in overall professional development. The education profession has generally underestimated the conceptual role of teachers; by so doing, we have not only missed opportunities to nurture and use local intelligence and creativity, but we have also turned the profession into a rank-and-file organization that replaces self-motivation with greater and greater amounts of supervision.

Complicated teacher evaluation systems have been adopted by some states and districts that give higher ratings to persons adhering to formula-driven teaching-by-prescription than to creative and responsive, student-centered teaching! In one state that adopted such an evaluation system, several teachers acknowledged as among the very best in a particular district actually earned the lowest ratings because they did not use the prescribed steps in every lesson. The knowledge seminars provide opportunities for enhancing the professionalization of teaching by allowing practitioners to study and to examine the theoretical issues and research findings that are the foundation of their work.

Know-How Workshops

This dimension of the professional development triangle is probably the most familiar to teachers and other educational personnel. Know-how workshops usually focus on the acquisition of new skills, teaching and management techniques, and the use of specified sets of instructional materials. Most of the training in this area has been carried out by having persons present information in workshop settings. Equally valuable, but less frequently used approaches, are observations of particular techniques in classrooms where the technique has been perfected, or participation in demonstration lessons in which adult audience members assume the roles of students. The effectiveness of all three approaches can be enhanced by using them in conjunction with one another; and effectiveness will be further enhanced if know-how workshops include, whenever possible, demonstration teaching and opportunities for participants to practice a particular technique.

One of the more fortunate results of the school improvement initiative has been a rapidly growing body of staff development materials. The use of video training tapes and interactive satellite communication links has made high levels of professional training available to schools that cannot afford expensive consultants or schools that lack the local expertise necessary for new initiatives.

Professional development that focuses on the acquisition of know-how has been a mainstay of teacher training, and it has also been the subject of a fair amount of criticism and wasted time. There are few teachers who cannot add their own horror stories to the list of tales about disappointing workshops, boring presenters, and forced attendance at training sessions on topics in which they had little interest. Although it will be difficult, if not impossible, to overcome all of the criticism about inservice training, there are at least four specific issues to be considered if we are to avoid past mistakes and therefore increase the impact of training recommended for the know-how dimension of the staff development model. First, all persons in the school community should be involved in planning inservice training, either directly or indirectly through the representatives of their respective teams. Second, input about the quality of a trainer or training package should be sought from individuals or groups who have had firsthand experience with the trainer or training package being considered. Third, time should be made available for a post-learning analysis of the training session in order to consider the value of the training within the overall context of the school's goals. Finally, administrators and parents, as well as teachers, should participate in the know-how workshops, and teacher and parent representatives should participate in workshops that are specifically targeted for administrators.

Two ground rules should guide all know-how workshops. First, a workshop should be offered only if it fits with an already adopted model or larger plan for school improvement. This ground rule will help prevent schools from falling prey to the flavor-of-the-month approach to staff development. This ground rule helps guarantee continuity and integrity to a comprehensive approach to school improvement rather than an ad hoc approach to staff development.

A second ground rule is that any know-how training must be recommended by the steering committee and approved by a majority of the faculty within a given building. This ground rule guarantees staff involvement rather than top-down decision making, and it helps to link the knowledge seminars with know-how workshops. When an entire faculty examines training opportunities within the context of a general plan or model, and when there is a perceived need based on discussions of theoretical and pedagogical issues, there is greater likelihood that professional development will have the kind of payoff that we have hoped for but seldom achieved.

The fit or need for inservice can be assessed in a dialogue among educators or with the assistance of inventories. Schlichter and Olenchak (1992) developed an instrument for identifying inservice needs in schools using the SEM. Through extensive interviews and reviews of literature on the model and on enrichment teaching practices, the authors developed an item pool that they field tested subsequently in three schools. Measures of central tendency and dispersion were calculated, and a factor analysis was conducted to determine the number of significant factors and the loadings defining each factor. Four areas were identified as major categories that should be considered in preparing for staff development: Preparing for School Change, Focusing Type III Investigations, Organizing and Providing Enrichment for All Students, and Stimulating the Interests of Each Individual Student. The research resulted in a final instrument consisting of 24 items based on a 5-point Likert response format. The instrument, entitled *Schoolwide Enrichment Teachers' Ratings of Appraised In-service Needs* (SE-TRAIN) is included in Appendix C. In addition to this model-specific approach to examining inservice needs, general approaches such as the Concerns-Based Adoption Model (CBAM) (Hall, George, and Rutherford 1979) can be customized to provide direction to staff development needs. CBAM uses a 35-item survey instrument, *Stages of Concern Questionnaire*, to examine the following seven stages of concern with regard to adopting new practices: awareness about the practice; information about what the uses of the practice entail; personal concerns and uncertainties; management concerns about time and logistics; consequence concerns about the impact upon students; implications about collaboration; and refocusing concerns about new ideas to replace or alter the practice. The instrument yields an individual profile that can be used for diagnostic purposes about both the adoption of a new practice and the nature of support required during the implementation of an innovation.

Application Situations

Our efforts to improve teaching have profoundly violated what we know about learning by failing to provide teachers with opportunities to apply what they have learned about good teaching. Almost every teacher has been subjected to hundreds of hours of training and yet, very little of that training has produced lasting changes in what takes place in classrooms. External regulations, the influence of textbooks and standardized testing, and the tendency of our profession to jump on almost every fad and bandwagon that comes down the road are undoubtedly reasons for the limited impact of training. But another reason we do not make use of newly acquired skills over longer periods of time is that limited opportunities exist in the present school structure to practice and refine new skills in a supportive and nonthreatening environment. Using a metaphor called "polishing the stone," Stigler and Stevenson (1991) report that one of the characteristics of successful Asian teachers is that they devote time to refining and honing their lessons to a high state of perfection. Furthermore, not only do they discuss with their colleagues the art and science of good teaching, and engage in a continuous inquiry about their own teaching activities, but also national television in Japan presents programs that show how master teachers handle particular lessons or concepts (Stigler and Stevenson 1991; Stevenson and Stigler 1992).

The third dimension of the SEM professional development model is designed to provide application situations and opportunities to discuss concerns and issues related to newly initiated teaching methods. This type of *reflective teaching* capitalizes on the knowledge base and know-how phases discussed earlier, and it draws upon the same principles of learning that are advocated for students. One vehicle for application situations is built into the SEM in the form of the enrichment clusters. Our own experience, and the experience of numerous teachers with whom we have worked over the years, provided the clue for this connection between reflective teaching and the lack of structure that characterizes enrichment clusters.

Anyone who has ever taught in a special program (e.g., Saturday enrichment classes, 4-H program, preparation for science fairs, play or musical production), or who has served as a leader or coach in an extracurricular activity, operates by a different set of rules from those present in formal classroom instruction. First, the major goal is to produce a high-quality product or service. Second, there are no mastery tests or grading requirements hanging over the teacher's heads. Third, the adult's role is more like that of a guide and compatriot rather than a direct frontal instructor. These types of situations result in qualitatively different relations between young people and adults,[1] and they require that a different kind of learning paradigm be used. Many of our colleagues have reported that teaching in such an environment has enabled them to develop skills that are readily applicable to regular classroom teaching situations. Because the enrichment clusters are purposefully designed to provide a different type of learning, they can also serve as true laboratories for teachers to practice and refine new skills in a climate free from the constraints usually placed on the regular curriculum.

There is, however, one additional component necessary to capitalize on these laboratory situations, and to ensure that they are a systematic, rather than random, part of professional development. Teachers need an opportunity to discuss and reflect upon all of their teaching practices. To do this, time must be made available, and procedures initiated so that discussions about one another's teaching can be carried out in an open and trusting atmosphere. This is a difficult task, especially in a profession that historically has treated what goes on in the privacy of one's own classroom as a very personal matter. Such follow-up discussions are important in order to overcome two major

> . . . enrichment clusters . . . can also serve as true laboratories for teachers to practice and refine new skills in a climate free from the constraints usually placed on the regular curriculum.

taboos of teaching: "Thou shall not enter thy neighbor's classroom while she or he is teaching," and "Thou shall not discuss craft with one's colleagues." There are no formulas or easy solutions for overcoming these ancient taboos; however, a number of specific strategies are emerging from recent studies on team building that provide guidance for creating a nucleus of committed people in each school that can lead the way toward more consultation and sharing between and among members of the faculty.

Team building is an excellent way of overcoming the isolation and sense of inconsequentiality that many teachers experience. Teams can consist of two persons such as the type recommended in the peer coaching model (Glatthorn 1987; Joyce and Showers 1982; Showers, Joyce, and Bennett 1987), or they can be slightly larger based on individual preferences. The most important consideration in forming teams that focus on the teaching process is that persons have a choice in determining their own team's make-up. This approach will help overcome problems usually associated with school committees that are formed along traditional lines. Since the function of the teams is to examine the most personal part of our professionalism, that is, our teaching, it is essential that persons be on a team with people they trust.

This approach to school improvement is based, in part, on lessons that have been learned from successful practices in business and industry, where teams have been formed to tackle difficult problems related to efficiency, effectiveness, and motivation. Although a good deal of the emerging literature on democratic school governance focuses on policy and management issues, the team approach is especially applicable to the direct improvement of teaching. The major reality that catapulted team building to the forefront of private and public organizations is that persons closest to the work know best how to perform and improve the work they are doing. At the heart of the work of schools, and of the SEM, is the act of learning. In a later section, we will discuss team building issues related to democratic school governance. Although there are commonalities in all processes based on the use of teams, our concern here is with the application of team strategies to the learning process.

THE SCHOOLWIDE ENRICHMENT MODEL WEB SITE

One of the advantages of a school improvement process based on a unified model is that categorical components of the model can be shared among model users in an organized rather than random fashion. To facilitate this process we have developed a Schoolwide Enrichment Model Web site (www.gifted.uconn.edu) that includes information on SEM and lists of resources that support SEM. Communication vehicles include newsletters, a computer bulletin board, training institutes, videotapes, teleconferences, and articles related to SEM.

PARENT ORIENTATION, TRAINING, AND INVOLVEMENT

A growing body of literature points out the crucial role that parents need to play in their children's education. Accordingly, we have developed and acquired materials and procedures that promote the parental advocacy and support system necessary for improved cooperation between home and school. Print and audiovisual materials have been developed that provide orientation for parents about SEM concepts such as curriculum compacting, the role of interest and effort in learning, the overall goals and components of the model, and ways in which parents can become involved in their own children's work as well as in various aspects of the enrichment program in general. Vehicles such as the *Community Talent Miner* (Renzulli and Reis 1985) are designed to query parents about special areas of expertise, cultural experiences, and know-how that can serve as enrichment resources to the school.

Our goal in this organizational component is to integrate parents and other community resources into the educational program rather than simply using parents for miscellaneous busy work. Improved communication with parents is the key to making better connections between the home and school cultures, but it is also necessary to have an organizational plan for building the parent component of the model. The plan that we have developed focuses on the following three dimensions of parent involvement: parent orientation about schoolwide enrichment and roles that parents can play in decision-making processes that affect their children's education, direct involvement with their children at home, and involvement in enrichment activities at school. This plan is based on parent involvement programs that have proven successful in various types of schools around the country.

One such plan is James Comer's (1988, 1990) model, developed specifically to help parents and teachers in inner-city schools work together to overcome barriers created by rigid school structures and limited cooperation between and among parents, schools, and other social service agencies and specialists. Because poor minority children from nonmainstream families often feel disconnected from schools, Comer emphasized psychological development and interpersonal factors rather than traditional reform initiatives that tend to favor curriculum and instruction. The program supports children's learning and development by building bonds among children, parents, and school personnel. Social gatherings help to promote better relations between parents and staff, and life-skill training programs for students help them to develop mainstream social skills for interacting with peers and adults.

The centerpiece of Comer's plan is a core management team for each school that includes community-elected parents and teachers, the principal, a mental-health specialist, and a member of the classified support staff. The principal has ultimate authority, but consensus is encouraged and the focus is on problem solving rather than accusing and blaming others for past problems. Each school also has an intervention team consisting of a teacher, psychologist, and social worker. The team identifies patterns of troublesome behavior in individual students, and intervention strategies are based on total team input that takes into consideration the personal and social as well as academic needs of the developing child. Although initial problems and resistance to this innovative plan were experienced in the early stages of implementation, parents and staff realized the benefits of solving school problems by overcoming the misalignment between home and school, and positive results began to emerge. Follow-up studies (Comer 1988) of schools using Comer's model showed that participating schools improved in achievement and attendance, and there was a decrease in the incidence of behavior problems.

A five-state study conducted by the Southwest Educational Development Laboratory used key informants, site visits, and evaluation questionnaires to examine factors that contributed to successful programs of parent involvement. The programs identified as promising featured several types of parent involvement and included many roles for parents: audience, home tutor, program supporter, co-learner, advocate, and decision maker (Williams and Chavkin 1989). Some of the programs were affiliated with national coalitions such as the National School Volunteer Program, and others were described as small, homegrown efforts. Regardless of size and affiliation, however, all of the promising programs had the following seven essential elements:

1. Written policies that legitimize parent involvement and frame the context for program activities.
2. Administrative support in the form of funds, resources (materials, meeting space, duplication and communication equipment), and designated people to carry out program efforts.
3. Ongoing training for the development of parenting skills, and training on skills for teacher and parent cooperation.
4. A "partnership approach" to joint planning, goal setting, defining roles, setting school standards, developing instructional and school support efforts, and program assessment.
5. Two-way communication that allowed parents to feel comfortable coming to school, sharing ideas, and voicing concerns.
6. Networking with other schools with parent involvement initiatives in order to share information, resources, and technical expertise.
7. Regular (formative) evaluation activities at key stages so that modifications and revisions can be made when needed rather than waiting until the end of the year (Williams and Chavkin 1989, 18–20).

Although everyone talks about parent involvement in decision making, very little guidance exists in the literature about specific procedures for promoting this kind of involvement; to be very frank, the education establishment has paid only lip service to opening doors to important decision making on the parts of parents. Boards of education are *supposed* to be major policy-making bodies, but in reality, most of the decisions they make are carefully crafted and steered within limited boundaries set by external regulations and district administrators. Persons in positions of power and authority at state and district levels and in collective bargaining units determine almost all of what happens in today's classrooms. It is not our intent to minimize the roles that these forces should play in the overall education of young people; however, if we are sincere about parent involvement, then it is necessary to create honest vehicles for parental participation in decision making as well as functionary activities. And, just as parents must learn about the techniques and responsibilities for decision making, so also must professional educators learn the know-how of sharing power with nonprofessional groups and individuals.

> In order to help parents take a more active part in their children's education, the school must also take a more active role in providing specific services and resources for parents.

There is no easy formula for creating a more viable role for parents in school decision making, but some of the materials listed in the Resource Guide are designed to provide guidance for both parents and professional educators in the delicate task of opening up the school to a more meaningful role for parents. These materials include books and articles by leaders at the national, state, and local level who are creating new partnerships between schools and families.

The best efforts to improve our schools will not be maximally effective unless parents become more directly involved in their children's education. We are not recommending that parents fulfill the role of teacher-at-home, nor do we expect parents to master the subject matter that their children are expected to learn. Parents can, however, provide the physical environment and psychological support at home that is necessary for improved school performance. Obvious support activities such as a fixed time and place to study, a daily routine that ensures both the completion of homework and a parental review of each day's assignments, periodic visits to school, and becoming acquainted with teachers are far less common in our society than they were a few decades ago. In order to help parents take a more active part in their children's education, the school must also take a more active role in providing specific services and resources for parents.

IMPLEMENTING DEMOCRATIC SCHOOL MANAGEMENT AS A PLAN FOR CHANGE

National, state, and local concerns for school improvement, perhaps for the first time in the history of education, have opened the door to more democratic school governance procedures. Everyone who has a stake in effective schools realizes that practical strategies for attracting, organizing, and making the best use of human resources are, without question, the hallmark of successful organizations. Many of these strategies originated in the private sector and in overseas corporations, but they are rapidly being embraced by US schools. Although we have not adopted a single model for school management, a set of criteria for democratic management has been developed (see Goal 5 in chapter 2), and we will recommend the essential components of a plan for initiating a democratic school management process.

The Seven Cs of School Change

The essence of this plan is built around what we call the Seven Cs of School Change and the use of these Cs by a school governing council. The Seven Cs consist of the following components:

1. Consensus
2. Compromise
3. Communication
4. Collegiality
5. Commitment
6. Creativity
7. Courage

The school governing council should consist of the principal, an equal number of elected teachers and parents, an appointed member from the special service staff (e.g., school psychologist, social worker, nurse), and an appointed member of the nonprofessional staff (e.g., custodian, security guard, cafeteria worker). The principal should chair the council and be responsible for setting up a regularly scheduled meeting and soliciting agenda items from all staff members and parents of students in the school. There may also be times when agenda items are solicited from students or members of the community at large.

The first, and perhaps most important, C for the council to consider is *consensus.* The difficult task of sharing power and decision making must begin with a willingness to establish a governance group in each school that honors the opinions of all members of the council. A second but related C is *compromise.* Each group (teachers, parents, administrators) brings to the table its own agenda and accumulated history of grievances that it is prone to blame on one or more of the other groups. Many school improvement initiatives have faltered or become ineffective because ground rules were not established to ensure consensus and compromise at the very outset of the governance process. One of the first decisions that the council should make is whether or not it should obtain professional assistance in learning how to conduct a democratic governance process that is based on consensus and compromise.

The third C is *communication.* All council meetings should be open to the staff and public, and a summary of the minutes of meetings should be included in a regularly published newsletter. A budget for communication, reproduction, and distribution services should be made available to the council, and a council work space should be provided so that parents feel they have a home base when they come to the school. Each newsletter should have a clip-and-mail coupon that encourages readers to react to actions by the council and to make suggestions about issues or services that readers would like the council to consider.

The fourth C, *collegiality,* should help define the larger mission of the council. This mission transcends the traditional constituencies of school organizations (i.e., parents representing parents, teachers representing teachers, etc.). Collegiality means that members of the council are tied together in the larger mission of working together to make a difference in the lives of students. Colleagues are persons who talk with one another and collaborate in order to better serve the interests of their common clients. Far too many school organizations and legislative bodies view themselves as representatives of vested interest peer groups rather than participants who share a common vision. All council activities should address the questions, "Is this good for our students?" or "Is this good for our school?" rather than questions relating to the satisfaction of one's fellow teachers, parents, or administrators. Admittedly, this is a difficult transition for any leadership group to make; however, all of the adults associated with a school should know beforehand that the council will have this kind of orientation.

The fifth and sixth Cs are *commitment* and *creativity*. Involvement on a school council that is going to accomplish anything important requires a commitment of time and energy that goes beyond the time spent in meetings. Background reading, meetings with subgroups, attendance at leadership training activities, preparing material for distribution to others, writing proposals, and working one-on-one with reluctant individuals are all commitments of time that persons should be willing to make if they choose to serve on a school council. The most effective meetings are those that draw upon activities that have taken place in preparation for the meeting.

Persons who become involved in school councils should also be willing to explore ways of expanding their own creative ability. One of the main reasons that schools have not changed is that we have tried to address present-day school concerns and problems with endless variations of the same solutions. Albert Einstein once said, "Problems cannot be solved at the same level of consciousness that created them." As schools have become more structured and subjected to an endless proliferation of regulations, we have used these very structures and regulations as defenses against change. "We can't change the schedule because it won't meet state requirements." "The teachers' union will never let you have a staff development session that is not over by 4:20." "Who will pay the custodians if we have a Saturday morning enrichment program?" "If it doesn't cover one of the standards on the state list, the director of curriculum will never buy it." None of these is an insurmountable problem; however, we often *act* as if they are as inevitable and omnipresent as the phases of the moon. The result has been that we tinker with the status quo rather than use our imaginations to change it.

Edward de Bono (1985) developed a planned strategy for improving the efficiency of meetings. De Bono's plan is also built around his work in the area of creativity training. We recommend that the school council consider engaging in some type of systematic creativity training such as de Bono's Six Thinking Hats model, or other approaches that are listed in the Resource Guide. It would be unthinkable to put together a talent development program for students without a creative thinking and problem-solving component, and we believe that such a component is equally important for adults who are responsible for both program development and for overcoming the traditional roadblocks that have stood in the way of most efforts to improve schools.

The last C in our Seven Cs of School Improvement is *courage*. The activities described here and, indeed, throughout this book, are not radical or revolutionary; they do, however, require that some people have the courage to examine what is widely recognized as one of the most intransigent and bureaucratized public service agencies in our society. Radical changes have taken place in our society during the last quarter of the twentieth century. The emergence of a global economy and the transfer of manufacturing jobs to other nations; the development of sophisticated communication systems and information technologies; and the rise of feminism, multiculturalism, and concerns for planetary ecosystems have all played a part in bringing about massive cultural changes. As this trend accelerates, the ways that we modify our education system become the most crucial factors in determining whether schools will play a role in shaping society or whether they will become obsolete. To change the system, even through a gentle and evolutionary process, persons at all levels of involvement need to summon up the courage to think and act in ways that may be discomforting.

Creating More Effective Leadership and Management Techniques

School leadership and management are the hottest new topics to emerge from current efforts to restructure schools. Buzz words about structural changes such as teacher empowerment, total quality management, site-based management, and transformational leadership jump off the pages of educational publications, and leadership training has recently become a cottage industry. The critical importance of leadership and management is indisputable, but if real and lasting change is to take place, specific and practical ways of implementing structural changes must be devised. In spite of all the school improvement literature, most schools seem to operate in much the same way they have operated over the past several decades in ways in which teachers promote achievement (Murphy 1991, 76–77).

With so much material about educational leadership and management available and with conflicting and unsubstantiated approaches to contend with, it is difficult to draw any firm conclusions from the mountain of recommendations. Some of the rapidly growing literature on leadership and school management that we have found to be particularly helpful is listed in the Resource Guide. We will not attempt to reinvent this literature, nor give new names to concepts or practices that are already defined in various books, articles, and reports. We will, however, describe three major considerations that must be addressed when examining present and possible future leadership activities necessary for the successful operation of a SEM program.

Focus on the Act of Learning

The first consideration is that all leadership activities must be directly related to the act of learning. A focus on the act of learning (along with the schoolwide enrichment goals discussed in chapter 2) is the centerpiece of the SEM. Adoption of this model means that a majority of the school community has reached consensus on a common purpose and a shared vision about learning. Every decision should be examined by asking: How will this affect what happens in the interaction that takes place between and among learners, teachers, and curriculum? Conventions such as traditional scheduling, budgeting, single textbook adoption, school hours, large-scale testing, grading policies, tenure rules, decisions about staff development, and collective bargaining agreements should be subjected to the act-of-learning question rather than administrative expedience or mere convenience. Even state regulations should be questioned, and waivers should be sought if they impinge upon a school's act-of-learning mission. As the responsibility for improved student performance is moved closer to classrooms where actual learning takes place, power and authority should also be moved down the bureaucratic pipeline into the hands of those responsible for producing agreed-upon results. Leadership training in the use of authority must be provided, just as training should be provided to those persons who must learn how to share authority and power with others. All of the Seven Cs of school change mentioned previously will be required to bring about the evolution of shared decision making necessary to focus on learning rather than on organizational expediency. Certainly, though, the courage to venture into uncharted waters will be an essential ingredient.

Reflecting on Your School's Personality

A second consideration for a successful SEM program is a school's personality and the ways in which a school collectively views itself. One of the best ways to begin a systemic improvement process is for members of the school's nuclear family to focus in on the school's desire for change versus the desire to create the appearance of change. Although the level of change varies from one school type to another, an honest appraisal of predominant characteristics is the starting point for school improvement.

There are two potential school syndromes that should be reflected upon. The first has to do with adopting any school improvement plan based on ideas that originated outside the school. Schools with high self-esteem but low desire for actual change may feel they will lose face if the idea is not their own. This syndrome results in competition between schools to come up with something different, even if what they come up with is of questionable value. In most cases, this kind of one-upmanship competition is mainly for show, or a desire for the *appearance* of change.

The second syndrome is usually found in schools that have both low and high self-esteem, but that also have a low desire for actual change. In low self-esteem schools it might best be described as the "It-Won't-Work-Here" syndrome. In high self-esteem schools it is manifested in the "We're-Already-Doing-That" syndrome. In both cases, the hidden message to persons who want to bring a plan for change to the attention of the school's nuclear family is "Keep your ideas to yourself." Fear of looking bad by calling attention to possible modifications in the status quo has caused more than one individual or group to actually conceal, misrepresent, or even subvert the efforts of persons who want to examine a school improvement process.

The personalities of entire schools do not change easily; we would be fooling ourselves if we thought than any model or plan for school improvement could overcome the accumulated history that results in determining where a school stands on the continuum of change. It is, however, worthwhile for schools to examine where they are on the continuum of school change. Even if the probability for real change is low, an honest appraisal of a school's personality and level of self-esteem will at least place the issue about readiness for change on the table. A confrontation with a difficult problem or issue is always the first step toward alternative courses of action; therefore, we recommend that all schools take the time to examine where they fall in the continuum of change.

What Happens When Democratic Management Is Absent?

The third leadership consideration necessary for implementing the SEM (or any other model, for that matter) addresses two issues that everyone is familiar with but that are seldom covered in polite conversation or the written material about school improvement. These issues are the personalities of individuals, especially those in positions of power and authority, and the politics of self-protection, job enhancement, or the exercise of power for egotistic (or even pathological) reasons. Anyone who has worked in schools or other bureaucracies knows that competence, initiative, creativity, service to clients, and the stated goals of the organization are not always the criteria upon which decisions are made and resources allocated. Almost everyone can add her or his own "horror story" to the list of questionable practices and decisions that have been made because politics and personalities have overshadowed actions that are in the best interest of students. One of the best enrichment programs we have ever observed was eliminated almost overnight when a new assistant superintendent arbitrarily decided to cut the program from the budget. A subsequent investigation by interested teachers and parents revealed that the assistant superintendent harbored a grudge against the program director dating back to the time when they were both students in high school!

Unfortunately, personalities and the politics of self-protection and enhancement will always be present in organizations; they are, unquestionably, the most complex variables in the change process. Equally unfortunate is the sad reality that even the most noble goals and worthwhile practices do not change personalities. It is for this reason that a democratic governance process is necessary. Programs that earn their merit following a reasonable experimental period should be protected from capricious and arbitrary decisions at the policy level. The essence of a democratic system of governance is that no single individual can circumvent the interests of the majority or the reasoned interests of a minority not fairly represented in governing bodies. And the role of policy in an organization is to take a stand on matters of importance so that they are not subject to the whim or will of persons with temporary influence or an idiosyncratic ax to grind. Policies should be enacted only after considered study, dialogue, and debate, and final policy should be adopted only following experimental or pilot periods during which changes in practice are field tested and evaluated.

Although democratic management will help create the motivation and commitment necessary for bringing about *any* change in our schools, it would be unrealistic to assume this goal could be achieved in all schools and districts. Personalities, politics, and vested interests are not stronger than good ideas, but they have a way of gaining control of power over the decision-making process that influences so much of what happens in our schools and classrooms. What happens when a majority of the school's nuclear family wants to implement the SEM but they come up against a road block of an authority person(s) unwilling to support the plan? It is at this point that only two alternatives are available to scrapping the plan and returning to business as usual. The first alternative is "friendly persuasion." We may need to redouble efforts to inform and influence authority figures about the rationale, feasibility, and advantages of pursuing a model that has the support of a significant majority of persons in the nuclear family. This is the best alternative because everything will operate more effectively and harmoniously if persons in positions of authority are at least willing to accept the plan on an experimental basis for a specified period of time.

The second alternative, called "the end run strategy," is recommended *only* when all efforts to achieve support through the Seven Cs of school change have failed. As its name implies, the end run strategy is designed to go around a road block; more than anything, it requires courage on the parts of persons who are advocating a school improvement model. We will illustrate the end run strategy by presenting an actual case study that involved a dictatorial and recalcitrant school superintendent whom we will call Moe Steel. Moe can best be described as a clever, street smart, and very articulate administrator who surrounded himself with yes men, and who managed to keep a fairly sophisticated school board under his control by feeding them contemporary jargon and educational double-talk. Many board and community members respected Moe because he ran a tight ship, kept school costs down and problems contained, and could tell you at a moment's notice enrollment projections, the basketball team's record, and the best vendors from whom to buy toilet tissue. Moe said that any changes in "his schools" would be based only on his beliefs, which were essentially a regimented, one-size-fits-all curriculum. He defended his beliefs by talking about "uniform standards," "curriculum alignment," and other flavor-of-the-month terms that he used to justify the status quo.

A group of parents and teachers in the district expressed an interest in the SEM, and a building principal said that she would be interested in piloting the model in her school. But because they feared recriminations, the teachers and principal said that they wanted to keep a low profile until Moe gave permission for the plan to proceed. Moe, of course, stopped the plan dead in its tracks, using every bureaucratic ploy in his bag of tricks. At this point, the parents and two courageous teachers approached a school board member and provided him with information about the SEM. The board member enthusiastically supported the plan and assumed the role of champion[2] of the group. Following an effective presentation to the board that was arranged by the supportive board member, it looked as though there was enough support to gain a favorable vote for a pilot SEM program. When Moe sensed that the vote might go against him, he invoked one of his favorite ploys: "Let's do a study to see if we really need this program."

The board followed Moe's advice, and a consultant was retained to conduct a needs assessment study. Two local newspapers reported the story, and up to this point, everyone involved received favorable comments from the press. The newspaper stories also resulted in more parent and teacher support for suggested changes in the school program. Although it was clear that the study was initiated by the board rather than the administration, Moe immediately began to conspire so that he could steer and micro-manage the study. Fortunately, the consultant in charge of the study did not buckle under to Moe's demands and intimidation tactics, but Moe used his position to sabotage the study and intimidate school personnel. He would not allow questionnaires to be distributed unless he edited them, and he would not allow teachers to be interviewed unless administrators were present. These activities were reported by the consultant at a subsequent board meeting, and this time both the board and the press questioned Moe's actions. A reprimand was issued, the study was completed without additional interference, and the SEM was eventually implemented at a number of schools in the district. A year later, Moe Steel moved on to a new job.

We do not consider this case history of an end run strategy to be a success story. Many people were caught in the cross fire and the intrigue that resulted from the differences of opinion that could have been negotiated and minimized through communication and compromise. But the example does point out that when persons in positions of authority are unresponsive to the sincere interests of their constituents, there is recourse to higher authority. If a democratic management plan had been in place prior to the events described here, a good deal of unpleasantness and wasted energy would have been avoided—that would have been the best success story of all!

CONCLUDING THOUGHTS

The issues raised in the case history of Moe Steel are a subset of those related to democratic school governance. They are also tied to the professionalism objectives of SEM: the need to promote continuous, reflective growth among the members of the nuclear school family and the need to create a community of learners. Furthermore, these goals are related to the first two goals of this plan for school improvement: enhancing the creative productivity and achievement levels of students. Specifically, systematic reform begins when all members of the school family are treated as equal partners pursuing a common mission. The work among the equal partners must be based on the premise that all involved strive for continuous improvement, actively seek job-related knowledge, and share, though collaboration, their experiences and expertise. When members of the nuclear school family learn to trust and respect each other, encourage and challenge one another to stimulate optimal performance, share a common vision and choose to work together, educational opportunities for students will improve. And when educational opportunities for students improve, talent development for all students becomes a realistic goal. Roland Barth (1990) captured the essence of the meaning of collaboration when he wrote: "The relationships among the adults in schools are the basis, the precondition, the *sine qua non* that allow, energize, and sustain all other attempts at school improvement. Unless adults talk with one another, observe one another, and help one another, very little will change" (p. 32).

With collaboration as both a goal and a process, the nuclear school family can initiate long-sought, systemic reforms by freeing and allocating school time to the two essential elements discussed in this realistic plan for school improvement: teachers and students. Teachers need time to collectively re-create a vision of schools as places for talent development and time to plan learning activities that will engage, and re-engage, students. Students need time within the framework of enrichment clusters to discover that they can be producers of knowledge by adopting the role of the firsthand inquirer. By beginning with these steps, this plan for talent development focuses on those aspects of learning and development over which the schools have the most control, thereby providing the nuclear school family with the highest probability of achieving success.

In closing, we acknowledge the limitations that confront systemic school reform. Society's faith in the capacity of the nation's schools to improve the conditions of people, individually and collectively, is misplaced hope. Changing family structures, de facto segregation, insufferable housing conditions, poor nutrition and health care, limited employment and economic opportunities, and unfair treatment of women and minorities are all factors that contribute to inferior schools. We believe, therefore, that other institutions in society must share in the responsibility for addressing the multifaceted problem of developing the talent of all children. At the same time, we believe also that schools can do something now by concentrating on improving the quality of experiences for nuclear school family members provided between the opening and closing bells of the school day, and by working with parents on matters that affect student performance in school. Schools may not be powerful enough to restructure society, but they do have the potential to be powerful forces in the lives of young people.

ENDNOTES

1. It is interesting to note that studies of college graduates found that extracurricular activities were more consequential in determining adult accomplishments than were traditional academic predictors, including test scores, high school grades, and college grades (Munday and Davis 1974).
2. Conventional wisdom in politics says that action within a decision-making body, especially if the action is related to changes in the status quo, is much more likely to take place if one or more persons become "champions" of a particular cause or action.

Appendix A: Research Related to the Schoolwide

AUTHOR & DATE	TITLE OF STUDY	SAMPLES*
Cooper 1983	Administrator's attitudes toward gifted programs based on the Enrichment Triad/ Revolving Door Identification Model: Case Studies in Decision-Making.	8 districts $n = 32$
Baum 1985	Learning disabled students with superior cognitive abilities: A validation study of descriptive behaviors.	E $n = 112$
Karafelis 1986	The effects of the tri-art drama curriculum on the reading comprehension of students with varying levels of cognitive ability.	E, M $n = 80$
Schack 1986	Creative productivity and self-efficacy in children.	E, M $n = 294$
Starko 1986	The effects of The Revolving Door Identification Model on creative productivity and self-efficacy.	E $n = 103$
Burns 1987	The effects of group training activities on students' creative productivity.	E $n = 515$
Skaught 1987	The social acceptability of talent pool students in an elementary school using The Schoolwide Enrichment Model.	E
Baum 1988	An enrichment program for gifted learning disabled students.	E $n = 7$
Delcourt 1988	Characteristics related to high levels of creative/productive behavior in secondary school students: A multi-case study.	S $n = 18$
Emerick 1988	Academic underachievement among the gifted: Students' perceptions of factors that reverse the pattern.	H+ $n = 10$

*P = Primary Grades, K–2; E = Elementary grades, 3–5; M = Middle grades, 6–8; S = Secondary grades, 9–12

SkyLight Professional Development

Enrichment Model

MAJOR FINDING

- Administrator perceptions regarding the model included: greater staff participation in education of high ability students, more positive staff attitudes toward the program, fewer concerns about identification, positive changes in how the guidance department worked with students, and more incentives for students to work toward higher goals.
- Administrators found SEM to have significant impact on *all* students.

- SEM recommended as one vehicle to meet the unique needs of gifted students with learning disabilities because of the emphasis on strengths, interests, and learning styles.

- Students receiving experimental treatment did equally well on achievement tests as the control group.

- Self-efficacy was a significant predictor of initiation of an independent investigation, and self-efficacy at the end of treatment was higher in students who participated in Type III projects.

- Students who became involved with self-selected independent studies in SEM programs initiated their own creative products both inside and outside school more often than students who qualified for the program but did not receive services.
- Students in the enrichment group reported over twice as many creative projects per student (3.37) as the comparison group (.50) and showed greater diversity and sophistication in projects.
- The number of creative products completed in school (Type IIIs) was a highly significant predictor of self-efficacy.

- Students receiving process skill training were 64% more likely to initiate self-selected projects (Type IIIs) than the students who did not receive the training.

- Students identified as above average for a SEM program were positively accepted by their peers.
- In schools where SEM had been implemented, a "condition of separateness" did not exist for students in the program.

- The Type III independent study, when used as an intervention with high ability, learning disabled students, was associated with improvement in the students' behavior, specifically the ability to self-regulate time on task; improvement in self-esteem; and the development of specific instructional strategies to enhance the potential of high potential, learning disabled students.

- Students completing self-selected investigations (Type IIIs) displayed positive changes in the following: personal skills required for project completion (e.g., writing), personal characteristics (e.g., increased patience), and decisions related to career choices.

- Reversal of academic underachievement through use of various components of SEM including: curriculum compacting, exposure to Type I experiences, opportunities to be involved in Type III studies, and an appropriate assessment of learning styles to provide a match between students and teachers.

(Appendix A continued on next page.)

Appendix A (continued)

AUTHOR & DATE	TITLE OF STUDY	SAMPLES
Olenchak & Renzulli 1989	The effectiveness of the Schoolwide Enrichment Model on selected aspects of elementary schools change.	P, E n = 236, teacher n = 1,698, student
Heal 1989	Student perceptions of labeling the gifted: A comparative case study analysis.	E n = 149
Olenchak 1990	School change through gifted education: Effects on elementary students' attitudes toward learning.	P, E n = 1,935
Imbeau 1991	Teachers' attitudes toward curriculum compacting with regard to the implementation of the procedure.	P, E, M, S n = 166
Newman 1991	The effects of the Talents Unlimited Model on students' creative productivity.	E n = 147
Olenchak 1991	Assessing program effects for gifted/learning disabled students.	P, E n = 108
Taylor 1992	The effects of The Secondary Enrichment Triad Model on the career development of vocational-technical school students.	S
Delcourt 1993	Creative productivity among secondary school students: Combining energy, interest, and imagination.	S n = 18 (longtudinal)
Hébert 1993	Reflections at graduation: The long-term impact of elementary school experiences in creative productivity.	S n = 9 (longitudinal)
Baum, Renzulli, & Hébert 1995	The Prism Metaphor: A New Paradigm for Reversing Underachievement	M n = 17
Kettle, Renzulli, & Rizza 1998	Products of mind: Exploring student preferences for product development using My Way...an Expression Style Instrument.	E, M n = 3532
Reis, Westberg, Kulikowich, & Purcell, 1998	Curriculum compacting and achievement test scores: What does the research say?	E, M n = 336

*P = Primary Grades, K–2; E = Elementary grades, 3–5; M = Middle grades, 6–8; S = Secondary grades, 9–12

MAJOR FINDING

- SEM contributed to improved teacher, parent, and administrator attitudes toward education for high ability students.

- SEM was associated with a reduction in the negative effects of labeling.

- Positive changes in student attitudes toward learning as well as toward gifted education and school in general.

- Group membership (peer coaching) was a significant predictor of posttest teacher attitudes.

- Students with training in the Talents Unlimited Model were more likely to complete independent investigations (Type IIIs) than the students who did not receive the training.

- Supported use of SEM as a means of meeting educational needs of a wide variety of high ability students
- SEM, when used as an intervention, was associated with improved attitudes toward learning among elementary, high ability students with learning disabilities. Furthermore, the same students (who completed a high percentage of Type III projects) made positive gains with respect to self-concept.

- Involvement in Type III studies substantially increased post-secondary education plans of students (from attending 2.6 years to attending 4.0 years).

- Students who participated in Type III projects, both in and out of school, maintained interests in college and career aspirations that were similar to those manifested during their public school years as opposed to previous reports of little or no relation between personally initiated and assigned school projects.
- Supports the concept that adolescents and young adults can be producers of information, as well as consumers.

- Five major findings: Type III interests of students affect post-secondary plans; creative outlets are needed in high school; a decrease in creative Type III productivity occurs during the junior high experience; the Type III process serves as important training for later productivity; non-intellectual characteristics with students remain consistent.

- The impact of creative productivity via Renzulli's Type III enrichment on underachieving students is encouraging. Researchers and teachers trained in the Enrichment Triad Model implemented interventions that, for most students, led to positive gains in achievement levels.

- Student preferences for creating potential products were explored through the use of an expression style inventory. Factor analytic procedures yielded the following 11 factors: computer, service, dramatization, artistic, audio/visual, written, commercial, oral, manipulative, musical, and vocal.

- Using curriculum compacting to eliminate between 40–50% of curricula for students with demonstrated advanced content knowlege and superior ability resulted in no decline in achievement test scores.

Appendix B: Taxonomy of Type II Process Skills

Deborah E. Burns, 1994

I. COGNITIVE TRAINING

A. Analysis Skills

Identifying characteristics
Recognizing attributes
Making an observation
Discriminating between same and
    different
Comparing and contrasting
Categorizing
Classifying
Criteria setting
Ranking, prioritizing, and sequencing
Seeing relationships
Determining cause and effect
Pattern finding
Predicting
Making analogies

B. Organization Skills

Memorizing
Summarizing
Metacognition
Goal setting
Formulating questions
Developing hypotheses
Generalizing
Problem solving
Decision making
Planning

C. Critical Thinking Skills

Inductive thinking
Deductive thinking
Determining reality and fantasy
Determining benefits and drawbacks
Identifying value statements

Identifying points of view
Determining bias
Identifying fact and opinion
Determining the accuracy of presented
    information
Judging essential and incidental
    evidence
Determining relevance
Identifying missing information
Judging the credibility of a source
Determining warranted and unwar-
    ranted claims
Recognizing assumptions
Recognizing fallacies
Detecting inconsistencies in an
    argument
Identifying ambiguity
Identifying exaggeration
Determining the strength of an
    argument

D. Creativity Skills

Fluent thinking
Flexible thinking
Original thinking
Elaborational thinking
Developing imagery
SCAMPER modification techniques
Attribute listing
Random input
Brainstorming
Creative problem solving
Synectics

II. AFFECTIVE TRAINING

A. Intrapersonal Skills

Analyzing strengths
Clarifying values
Developing a personal framework for
 activism
Developing a sense of humor
Developing an ethical framework
Developing moral reasoning
Developing resiliency
Developing responsibility
Developing self-efficacy
Developing self-esteem
Developing self-reliance
Developing task commitment
Understanding integrity
Understanding self-management
Understanding image management
Understanding learning styles

B. Interpersonal Skills

Developing environmental awareness
Developing etiquette and courtesy
Developing multicultural awareness
Developing social skills
Understanding assertiveness
Understanding and developing leader-
 ship skills
Understanding conflict resolution
Understanding cooperation and
 collaboration
Understanding nonverbal communica-
 tion
Understanding stereotypes
Understanding tolerance, empathy, and
 compassion

C. Dealing with Critical Life Incidents

Coping with loss
Dealing with change
Dealing with dependency
Dealing with failure
Dealing with stress
Dealing with success
Making choices
Planning for the future

Understanding perfectionism
Understanding risk-taking

III. LEARNING HOW-TO-LEARN SKILLS

A. Listening, Observing, and Perceiving Skills

Following directions
Noting specific details
Understanding main points, themes,
 and sequences
Separating relevant from irrelevant
 information
Paying attention to whole-part relation-
 ships
Scanning for the "big picture"
Focusing on specifics
Asking for clarification
Asking appropriate questions
Making inferences
Noting subtleties
Predicting outcomes
Evaluating a speaker's point of view

B. Notetaking and Outlining Skills

Notetaking Skills
Selecting key terms, concepts, and ideas
Disregarding unimportant information
Noting what needs to be remembered
Recording words, dates, and figures to
 aid in recall
Reviewing notes and highlighting the
 most important items
Categorizing notes in a logical order
Organizing notes so that information
 from various sources can be added
 later

Outlining and Webbing
Using outlining skills to write material
 that has unity and coherence
Selecting and using a system of nota-
 tion (e.g., Roman numerals)
Deciding whether to write topic
 outlines or sentence outlines
Stating each topic or point clearly
Developing each topic sufficiently

C. Interviewing and Surveying Skills

Identifying information being sought
Deciding on appropriate instruments
Identifying sources of existing instruments
Designing instruments (e.g., checklists, rating scales, interview schedules)
Developing question wording skills (e.g., factual, attitudinal, probing, follow up)
Sequencing questions
Identifying representative samples
Field testing and revising instruments
Developing rapport with subjects
Preparing a data-gathering matrix and schedule
Using follow-up techniques

D. Analyzing and Organizing Data Skills

Identifying types and sources of data
Identifying and developing data-gathering instruments and techniques
Identifying appropriate sampling techniques
Developing data-recording and coding techniques
Classifying and tabulating data
Preparing descriptive (statistical) summaries of data (e.g., percentages, means, modes, etc.)
Analyzing data with inferential statistics
Preparing tables, graphs, and diagrams
Drawing conclusions and making generalizations
Writing up and reporting results

IV. USING ADVANCED RESEARCH AND REFERENCE MATERIALS

A. Preparing for Type III Investigations

Developing problem-finding and focusing skills
Identifying variables

Stating hypotheses and research questions
Identifying human and material resources
Developing a management plan
Developing time management skills
Selecting appropriate product formats
Obtaining feedback and making revisions
Identifying appropriate outlets and audiences
Developing an assessment plan

B. Library Skills

Understanding library organizational systems
Using information retrieval systems
Using interlibrary loan procedures
Understanding specialized types of information in reference books, such as:
  abstracts
  almanacs
  annuals
  anthologies
  atlases
  bibliographies
  books of quotations, proverbs, maxims, and familiar phrases
  concordances
  data tables
  diaries
  dictionaries and glossaries
  digests
  directories and registers
  encyclopedias
  handbooks
  histories and chronicles of particular fields and organizations
  indexes
  manuals
  periodicals
  reader's guides
  reviews
  source books
  surveys
  yearbooks

Understanding the specific types of information in nonbook reference materials, such as:
- art prints
- audio tapes
- CD Roms
- charts
- data tapes
- film loops
- films
- filmstrips
- filmstrips with sound
- flashcards
- globes
- maps
- microforms
- models
- pictures
- realia
- records
- slides
- study prints
- talking books
- transparencies
- video tapes, discs

C. Community Resources

Identifying community resources, such as:
- art and theater groups
- clubs, hobby, and special interest groups
- college and university services and persons
- governmental and social service agencies
- museums, galleries, science centers, places of special interest or function
- private and community colleges
- private business
- private individuals
- professional societies and associations
- senior citizen groups
- service clubs
- universities

V. DEVELOPING WRITTEN, ORAL, AND VISUAL COMMUNICATION TECHNIQUES

A. Visual Communication Skills

- Audio tape recordings
- Filmstrips
- Motion pictures
- Multimedia images
- Overhead transparencies
- Photographic print series
- Slide series
- Video tape recordings

B. Oral Communication Skills

- Organizing material for an oral presentation
- Vocal delivery
- Appropriate gestures, eye movement, facial expression, and body movement
- Acceptance of the ideas and feelings of others
- Appropriate words, quotations, anecdotes, personal experiences, illustrative examples, and relevant information
- Appropriate use of the latest technology
- Obtaining and evaluating feedback

C. Written Communication Skills

- Planning the written document (e.g., subject, audience, purpose, thesis, tone, outline, title)
- Choosing appropriate and imaginative words
- Developing paragraphs with unity, coherence, and emphasis
- Developing "technique" (e.g., metaphor, comparison, hyperbole, personal experience)
- Writing powerful introductions and conclusions
- Practicing the four basic forms of writing (exposition, persuasion, description, and narration)

Applying the basic forms to a variety of genre (e.g., short stories, book reviews, research papers, etc.)

Developing technical skills (e.g., proofreading, editing, revising, footnoting, preparing bibliographies, writing summaries and abstracts)

Appendix C: SE-Train

Schoolwide Enrichment Teachers' Rating of Appraised In-service Needs

INSTRUCTIONS: The following statements should be considered as they relate to *you* and to *your perceptions* regarding in-service needs connected to the Schoolwide Enrichment Program with which your school has been involved. Please rate each item on the scale of A (strongly agree) to E (strongly disagree). Although the demographic information is needed to assist in analyzing the results of this survey, all responses are anonymous. The results of the information provided through this survey will be used to help your school formulate future Schoolwide Enrichment training programs that are based on actual needs of teachers and other instructional staff members in your school.

DEMOGRAPHIC INFORMATION

Your role in school *(circle the ONE that BEST pertains)*

Classroom teacher	Special program teacher	Instructional aide
Media/librarian	Counselor	Administrator

Other instructional position _____

Grade level you *primarily* serve *(circle the ONE that BEST pertains)*

Preschool	Kindergarten	1st
2nd	3rd	4th
5th	6th	All of the above
K-2	3-5	3-6

Other levels _____

Total years you have worked in education (teacher, administrator, counselor, media/librarian, therapist, specialist, aide, etc.) _____ year(s)

The highest degree/course work you held *(circle the **ONE** that **BEST** pertains)*

Diploma	AD	BA
BS	BA plus	BS plus
MA plus	MS plus	Specialist
Specialist plus	EdD	PhD

Training you have had in education of the gifted and talented *(circle the **ONE** that **BEST** pertains)*

undergraduate course(s)	1 course	2 courses	3 or more courses
graduate course(s)	1 course	2 courses	3 or more courses
In-service session(s)	1 session	2 sessions	3 or more sessions

Training you have had in Schoolwide Enrichment as either the *entire* content or *potential* content of the course(s) or session(s) *(circle the **ONE** that **BEST** pertains)*

undergraduate course(s)	1 course	2 courses	3 or more courses
graduate course(s)	1 course	2 courses	3 or more courses
In-service session(s)	1 session	2 sessions	3 or more sessions

		Strongly Agree				Strongly Disagree

1. I am able to show other teachers how to use curriculum compacting.   A   B   C   D   E

2. Encouraging students to do original work is important to me.   A   B   C   D   E

3. Good teachers are able to guide students into Type III activities.   A   B   C   D   E

4. The debriefing technique is a crucial skill for classroom teachers to use.   A   B   C   D   E

5. Students' interests are used as means for developing exploratory activities.   A   B   C   D   E

6. I try to use a variety of instructional strategies to address different learning styles of students.   A   B   C   D   E

7. Students who are really gifted are able to identify outlets for their interest without a lot of teacher attention.   A   B   C   D   E

8. My teaching reflects attention to development of a wide array of thinking skills.   A   B   C   D   E

9. Curriculum compacting is viewed as a priority by the principal in our school.   A   B   C   D   E

10. My knowledge and skill in using a specific thinking skills model is a key to my success in providing Type IIs.   A   B   C   D   E

11. I can identify student behaviors suggesting the need for an Action Information Message.   A   B   C   D   E

12. I can help students find a variety of outlets for their independent projects.   A   B   C   D   E

13. Type IIIs often necessitate instruction in specific process skills.   A   B   C   D   E

	Strongly Agree				Strongly Disagree
14. Type I enrichment is aimed at inviting students to do more than explore.	A	B	C	D	E
15. I am comfortable in my ability to identify students for the Talent Pool.	A	B	C	D	E
16. Type IIs include a variety of skills, some of which have been addressed in schools for years.	A	B	C	D	E
17. I can explain the nature and purpose of Type I enrichment to others.	A	B	C	D	E
18. Even though there's always room for improvement, I feel I know how to stimulate students to pursue interests beyond an introductory level.	A	B	C	D	E
19. All students can benefit from regular instruction in thinking skills.	A	B	C	D	E
20. Children best get identified for gifted programs when teachers and parents work together.	A	B	C	D	E
21. I think it's important to be able to explain the three-ring conception of giftedness.	A	B	C	D	E
22. Students in my classes can identify procedures for decision making, planning, and predicting.	A	B	C	D	E
23. Compacting should be offered to any student who can demonstrate mastery in an area of the curriculum.	A	B	C	D	E
24. I have developed some ways to help students keep on task with their investigations.	A	B	C	D	E

Resources

▶   ▶   ▶   ▶   ▶   ▶   ▶   ▶   ▶   ▶

Before going into the substance of the Schoolwide Enrichment Model, there is one very important caution about the change process that readers should consider. No single book, article, workshop, or presentation can provide all of the background information or knowledge necessary to implement a program such as the one described here. For this reason, I have included a series of resources that will help interested persons obtain the practical know-how that has emerged over the years from schools and classrooms using the SEM. Because of space limitations, the list is selective and, of course, new resources are always under development. But thanks to the Internet, it is now possible to update information and to share new resources as they come online.

The resources are divided into two categories. The list entitled Resources for the Implementation of the Schoolwide Enrichment Model should be thought of as a starter kit for persons interested in embarking on a school improvement process based on this model. I have tried to keep this list as short and as practical as possible. The second list, Resources that Supplement the Schoolwide Enrichment Model, consists of materials that we have found helpful in expanding the basic dimensions of the model. Readers are invited to share with the author resources with proven effectiveness so that they can be entered into the various data bases at our Web site. This approach will allow the creative ideas of many individuals and schools faculties to help others who are looking for new and improved ways of making schools more enriching places for young people.

RESOURCES FOR THE IMPLEMENTATION OF THE SCHOOLWIDE ENRICHMENT MODEL

TITLE: *Total Talent Portfolio: A Systematic Plan to Identify and Nurture Gifts and Talents* (1998)
AUTHOR: Purcell, J. H., and Renzulli, J. S.
DESCRIPTION: This book provides a systematic vehicle, the Total Talent Portfolio, to gather, record, and act upon the best information teachers can learn about each young person's strengths and abilities. The portfolio is designed to help teachers, students, and parents collect, organize and keep several types of information that illustrate a student's strength areas.
PUBLISHER: Creative Learning Press

TITLE: *The Enrichment Triad Model* (1977)
AUTHOR: Renzulli, J. S.
DESCRIPTION: In this book Dr. Renzulli addresses some of the age-old questions that haunt persons attempting to develop defensible programs for exceptional youth. He draws a distinction between enrichment activities that are good for all children and those that are relatively unique to those with high abilities. Three types of enrichment (Type I, Type II, and Type III) are introduced along with recommendations for their use in the school setting.
PUBLISHER: Creative Learning Press

TITLE: *The Schoolwide Enrichment Model: A How-to Guide for Educational Excellence* (2/e) (1997)
AUTHOR: Renzulli, J. S., and Reis, S. M.
DESCRIPTION: In its second edition, The Schoolwide Enrichment Model contains updated information about how to achieve educational excellence in today's schools. Drs. Renzulli and Reis offer practical, step-by-step advice for implementing successful SEM programs in the K-12 setting.
PUBLISHER: Creative Learning Press

TITLE: *The Schoolwide Enrichment Model: A Videotape Training Program for Teachers* (1987)
DESCRIPTION: This videotape training program is based on the Schoolwide Enrichment Model and features Drs. Joseph Renzulli and Sally Reis. It consists of nine tapes in which various components of the model are described. Each tape is approximately 25-30 minutes long and can easily be incorporated into any workshop program.

Tape 1(26 Minutes): Orientation and Overview of The Schoolwide Enrichment Model

Tape 2 (35 minutes): The Conception of Giftedness Underlying The Schoolwide Enrichment Model

Tape 3 (23 minutes): Forming the Talent Pool in a Schoolwide Enrichment Program

Tape 4 (28 minutes): Introduction and Overview of Curriculum Compacting

Tape 5 (25 minutes): An In-Depth Look at Curriculum Compacting

Tape 6 (30 minutes): Type I Enrichment: General Exploratory Activities

Tape 7 (30 minutes): Type II Enrichment: Group Training Activities

Tape 8 (30 minutes): Type III Enrichment: Investigations Into Real Problems

Tape 9 (26 minutes): Implementing The Schoolwide Enrichment Model at the Secondary Level

PUBLISHER: Creative Learning Press

TITLE: *Interest-A-Lyzer Family of Instruments: A Manual for Teachers* (1997)

AUTHOR: Renzulli, J. S.

DESCRIPTION: This manual describes the six interest assessment tools that comprise the *Interest-A-Lyzer* Family of Instruments. Dr. Renzulli discusses the importance of assessing student interests and provides suggestions for administering and interpreting these instruments.

PUBLISHER: Creative Learning Press

TITLE: *The Complete Triad Trainers In-service Manual* (1991)

AUTHOR: Renzulli, J. S., and Reis, S. M.

DESCRIPTION: Based on *The Enrichment Triad Model and The Schoolwide Enrichment Model,* this book offers advice and organizational tips that will help practitioners conduct successful workshops in any subject or field.

PUBLISHER: Creative Learning Press

TITLE: *The Triad Reader* (1986)

AUTHOR: Renzulli, J. S., and Reis, S. M.

DESCRIPTION: This resource book is a collection of articles, background information, and practical ideas about implementing enrichment programs for students. Included in this publication are articles on teacher training, curriculum compacting, how-to books, learning styles, mentorship programs, community resources, program evaluation, secondary enrichment programs, and schoolwide enrichment teams.

PUBLISHER: Creative Learning Press

CONFERENCES: **Confratute** is an annual summer institute on enrichment learning and teaching at the University of Connecticut. Confratute combines the best aspects of a **Conf**erence and an **Inst**itute and features presentations by the nation's best-known leaders in gifted education, talent development, and creativity. Strands at Confratute include sessions devoted to meeting the needs of gifted students in the regular classroom, schoolwide enrichment model, curriculum modification, differentiated instruction, thinking skills, technology, social/emotional issues, middle school and secondary programs, creativity, program administration, as well as strands for curriculum enrichment and arts development.

FOR REGISTRATION INFORMATION CONTACT: Confratute 2001, University of Connecticut, 2131 Hillside Rd., U-7, Storrs, CT 06269-3007; www.gifted.uconn.edu; or call (860) 486-4826.

Futher information about the Schoolwide Enrichment Model is available from www.gifted.uconn.edu

Curriculum Modification

TITLE: *Curriculum Compacting* (1992)
AUTHOR: Reis, S. M., Burns, D. E., and Renzulli, J. S.
DESCRIPTION: *Curriculum Compacting* is an easy-to-read book of 170 pages. It is designed for educators who want to free up students' classroom time by eliminating curricular material students already know as well as needless curriculum repetition while, at the same time, promoting educational accountability. The book contains four chapters: History and Rationale for Compacting; An Overview of Curriculum Compacting; Record Keeping and Enrichment Options; Challenges, Recommendations and Questions. Step-by-step instructions for the curriculum compacting process are included, as are many examples, key forms, and lists of resources.
PUBLISHER: Creative Learning Press

TITLE: *Curriculum Compacting: A Process for Modifying Curriculum for High Ability Students* (1992)
AUTHOR: Reis, S. M., Burns, D. E., and Renzulli, J. S.
DESCRIPTION: A videotape, facilitator's guide, and teacher's manual describe procedures for basic skill and content curriculum for elementary teachers.
PUBLISHER: The National Research Center on the Gifted and Talented

TITLE: *It's About Time* (1986)
AUTHOR: Starko, A.
DESCRIPTION: *It's About Time* is a how-to guide that describes compacting procedures and provides readers with guidelines for inservice strategies on this topic. Included in the book are simulations and frequently asked questions about curriculum compacting.
PUBLISHER: Creative Learning Press

Developing the Gifts of All Students

TITLE: *Nurturing the Gifts and Talents of Primary Grade Students* (1998)
AUTHOR: Baum, S. M., Reis, S. R., and Maxfield, L. M. (eds.)
DESCRIPTION: Compiled from experts in the field of primary education, this book provides educators and parents with relevant and practical information that addresses the needs of primary grade youngsters with advanced abilities, unique talents, and in-depth interests.
PUBLISHER: Creative Learning Press

TITLE: *Developing the Gifts and Talents of All Students in the Regular Classroom: An Innovative Curricular Design Based on the Enrichment Triad Model* (1995)
AUTHOR: Beecher, M.
DESCRIPTION: This book presents an innovative K-12 curriculum model designed for teachers who are searching for ways to reach all students in their heterogeneous classrooms. Based on the Enrichment Triad Model and principles of differentiated curriculum, it addresses interest-based learning, interest development centers, and Type I, II, and III enrichment.
PUBLISHER: Creative Learning Press

RESOURCES THAT SUPPLEMENT THE SCHOOLWIDE ENRICHMENT MODEL
Identifying Student Abilities

TITLE: *My Books of Things and Stuff* (1982)
AUTHOR: McGreevy, A.
AGE LEVEL: Grades K-6
DESCRIPTION: An interest questionnaire for young children that includes over 40 illustrated items focusing on the special interests and learning styles of 6-11 year olds. It also contains a teacher's section, an interest profile sheet, sample pages from a journal, and a bibliography of interest-centered books and magazines.
PUBLISHER: Creative Learning Press

TITLE: *Thinking Smart: A Primer of the Talents Unlimited Model* (1993)
AUTHOR: Schlichter, C. L., and Palmer, W. R.
DESCRIPTION: Talents Unlimited is a classroom-based model designed to develop creative and critical thinking skills. It is based on the work of Calvin Taylor's multiple talent theory which proposes that students have talents in creative and productive thinking, decision making, planning, forecasting, communication, and academics. In this handbook, thirteen chapters explain various aspects of the model including: theory and research, classroom and school applications, evaluations, and new directions. This book is designed to help teachers develop talents in all students.
PUBLISHER: Creative Learning Press

Interdisciplinary Learning

Interact Company
1825 Gillespie Way #101
El Cajon, CA 920202-1095
(800) 359-0961
GRADE LEVEL: K-12, depending on the simulation

DESCRIPTION: Interact offers creative and complete units of instruction that incorporate traditionally taught material into a simulated environment in the classroom. Students organize into small groups and role-play either an actual person or characterization of a person in history; or social, economic, or political situations today. Sample simulations include Math Quest, Internet Cruises, Homefront (an interaction unit analyzing American society during WW II), and Debbie's Desert.

TITLE: *Interdisciplinary Curriculum Design and Implementation* (1989)
EDITOR: Hayes-Jacobs, H.
DESCRIPTION: This yearbook is published by the Association for Supervision and Curriculum Development. The authors provide a rationale for interdisciplinary teaching, guidelines for selecting and developing interdisciplinary content, and questions that can assist teachers and curriculum writers in incorporating process skills into interdisciplinary content.
PUBLISHER: Association for Supervision and Curriculum Development

GEMS

WEB SITE: http://www.lhs.berkeley.edu/GEMS/
DESCRIPTION: Great Explorations in Math and Science (GEMS) is a resource that provides over 60 teacher's guides and handbooks, offers specialized workshop opportunities, and maintains a national network of teacher-training sites and centers to advance inquiry-based science and mathematics education. GEMS curricular units are designed for hands-on, in-depth learning in science and mathematics for students in grades K-10. Specifically, each of the more than 30 units is focused on a single topic or theme, and the activities within a unit build upon each other. Additionally, the materials are organized by major concepts and skills. For example, the Earthworms unit focuses on the following themes: systems and interaction, stability, effects of temperature, the circulatory system, and adaptation. Participating students are provided practice in observing, measuring, experimenting, predicting, averaging, graphing, interpreting data, and inferring from data.
PUBLISHER: Lawrence Hall of Science, University of California-Berkeley

Great Books Foundation

WEB SITE: http://www.greatbooks.org/
DESCRIPTION: Established in 1947, the Great Books Foundation provides reading and discussion programs for children in grades K–12 and adults. Readings include fiction and nonfiction selections by grade level, and discussions are student-oriented around questions of enduring human significance: Why are there wars? Is there a "real me" apart from the self I present to others? The Great Books Program has a threefold purpose: (1) to build skills in shared inquiry, (2) to encourage reflective and interpretive reading, and (3)

to stimulate original thought. Essentially, the program helps teachers and students construct meaning about their lives through literature and the lives of others.

FOR INFORMATION ABOUT THE PROGRAM AND/OR TRAINING: The Great Books Foundation, 35 East Wacker Drive, Suite 3500, Chicago, IL 60601-2298, (800) 222-5870.

TERC

WEB SITE: http://www.terc.edu/
DESCRIPTION: TERC is a nonprofit research and development organization devoted to improving mathematics, science, and technology teaching and learning.

Problem-Based Learning

DESCRIPTION: A series of interdisciplinary units created by researchers and teachers at the Center for Problem-Based Learning. The instructional units are loosely structured problems that provide students with the opportunity to become first-hand professional researchers.

FOR MORE INFORMATION: The Center for Problem-Based Learning, Illinois Mathematics and Science Academy, 1500 West Sullivan Road, Aurora, IL 60506-1000, (630) 907-5956/7, http://www.imsa.edu/team/cpbl/cpbl.html

Resources to Support Type IIs

TITLE: *Writing for Kids* (1985)
AUTHOR: Benjamin, C. L.
AGE LEVEL: Grades 3-6
DESCRIPTION: This guidebook contains clear explanations on how children can come up with ideas, choose words, move from sentences to paragraphs to finished works, and edit their own writing. Directions are included for making books of various sizes.
PUBLISHER: HarperCollins

TITLE: *A Student's Guide to Conducting Social Science Research* (1999)
AUTHOR: Bunker, B., Pearlson, H.,and Schulz, J.
AGE LEVEL: Grades 1-6
DESCRIPTION: This book provides experience with data-gathering techniques through hands-on activities. The authors discuss the relationship between research and life-experiences and provide a nine-step approach to research. Chapters present information about research design, surveys, observations, experiments, and more.
PUBLISHER: Creative Learning Press

TITLE: *Usborne Guide to Photography* (1987)
AUTHOR: Butterfield, M., and Peach, S.
AGE LEVEL: 3-8
DESCRIPTION: This step-by-step guide offers advice on all aspects of photography, from operating a camera to developing film.
PUBLISHER: Educational Development Corporation

TITLE: *How to Write and Give a Speech* (1992)
AUTHOR: Detz, J.
AGE LEVEL: Grades 7-12
DESCRIPTION: This guidebook takes students from the beginning of the speech writing process to the nitty-gritty details of the presentation. Included are sections on assessing the audience, researching and writing the speech, style, uses of humor, delivery, and preparing for the delivery.
PUBLISHER: St. Martin's Press

TITLE: *Sciencewise* (1999)
AUTHOR: Holley, D.
AGE LEVEL: Grades 8-12
DESCRIPTION: This text contains fifty-four creative, unique, and relatively easy-to-execute labs with high-order thinking questions; full lab instructions and lessons are included. Demonstrations and labs address a variety of science concepts. Labs may be used as the foundations for complex lessons or as discrete lessons in themselves.
PUBLISHER: Critical Thinking Books and Software

TITLE: *The Kids' Guide to Service Projects* (1995)
AUTHOR: Lewis, B.
AGE LEVEL: Grades 5-12
DESCRIPTION: This book provides ideas for simple activities through large-scale projects. A multitude of resources and contacts are provided. Working through the process presented will develop students' skills in all areas of development and lead them down the road of exploration and service.
PUBLISHER: Free Spirit Press

TITLE: *How to Make Visual Presentations* (1982)
AUTHOR: McBride, D.
AGE LEVEL: Grades 7-12
DESCRIPTION: This guidebook provides information about and tips regarding visual presentations in a variety of contexts. It includes sections on: overhead projectors, charts, slides, and movies/video. General tips are provided about charts, graphs, diagrams, and illustrations, as well as lettering.
PUBLISHER: Art Direction Book Company

TITLE: *What Next? Futuristic Scenarios for Creative Problem Solving* (1994)
AUTHOR: Myers, R. E., and Torrance, E. P.
AGE LEVEL: Grades 6-12
DESCRIPTION: More than 50 activities address creative problem solving in fun and original ways. The focus for delivery is study of the future. Students will be actively engaged in hypothesizing, brainstorming, and problem solving as well as delving into literature and real-world scenarios.
PUBLISHER: Zephyr Press

TITLE: *Joining In: An Anthology of Audience Participation Stories & How to Tell Them* (1998)
AUTHOR: Miller, T.
AGE LEVEL: Grades 4-11
DESCRIPTION: This book is an anthology for those who are interested in audience participation stories. Eighteen classic stories are included, each containing the teller's recommendations about actions and strategies for dealing with audience responses. Historical perspectives are provided on each story.
PUBLISHER: Yellow Moon Press

TITLE: *The Art of Construction* (1990)
AUTHOR: Salvadori, M.
AGE LEVEL: 5-12
DESCRIPTION: Using historical examples from caves to skyscrapers, this resource takes students through the principles of engineering and architecture. Many projects use household items and hands-on understanding of all aspects of structure and design.
PUBLISHER: John Wiley and Company

TITLE: *Kidtech: Hands-on Problem Solving with Design Technology* (1997)
AUTHOR: Miller, L.
AGE LEVEL: 5-8
DESCRIPTION: This book includes sixty activities that integrate technology and real-world problems into the curriculum. Students use their creativity, critical thinking skills, and confidence to design and build toys, a personal cooling device, moving ads, and more.
PUBLISHER: Dale Seymour

Research Methodology

TITLE: *Chi Square, Pie Charts and Me* (1987)
AUTHOR: Baum, S., Gable, R. K., and List, K.
AGE LEVEL: Grades 4-12
DESCRIPTION: This book is designed for students and teachers because it provides easy-to-understand descriptions of the research process, types of re-

search, management plans, and statistical techniques. Examples of research done by students are provided.
PUBLISHER: Royal Fireworks Press

TITLE: *How to Conduct Surveys: A Step-by-Step Guide* (1998)
AUTHOR: Fink, A., and Kosecoff, J.
AGE LEVEL: Grades 8-12
DESCRIPTION: This guidebook contains information about all aspects of conducting surveys. Included are chapters on survey design, data analysis, and presentation of results. Examples are provided to illustrate positive and negative examples of points being made.
PUBLISHER: Sage Publications

TITLE: *Looking for Data in All the Right Places* (1992)
AUTHOR: Starko, A., and Schack, G.
AGE LEVEL: Grades 3-12
DESCRIPTION: The author of this book invites students to go out into the real world to gather and analyze data and share their results. Chapters are devoted to steps in the research process and include finding a problem, focusing a problem, formulating research questions and hypotheses, choosing research designs, gathering data, analyzing data, and sharing results.
PUBLISHER: Creative Learning Press

TITLE: *Research Comes Alive! A Guidebook for Conducting Original Research with Middle and High School Students* (1998)
AUTHOR: Schack, G. M., and Starko, A. J.
DESCRIPTION: The sequel to *Looking for Data in All the Right Places,* this is a comprehensive guide to conducting research with middle and high school students. The authors cover how to develop a research question, different types of research, different types of data-gathering techniques, techniques for analyzing data, and outlets for sharing information.
PUBLISHER: Creative Learning Press

TITLE: *Like It Was: A Complete Guide to Writing Oral History* (1988)
AUTHOR: Brown, S. C.
AGE LEVEL: Grades 6-12
DESCRIPTION: The author's history of the Civil Rights Movement serves as a backdrop to this guidebook. Clear directions are included about using a recorder, conducting the interview, and transcribing and developing a product, such as short articles and full-length biographies.
PUBLISHER: Teachers and Writers

TITLE: *The Most Excellent Book for How to Be a Puppeteer* (1996)
AUTHOR: Lade, R.
AGE LEVEL: 3-12

DESCRIPTION: A complete resource that contains instructions for making different types of puppets, hints, and tips for making theaters.
PUBLISHER: Copper Beech Books

TITLE: *How to Do a Science Fair Project* (1998)
AUTHOR: Webster, D.
AGE LEVEL: 3-7
DESCRIPTION: An introduction to scientific interpretation for young children.
PUBLISHER: Franklin Watts

TITLE: *The Whole Cosmos Catalog of Science Activities* (1991)
AUTHOR: Abruscato, J., and Hassard, J.
AGE LEVEL: Grades 3-9
DESCRIPTION: This oversized guidebook provides readers with puzzles and games related to a variety of science topics. Sections include life sciences, earth sciences, physical sciences, aerospace sciences, and science fiction.
PUBLISHER: Scott Foresman Trade

How-To Books Especially Appropriate for Enrichment Clusters

TITLE: *Kid Vid: Fundamentals of Video Instruction* (1996)
AUTHOR: Black, K.
GRADE LEVEL: Grades 4-12
DESCRIPTION: Nine easy lessons are contained in this book about video production. Topics include scripting, story boarding, program treatment, production, editing, and evaluation. Appendices provide useful items, including sample scripts, storyboarding sheets, video production proposals, and suggested materials for the classroom.
PUBLISHER: Zephyr Press

TITLE: *Usborne Guide to Fashion Design* (1988)
AUTHOR: Everett, F.
AGE LEVEL: Grades 6-12
DESCRIPTION: The author of this guide books takes readers behind the scenes to learn how clothes are designed, made, and sold. In addition to learning about the business and artistic aspects of fashion design, readers will learn about the materials and skills used by fashion illustrators.
PUBLISHER: Educational Development Corporation

TITLE: *How to Make Pop-Ups* (1998)
AUTHOR: Irvine, J.
AGE LEVEL: Grades 3-12

DESCRIPTION: Clear directions and illustrations characterize this guidebook that details pop-up strategies for making different kinds of cards. Material lists are supplied as are tips on getting started. More advanced activities include the creation of a pop-up book.
PUBLISHER: William Morrow

TITLE: *Show Time* (2000)
AUTHOR: Barry-Winters, L.
AGE LEVEL: Grades K- 4
DESCRIPTION: Rising stars will shine through more than 80 activities that help young performers develop skills as singers, dancers, and actors. From small groups to whole classrooms, kids will have fun playing directors, choreographing, discovering how to put on a musical or variety show, and learning the differences among musical compositions from up-tempo songs to slow ballads.
PUBLISHER: Independent Publishers

TITLE: *Conversations in Paint* (1996)
AUTHOR: Dunn, Charles
AGE LEVEL: Grades 7-12
DESCRIPTION: A fresh introduction to the fundamentals, *Conversations in Paint* is part painter's sketchbook, part philosopher's journal, part instructor's primer. Watercolor illustrations and engaging text will inspire novices and give new insight to the experienced painter.
PUBLISHER: Workman Publishing

TITLE: *The Young Journalist's Book* (2000)
AUTHOR: Gutherie, D. and Bentley, N.
AGE LEVEL: Grades 1-4
DESCRIPTION: This guide teaches the ins and outs of newspaper writing and explains the steps involved in producing a newspaper. Students learn about proofreading, writing an editorial page, special sections, layout, classifieds, and more! Great resource for the budding Helen Thomas.
PUBLISHER: Millbrook

TITLE: *The Usborne Book of Puppets* (1998)
AUTHOR: Haines, K., and Harvey, G.
AGE LEVEL: Grades 2-4
DESCRIPTION: Create lively, expressive puppets with simple and inexpensive materials such as plastic bottles, old socks, newspaper, and cardboard. Kids will have fun bringing to life finger puppets, glove puppets, rod puppets, shadow puppets. Once the puppets are made, this book has ideas for making a simple puppet stage and gives tips on the art of puppetry.
PUBLISHER: Educational Development Corporation

TITLE: *An Introduction to Drawing* (1998)
AUTHOR: Horton, J.
AGE LEVEL: Grades 6-12
DESCRIPTION: Whether you have taken art classes or never held a drawing pen, this book shows you everything you need to know about working in this medium. Easy to follow projects, shown as they were created, teach the essentials while inspiring students to tackle complex techniques.
PUBLISHER: DK Publishers

TITLE: *Growing Money* (1999)
AUTHOR: Karlitz, G.
AGE LEVEL: Grades 4-12
DESCRIPTION: A complete investing guide for kids, *Growing Money* explains the difference between stocks and bonds, how to read the financial pages, the lowdown on savings, banks, the buying and selling of stocks, and more. Students will learn how to take the money they have and make it grow.
PUBLISHER: Penguin/Putnam

TITLE: *The Kids' Natural History Book* (2000)
AUTHOR: Press, J.
AGE LEVEL: Grades 1-6
DESCRIPTION: Scientific concepts take on real meaning with a geologic time rap, a dinosaur clothesline timeline, a huge animal kingdom button sort, and an investigation of the dino-bird connection (and how to use the Internet for late-breaking news). Brimming with hands-on discoveries, crafts, and games, children can bring to life 570 million years of history.
PUBLISHER: Williamson Publishing

TITLE: *Janice VanCleave's Science Bonanzas* (various)
AUTHOR: VanCleave, J.
AGE LEVEL: Grades 4-8
DESCRIPTION: Titles in this series include *200 Gooey, Slippery, Slimy, Weird & Fun Experiments*, 1993; *201 Awesome, Magical, Bizarre & Incredible Experiments*, 1994; and *202 Oozing, Bubbling, Dripping & Bouncing Experiments*, 1996. Why do bubbles escape from soda? Why is Venus so hot? Why does a person snore? Students discover the answers to fascinating science mysteries by exploring the fun-filled activities featured in VanCleave's exciting activity books. Young scientists investigate scientific principals in biology, chemistry, physics, earth science, and astronomy by conducting more than 200 low-cost, challenging experiments.
PUBLISHER: John Wiley

TITLE: *Science for Every Kid* (various)
AUTHOR: VanCleave, J.
AGE LEVEL: Grades 4-8

DESCRIPTION: Titles in this series include *Ecology,* 1996; *The Human Body,* 1995; and *Oceans,* 1996. Packed with project ideas, exercises, fascinating facts, step-by-step instructions, and detailed diagrams and illustrations, these award-winning books invite young scientists to find fun, exciting ways to explore the world around them. They show youngsters how to investigate scientific principles, conduct experiments, and discover answers to intriguing questions.
PUBLISHER: John Wiley

TITLE: *Jim Wiese's Science Activity Books* (various)
AUTHOR: Weise, J.
AGE LEVEL: Grades 4-8
DESCRIPTION: Titles in this Series include *Cosmic Science,* 1997; *Detective Science,* 1996; and *Rocket Science,* 1995. Youngsters can learn how to crack secret codes, build a rocket boat, make a solar hot dog cooker, dust for fingerprints, create constellations, and much more. These outstanding science activity books contain dozens of safe inexpensive experiments and projects, useful explanations, fascinating facts, activity extension ideas, and detailed illustrations and diagrams. Young scientists will enjoy exploring different areas of science with this collection of wacky, gravity-defying, case-breaking activities.
PUBLISHER: John Wiley

Social Action

TITLE: *The Kid's Guide to Social Action* (Revised 1995)
AUTHOR: Lewis, B.
AGE LEVEL: Grades 4-12
DESCRIPTION: This guidebook explains "power skills"—letter writing, interviewing, speechmaking, fund-raising and media coverage—that can be used by students to make a difference. Examples of real students who have been successful in campaigns related to social issues are included. Samples of actual projects and blank forms help others get started.
PUBLISHER: Free Spirit Publishing

Type III Skills

TITLE: *Pathways to Investigative Skills: Instructional Lessons for Guiding Students from Problem Finding to Final Product* (1990)
AUTHOR: Burns, D. E.
AGE LEVEL: Grades 3-12
DESCRIPTION: This is an all-in-one teacher resource book written by one of the nation's leading experts on thinking skills. It consists of ten step-by-step lessons designed to teach children about interest finding, problem finding, topic webbing, topic focusing, and creative problem solving. The numerous resources provided in this notebook include the following:

- 28 slides and a script for a slide show featuring Type III projects completed by students.
- 9 classroom posters (11" x 17").
- A pathways planning sheet that keeps students on target and helps them visualize their goals.
- Blackline masters needed in each lesson.
- A 273-item interest-finder form.
- A one-page summary of each lesson with goals, key ideas, and materials needed.

PUBLISHER: Creative Learning Press

Educational Change

TITLE: *Change Forces, The Sequel* (1999)

AUTHOR: Fullan, M.

DESCRIPTION: Michael Fullan continues with his revolutionary new intellectual base for building management systems for complex human and social organizations. The development of chaos theory and methods of modeling complex nonlinear systems is moving beyond the realm of fractals, imaging, and mathematical theories and into the practical world that needs a useful understanding of how management models and complex organizations interact. This latest book brings us up to date with some of the latest thinking in the field of "change management" and how it can help lead us toward truly lasting and powerful educational reform.

PUBLISHER: Taylor and Francis

TITLE: *The Copernican Plan: Restructuring the American High School* (1989)

AUTHOR: Carroll, J. M.

DESCRIPTION: Carroll's thinking is very specific and imaginative about restructuring secondary schools. He restructures the way schools use time through altering the school schedule, making smaller classes, focusing on individualized learning, and changing teaching methods.

PUBLISHER: The Regional Laboratory for Educational Improvement of the Northeast and Islands

TITLE: *The Fifth Discipline: The Art and Practice of the Learning Organization* (1995)

AUTHOR: Senge, P. M.

DESCRIPTION: Senge is concerned with building learning organizations that can overcome obstacles and recognize new opportunities. He argues that five disciplines (vital human dimensions) will distinguish learning organizations from the more traditional controlling organizations: systems thinking, personal mastery, mental models, building shared vision, and team learning. Although Senge's book is philosophical and his work has been with corporations, *The Fifth Discipline* has value for educators and school communities. If

schools are going to make the changes that many agree are necessary, they will have to become more like the learning organizations Senge describes.
PUBLISHER: Doubleday/Currency

TITLE: *Restructuring Schools: Capturing and Assessing the Phenomenon* (1991)
AUTHOR: Murphy, J. T.
DESCRIPTION: The purpose of Murphy's book is to chronicle what has been learned about restructuring. The first two chapters of the book review the rationale for restructuring and develop a model for this process that is explored in later chapters. Chapters 3-5 examine the major components of educational restructuring: work redesign, organization and governance structures, and the core technology of schools. Murphy's final chapter explores factors that will need to be addressed if restructuring is to be successful in schools.
PUBLISHER: Teachers College Press

Team Building and Collaboration

TITLE: *Team Building for School Change* (1993)
AUTHOR: Maeroff, G. I.
DESCRIPTION: Few would argue that although students have changed considerably over the last half century, schools continue to operate in much the same way as they did 50 years ago. This status quo condition related to the operation of schools remains in spite of massive school reform efforts in the last decade. Gene Maeroff, in his new book entitled, *Team Building for School Change: Equipping Teachers for New Roles,* suggests that one reason for the failure of school reform is the tendency of reformers and reform efforts to overlook the role of teachers in the change process. Maeroff compares school reformers to designers of new cars "who seek to overhaul the automobile without paying attention to the impact of the person who will sit behind the steering wheel" (p. 2).

To jump start meaningful and lasting educational change, Maeroff suggests that designated teachers and a building principal be trained as a team to deal with the changes that will be required to improve schools. His new book is not only a guidebook that explains how team members are selected and trained, but also an examination of the stages through which teams evolve as they develop lives of their own and an analysis of the obstacles the new team will encounter as it works to bring about changes in its respective district. Chapters include Selecting Teams, Bonding and Growing, The Team and the Principal, The Team Returns, Making Time for Teams, and Obstacles to Teams.

Maeroff's work leads to a deeper understanding of change, the dynamics of change in the educational setting, and contains some practical suggestions for those who wish to utilize teams to encourage change in their district. Most important, Maeroff's work is one of the few works to recognize teachers as the essential element in school improvement.
PUBLISHER: Teachers College Press

Staff Development

TITLE: *"The Virtues of Not Knowing."* In *The Having of Wonderful Ideas and Other Essays on Teaching and Learning* (1995)

AUTHOR: Duckworth, E.

DESCRIPTION: In this article Duckworth focuses attention away from the importance of knowing the right answer (which she believes is a passive virtue), and focuses on the virtues of not knowing. After all, she concludes, "what you do about what you don't know is, in the final analysis, what determines what you will ultimately know" (p. 68). If educators are going to make a difference in students' intellectual thoughts, they must relinquish the one-right-answer mentality and help children develop curiosity, patience, honest attempts, puzzlement, and wrong outcomes as legitimate elements in learning.

PUBLISHER: Teachers College Press

TITLE: *The Reflective Practitioner: How Professionals Think in Action* (1983)

AUTHOR: Schon, D.

DESCRIPTION: Schon argues that competent practitioners know more than they can say. He documents this belief with vignettes of practitioners who demonstrate reflection and intuitive knowing in the midst of action. Schon also argues that teachers must embark on the course of reflective practice, even though it may cause confusion and uncertainty, because the reflections ultimately increase teachers' capacities to contribute to student and organizational learning.

PUBLISHER: Jossey-Bass

Parenting and Parent Involvement in Schools

TITLE: *Awakening Your Child's Natural Genius* (1991)

AUTHOR: Armstrong, T.

DESCRIPTION: This book provides parents with strategies for bringing out the very best in their children. The author, a columnist for *Parenting Magazine*, divides his book into four parts. In the first section he deals with the learning environment of home and school. In the second and third parts, Academics the Natural Way and Growing Through Arts and Leisure, he explores ways families can explore and learn about academic content in enjoyable ways. In the final section of the book, Armstrong examines different strategies that will help parents maintain their children's uniqueness in school. The format for each of the chapters is practical. At the end of each chapter are tips for parents and lists of resources (i.e., organizations, books, articles) that parents can use to help develop the talents in their children.

PUBLISHER: Jeremy P. Tarcher, Inc.

TITLE: *College Comes Sooner Than You Think: The Essential Planning Guide for High School Students and Their Families* (1991)
AUTHOR: Featherstone, B. D., and Reilly, J. M.
DESCRIPTION: This book is written on the premise that few families take enough time to "shop" for colleges. Accordingly, students and parents are encouraged to act as consumers when they plan this important step in an adolescent's career. The chapters take families from defining priorities to planning the finances for the student's years in college. The planning forms are especially helpful as is the resource list in chapter 14. Also included is a complete list of references to related topics, including applications, athletes' information, career guidance, financial aid, résumé preparation, and testing.
PUBLISHER: Ohio Psychology Press

TITLE: *10 Traits of Highly Successful Schools: How You Can Know If Your School Is a Good One* (1999)
AUTHOR: McEwan, E.
DESCRIPTION: Aimed at parents, this book suggests a path to meaningful involvement in public education. McEwan provides criteria for measuring and evaluating the quality of your child's school.
PUBLISHER: Harold Shaw

TITLE: *How to Help Your Child with Homework* (1997)
AUTHOR: Radencich, M. C., and Schumm, J. S.
DESCRIPTION: This book is based on the premise that homework does not have to be unpleasant. The authors offer specific tips and techniques that can make homework more bearable for all who are involved. Separate chapters are devoted to academic areas (i.e., reading, spelling and writing, mathematics, science, and social studies) and each chapter contains specific strategies for working in the discipline. Additionally, other chapters are devoted to research projects and family games. A final chapter provides resources as well as forms, lists, charts, and game boards to help parents help children with homework.
PUBLISHER: Free Spirit Publishing

TITLE: *Parenting the Very Young Gifted Child* (Research Monograph No. 9308) (1996)
AUTHOR: Robinson, N. M.
DESCRIPTION: Although this monograph is about young high ability children, many of the topics and suggestions developed by Robinson can be used by parents to develop talent in all children. Two sections are especially useful: How Do Adults Promote the Development of Gifted Children? and What Other Aspects of Development Need Attention?
PUBLISHER: The National Research Center on the Gifted and Talented, Storrs, CT, The University of Connecticut, 2131 Hillside Road, U-7, Storrs, CT 06269-3007; www.gifted.uconn.edu

TITLE: *Reading With Young Children* (Research Monograph No. 9302) (1993)
AUTHOR: Jackson, N. E., and Roller, C. M.
DESCRIPTION: This monograph has a number of purposes. First, it summarizes the research literature about literary development. One of the important conclusions of the research is that children's reading and writing skills develop unevenly. Accordingly, the second part of this document contains recommendations and suggestions to enhance the reading skills of children at all stages of literacy development. The authors answer questions including, for example: What should adults do when they read with a child? Should talking be part of reading with a child? What kind of talk occurs during story reading? What kind of book choices make good reading? What do children learn from reading with adults?
PUBLISHER: The National Research Center on the Gifted and Talented, Storrs, CT, The University of Connecticut, 2131 Hillside Road, U-7, Storrs, CT 06269-3007; www.gifted.uconn.edu

TITLE: *Some Children Under Some Conditions: TV and the High Potential Kid* (Research Monograph No. 9206) (1992)
AUTHOR: Abelman, R.
DESCRIPTION: Abelman addresses controversial issues in this monograph: How Much TV Is Too Much? and Is TV Harmful? The author examines the relationship between high ability children and their television watching habits and presents these findings in the report. Equally important, he provides guidelines for parent decision making related to children's television viewing.
PUBLISHER: The National Research Center on the Gifted and Talented, Storrs, CT, The University of Connecticut, 2131 Hillside Road, U-7, Storrs, CT 06269-3007; www.gifted.uconn.edu

The following organizations also offer materials for parents:

National Coalition for Parent Involvement in Education
119 North Payne Street
Alexandria, VA 22314
(703) 683-6232

National Congress of Parents and Teachers
1201 16th Street., N.W., #619
Washington, DC 20036
(202) 822-7878

Parent Involvement Center
Chapter I Technical Assistance Center
RMC Research Corporation
400 Lafayette Road
Hampton, NH 03842
(603) 926-8888

Many of the titles in this Resource Guide can be obtained from the Creative Learning Press:

Creative Learning Press
P.O. Box 320
Mansfield Center, CT 06250
(888) 518-8004
www.creativelearningpress.com
clp@neca.com

References

Adler, M. J., and R. M. Hutchins. 1952. *The great ideas: A syntopicon of great books of the western world.* Chicago: Encyclopedia Britannica.

Albert, R. S., and M. A. Runco. 1986. The achievement of eminence: A model based on a longitudinal study of exceptionally gifted boys and their families. In R. J. Sternberg and J. E. Davidson (Eds.). *Conceptions of Giftedness* (pp. 332–357). Cambridge: Cambridge University Press.

Amabile, T. M. 1983. *The social psychology of creativity.* New York: Springer-Verlag.

Applebee, A. N., J. A. Langer, and I. V. S. Mullis. 1989. *Crossroads in American education.* Princeton: Educational Testing Service.

Ausubel, D. P. 1968. *Educational psychology: A cognitive view.* New York: Holt, Rinehart and Winston.

Bandura, A. 1977. Self efficacy: Toward a unifying theory of behavioral change. *Psychology Review,* 84(2):191–215.

Barth, R. 1990. *Improving schools from within: Teachers, parents, principals can make a difference.* San Francisco: Jossey-Bass.

Baum, S. 1985. *Learning disabled students with superior cognitive abilities: A validation study of descriptive behaviors.* Unpublished doctoral dissertation, University of Connecticut, Storrs.

Baum, S., L. J. Emerick, G. N. Herman, and J. Dixon. 1988. Identification, programs, and enrichment strategies for gifted learning disabled youth. *Roeper Review,* 12(1):48-53.

Baum, S., R. K. Gable, and K. List. 1987. *Chi squares pie charts and me.* Unionville, NY: Trillium Press.

Baum, S., J. S. Renzulli, and T. P. Hébert. 1995. *The Prism Metaphor: A New Paradigm for Reversing Underachievement* (CRS95310). Storrs, CT: The National Research Center on the Gifted and Talented, University of Connecticut.

Bloom, B. S., ed. 1954. *Taxonomy of educational objectives. Handbook I: Cognitive domain.* New York: Longman.

Brophy, J. E., and T. L. Good. 1974. *Teacher-student relationships: Causes and consequences.* New York: Holt, Rinehart & Winston.

Bruner, J. S. 1960. *The process of education.* Cambridge, MA: Harvard University Press.

———. 1966. *Toward a theory of instruction.* Cambridge, MA: Harvard University Press.

Bunker, B. B., H. B. Pearlson, and J. W. Schultz. 1999. *A student's guide to conducting social science research.* Mansfield Center, CT: Creative Learning Press.

Burns, D. E. 1987. *The effectiveness of group training activities on students' creative productivity.* Unpublished doctoral dissertation, University of Connecticut, Storrs.

Burns, D. E., and S. M. Reis. 1991. Developing a thinking skills component in the gifted education program. *Roeper Review*, 12(2):72–78.

Comer, J. P. 1988. Educating poor minority children. *Scientific American*, 259(5):42–48.

———. 1990. Home, school and academic learning. In J. I. Goodlad and P. Keating (Eds.). *Access to Knowledge: An Agenda for Our Nation's Schools* (pp. 23–42). New York: College Entrance Examination Board.

Conn, S. 1988. Textbooks: Defining new criteria. *Media and Methods*, 24(4):30–31.

Cooper, C. R. 1983. *Administrators' attitudes towards gifted programs based on enrichment triad/ Revolving Door Identification Model: Case studies in decision-making.* Unpublished doctoral dissertaion, University of Connecticut, Storrs.

de Bono, E. 1985. *Six thinking hats.* Boston: Little Brown and Company.

Delcourt, M. A. B. 1988. *Characteristics related to high levels of creative productive behavior in secondary school students: A multi-case study.* Unpublished doctoral dissertation, University of Connecticut, Storrs.

———. 1993. Creative productivity among secondary school students: Combining energy, interest and imagination. *Gifted Child Quarterly*, 37(1):23-31.

Dewey, J. 1913. *Interest and effort in education.* New York: Houghton Mifflin.

———. 1916. *Democracy and education.* New York: The Free Press.

Dunn, R., and K. Dunn. 1978. *Teaching students through their individual learning styles: A practical approach.* Englewood Cliffs, NJ: Prentice Hall.

———. 1992. *Teaching elementary students through their individual learning styles: Practical approaches for grades 3–6.* Boston: Allyn & Bacon.

———. 1993. *Teaching secondary students through their individual learning styles: Practical approaches for grades 7–12.* Boston: Allyn & Bacon.

Dunn, R., K. Dunn, and G. E. Price. 1975. *Learning style inventory.* Lawrence, KS: Price Systems.

———. 1978. Diagnosing learning styles: Avoiding malpractice suits against school systems. *Phi Delta Kappan*, 58:418–420.

Educational Opportunity Guide 2000: A Directory of Programs for the Gifted. Annual. Durham, NC: Duke University Talent Identification Program.

Educational Testing Service. 1991. *Performance at the top.* Princeton: Educational Testing Service.

Emerick, L. J. 1992. Academic underachievement among the gifted: Students' perceptions of factors that reverse the pattern. *Gifted Child Quarterly*, 36(3):140-146.

Flindt, M. 1978. *Gold Rush: A simulation of life and adventure in a frontier mining camp.* Lakeside, CA: INTERACT.

Fullan, M. G., and M. B. Miles. 1992. Getting reform right: What works and what doesn't. *Phi Delta Kappan*, 73(10):745–752.

Gagné, R. M., and L. J. Briggs. 1979. *Principles of instructional design*, 2d ed. New York: Holt, Rinehart, and Winston.

Gardner, H. 1983. *Frames of mind.* New York: Basic Books.

Glaser, R. 1990. Expert knowledge and the thinking process. *Chemtech*, 20: 394–397.

Glatthorn, A. A. 1987. Cooperative professional development: Peer-centered options for teacher growth. *Educational Leadership*, 45(3):31–35.

Goodlad, J. I. 1983. A study of schooling: Some findings and hypotheses. *Phi Delta Kappan*, 64:465–470.

———. 1984. *A place called school.* New York: McGraw Hill.

Gruber, H. E. 1986. The self construction of the extraordinary. In R. J. Sternberg and J. E. Davidson (Eds.). *Conceptions of Giftedness* (pp. 247–263). Cambridge: Cambridge University Press.

Gutiérrez, R., and R. E. Slavin. 1992. *Achievement effects of the nongraded elementary school: A retrospective review.* Baltimore, MD: Center for Research on Effective Schooling for Disadvantaged Students. (ERIC Document Reproduction Service No. ED 346 996)

Hall, G. E., A. A. George, and W. L. Rutherford. 1979. *Measuring stages of concern: A manual for the use of the Stages of Concern Questionnaire.* Austin: Research and Development Center for Teacher Education, University of Texas.

Hayes-Jacobs, H. 1989. The Interdisciplinary Model: A step-by-step approach for developing integrated units of study. In H. Hayes-Jacobs (Ed.). *Interdisciplinary curriculum: Design and implementation* (pp. 53–66). Alexandria, VA: Association for Supervision and Curriculum Development.

Heal, M. M. 1989. *Student perceptions of labeling the gifted: A comparative case study analysis.* Unpublished doctoral dissertation, The University of Connecticut, Storrs.

Hébert, T. P. 1993. Reflections at graduations: The long-term impact of elementary school experiences in creative productivity. *Roeper Review,* 16(1):22–28.

Hébert, T. P., M. F. Sorenson, and J. S. Renzulli. 1997. *Secondary Interest-A-Lyzer.* Mansfield Center, CT: Creative Learning Press.

Henderson, H., and J. M. Conrath. 1991. *CAPSOL style of learning assessment.* Mansfield, OH: Process Associates.

Henderson, H., W. Hartnett, and R. Wair. 1982. *Learning styles . . . An alternative for achievement. A guide to implementation.* Mansfield, OH: Madison Local Schools.

Herbart, J. F. 1965a. General theory of pedagogy, derived from the purpose of education. In J. F. Herbart (Ed.). *Writing an Education, Vol. 2* (pp. 9–155). Dusseldorf, Germany: Kuepper (Original work published in 1806).

———. 1965b. Outline of education lectures. In J. F. Herbart (Ed.). *Writing an education, Vol. 1* (pp. 157–300). Dusseldorf, Germany: Kuepper (Original work published in 1841).

Hoover, S. M., M. Sayler, and J. F. Feldhusen. 1993. Cluster grouping of gifted students at the elementary level. *Roeper Review,* 16(1):13–15.

Hunt, D. E. 1971. Matching models in education: The coordination of teaching methods with student characteristics. Canada: Ontario Institute for Studies in Education.

Imbeau, M. B. 1991. *Teachers' attitudes toward curriculum compacting: A comparison of different inservice strategies.* Unpublished doctoral dissertation, University of Connecticut, Storrs.

Jaeger, R. M. 1992. World class standards, choice and privatization: Weak measurement serving presumptive policy. *Phi Delta Kappan,* 74(2):118–128.

James, W. 1890. *The principles of psychology.* London: MacMillan.

Joyce, B., and B. Showers. 1982. The coaching of teaching. *Educational Leadership,* 45(3):4–10.

Kagan, J. 1966. Reflection-impulsivity: The generality and dynamics of conceptual tempo. *Journal of Abnormal Psychology,* 71(1):17–24.

Kaplan, S. N. 1986. The Grid: A model to construct differentiated curriculum for the gifted. In J. S. Renzulli (Ed.). *Systems and Models for Developing Programs for the Gifted and Talented* (pp. 180–193). Mansfield, CT: Creative Learning Press.

Karafelis, P. 1986. *The effects of the tri-art drama curriculum on the reading comprehension of students with varying levels of cognitive ability.* Unpublished doctoral dissertation, University of Connecticut, Storrs.

Kettle, K., J. S. Renzulli, and M. G. Rizza. 1998. Products of mind: Exploring student preferences for product development using *My Way . . . An Expression Style Instrument. Gifted Child Quarterly,* 42(1):49–60.

Krapp, A. 1989. The importance of the concept of interest in education research. *Empirische Paedagogik,* 3:233–255.

Kulik, J. A. 1992. *An analysis of the research on ability grouping: Historical and contemporary perspec-*

tives. (Research Monograph No. 9204). Storrs, CT: The National Research Center on the Gifted and Talented, University of Connecticut.

Kulik, J. A., and C. L. C. Kulik. 1987. Effects of ability grouping on student achievement. *Equity and Excellence,* 23(1–2):22–30.

Lockwood, A. T., and W. S. Secada. 1999, January. *Transforming education for Hispanic youth: Exemplary programs, policies, and schools.* Washington, DC: National Clearinghouse for Bilingual Education, The George Washington University.

Maeroff, G. I. 1993. *Team building for school change: Equipping teachers for new roles.* New York: Teachers College Press.

McCaslin, M., and T. Good. 1992. Compliant cognition: The misalliance of management and instructional goals in current school reform. *Educational Researcher,* 21(4):4–17.

McGreevy, A. 1982. *My book of things and stuff: An interest questionnaire for young children.* Mansfield Center, CT: Creative Learning Press.

Munday, L. A., and J. C. Davis. 1974. *Varieties of accomplishment after college: Perspectives on the meaning of academic talent.* Research Report No. 62. Iowa City, IA: American College Testing Program.

Murphy, J. T. 1991. *Restructuring schools: Capturing and assessing the phenomenon.* New York: Teachers College Press.

Newman, J. L. 1991. *The effects of the talents unlimited model on students' creative productivity.* Unpublished doctoral dissertation, The University of Alabama, Tuscaloosa.

Oakes, J. 1985. *Keeping track: How schools structure inequality.* New Haven, CT: Yale University Press.

Ogbu, J. U. 1974. *The next generation: An ethnography of education in an urban neighborhood.* New York: Academic Press.

———. 1985. Research currents: Cultural-ecological influences on minority school learning. *Language Arts,* 62(8):860–868.

———. 1987. Variability in minority school performance: A problem in search of an explanation. *Anthropology and Education Quarterly,* 18(4):312–334.

———. 1991. Immigrant and involuntary minorities in comparative perspective. In M. A. Gibson and J. U. Ogbu (Eds.). *Minority Status and Schooling: A Comparative Study of Immigrant and Involuntary Minorities* (pp. 3–33). New York: Garland Publishing.

———. 1992. Understanding cultural diversity and learning. *Educational Researcher,* 21(8):5–14.

Olenchak, F. R. 1990. School change through gifted education: Effects on elementary students' attitudes toward learning. *Journal for the Education of the Gifted,* 14(1):66-78.

———. 1991. Assessing program effects for gifted/learning disabled students. In R. Swassing and A. Robinson (Eds.). *NAGC 1991 Research Briefs.* Washington, DC: National Association for Gifted Students.

Olenchak, F. R., and J. S. Renzulli. 1989. The effectiveness of the schoolwide enrichment model on selected aspects of elementary school change. *Gifted Child Quarterly,* 33:36-46.

Osborne, J. H., B. F. Jones, and M. Stein. 1985. The case for improving textbooks. *Educational Leadership,* 42(7):9–16.

Paris, S., T. Lawton, J. Turner, and J. Roth. 1991. A developmental perspective on standardized achievement tests. *Educational Researcher,* 20(5):12–20.

Passow, A. H. 1982. *Differentiated curricula for the gifted/talented.* Ventura, CA: Leadership Training Institute on the Gifted and Talented.

Phenix, P. H. 1964. *Realms of meaning.* New York: McGraw-Hill.

Piaget, J. Ed. 1981. *Intelligence and affectivity: Their relationship during child development* (Trans.) Annual Reviews Monograph. Palo Alto, CA: Annual Review.

Raywid, M. A. 1993. Finding time for collaboration. *Educational Leadership,* 51(1):30–35.

Reis, S. M., D. E. Burns, and J. S. Renzulli. 1992. *Curriculum compacting: A guide for teachers.* Storrs, CT: University of Connecticut, The National Research Center on the Gifted and Talented.

Reis, S. M., and J. S. Renzulli. 1994. Research related to the schoolwide enrichment triad model. *Gifted Child Quarterly,* 38(10):7–20.

Reis, S. M., K. L. Westberg, J. M. Kulikowich, and J. H. Purcell. 1998. Curriculum compacting and achievement test scores: What does the research say? *Gifted Child Quarterly,* 42:123–129.

Renninger, K. A. 1989. Individual patterns in children's play interests. In L. T. Winegar (Ed.). *Social Interaction and the Development of Children's Understanding* (pp 147–172). Norwood, NJ: Ablex.

———. 1990. Children's play interests, representations and activity. In R. Fivush and J. Hudson (Eds.). *Knowing and Remembering in Young Children* (pp. 127–165). Emory Cognition Series (Vol. 3). Cambridge, MA: Cambridge University Press.

Renzulli, J. S. 1977a. *The enrichment triad model. A guide for developing defensible programs for the gifted.* Mansfield Center, CT: Creative Learning Press.

———. 1977b. *The Adult Interest-A-Lyzer.* Mansfield Center, CT: Creative Learning Press.

———. 1978. What makes giftedness? Reexamining a definition. *Phi Delta Kappan,* 60(3):180–184, 261.

———. 1983. Guiding the gifted in pursuit of real problems: The transformed role of the teacher. *Journal of Creative Behavior,* 17:49–59.

———. 1985. The three ring conception of giftedness: A developmental model for creative productivity. *South African Journal of Education* 5:1–18.

———. 1988. The Multiple Menu Model for developing differentiated curriculum for the gifted and talented. *Gifted Child Quarterly,* 32(3):298–309.

———. 1992. A general theory for the development of creative productivity through the pursuit of ideal acts of learning. *Gifted Child Quarterly,* 36(4):170–181.

Renzulli, J. S., and S. M. Reis. 1981. Student product assessment form. In J. S. Renzulli, S. M. Reis, and L. H. Smith (Eds.). *The Revolving Door Model.* (pp. 134–136). Mansfield Center, CT: Creative Learning Press.

———. 1985. *The schoolwide enrichment model: A comprehensive plan for educational excellence.* Mansfield Center, CT: Creative Learning Press.

———. 1994. Research related to the schoolwide enrichment model. *Gifted Child Quarterly,* 38(1):7–20.

———. 1997. *The schoolwide enrichment model: A how-to guide for educational excellence.* Mansfield Center, CT: Creative Learning Press.

Renzulli, J. S., and L. H. Smith. 1978. *The learning styles inventory: A measure of student preference for instructional techniques.* Mansfield Center, CT: Creative Learning Press.

Renzulli, J. S., L. H. Smith, C. Callahan, A. White, and R. Hartman. 1977. *Scales for rating the behavioral characteristics of superior students.* Mansfield Center, CT: Creative Learning Press.

Rogers, K. B. 1991. *The relationship of grouping practices to the education of the gifted and talented learner.* Research Monograph No. 9101. Storrs, CT: The National Research Center on the Gifted and Talented, University of Connecticut.

Schack, G. D. 1986. *Creative productivity and self-efficacy in children.* Unpublished doctoral dissertation, The University of Connecticut, Storrs.

Schack, G. D., and A. J. Starko. 1998. *Research comes alive! A guidebook for conducting original research with middle and high school students.* Mansfield Center, CT: Creative Learning Press.

Schiefele, U. 1989. Motivated conditions of text comprehension. *Zeitschrift Paeodgogik,* 34: 687–708.

Schlichter C. L., and F. R. Olenchak. 1992. Identification of in-service needs among schoolwide enrichment schools. *Roeper Review*, 14(3): 159–162.

Showers, B., B. Joyce, and B. Bennett. 1987. Synthesis of research on staff development: A framework for future study and a state-of-the-art analysis. *Educational Leadership*, 45(3):77–87.

Singal, D. J. 1991. The other crisis in American education. *The Atlantic Monthly*, 268(5):59–74.

Skaught, B. J. 1987. *The social acceptability of talent pool students in an elementary school using the schoolwide enrichment model.* Unpublished doctoral dissertation, University of Connecticut, Storrs.

Slavin, R. E. 1987. Ability grouping and school achievement in elementary schools: A best-evidence synthesis. *Review of Educational Research*, 57(3):293–336.

———. 1990. Ability grouping in secondary schools: A response to Hallinian. *Review of Educational Research*, 60(3):505–507.

Smith, L. H. 1976. *Learning styles: Measurement and educational significance.* Unpublished doctoral dissertation, University of Connecticut, Storrs, CT.

Smith, M. 1991. Put to the test: The effects of external testing on teachers. *Educational Researcher*, 21(4):4–17.

Starko, A. J. 1986. *The effects of the revolving door identification model on creative productivity and self-efficacy.* Unpublished doctoral dissertation, The University of Connecticut, Storrs.

Sternberg, R. J. 1984. Toward a triarchic theory of human intelligence. *Behavioral and Brain Sciences*, 7:269–287.

———. 1985. Human intelligence: Its nature, use and interaction with context. In D. Detterman (Ed.). *Current Topics in Human Intelligence.* Norwood, NJ: Ablex.

———. 1988. Mental self-government: A theory of intellectual styles and their development. *Human Development*, 31:197–224.

———. 1990. Thinking styles: Keys to understanding student performance. *Phi Delta Kappan*, 71(5):366–371.

Stevenson, H. W., C. Chen, and S. Y. Lee. 1993. Mathematics achievement of Chinese, Japanese, and American children: Ten years later. *Science*, 259:53–58.

Stevenson, H. W., S. Y. Lee, and J. W. Stigler. 1986. Mathematics achievement of Chinese, Japanese, and American children. *Science*, 231:693–669.

Stevenson, H. W., and J. W. Stigler. 1992. *The learning gap: Why our schools are failing and what we can learn from Japanese and Chinese education.* New York: Summit Books.

Stigler, J. W., and H. W. Stevenson. 1991. How Asian teachers polish each lesson to perfection. *American Educator*, 15(1):12–20, 43–47.

Taylor, L. A. 1992. *The effects of the secondary enrichment triad model and a career counseling component on the career development of vocational-technical school students.* Unpublished doctoral dissertation, University of Connecticut, Storrs.

Thorndike, E. L. 1935. *Adult interests.* New York: MacMillan.

Torrance, E. P. 1965. *Rewarding creative behavior.* Englewood Cliffs, NJ: Prentice Hall.

Walberg, H. W. 1984. Improving the productivity of America's schools. *Educational Leadership*, 41(8):19–27.

Ward, V. S. 1961. *Educating the gifted: An axiomatic approach.* Columbus, OH: Merrill.

Whitehead, A. N. 1929. The rhythm of education. In A. N. Whitehead (Ed.). *The Aims of Education* (pp. 46–59). New York: MacMillan.

Wiener, P. P., ed. (1973). *Dictionary of the history of ideas* (Vol. 1). New York: Charles Scribner.

Williams, D. L., and N. F. Chavkin. 1989. Essential elements of strong parental involvement programs. *Educational Leadership*, 47(2):18–20.

Yakes, N., and D. Akey, eds. Annual. *Encyclopedia of associations.* Detroit, MI: Gale Research Company.

Index

▶ ▶ ▶ ▶ ▶ ▶ ▶ ▶ ▶ ▶

There are
one-story intellects,
two-story intellects, and
three-story intellects with skylights.

All fact collectors, who have no aim beyond their facts, are

one-story minds.

Two-story minds
compare, reason, generalize,
using the labors of the fact collectors
as well as their own.

Three-story minds
idealize, imagine, predict—their best illumination
comes from above,

through the **skylight**.

—Oliver Wendell Holmes

SkyLight

PROFESSIONAL DEVELOPMENT

We Prepare Your Teachers Today
for the Classrooms of Tomorrow

Learn from Our Books and from Our Authors!

Ignite Learning in Your School or District.

SkyLight's team of classroom-experienced consultants can help you foster systemic change for increased student achievement.

Professional development is a process not an event. SkyLight's experienced practitioners drive the creation of our on-site professional development programs, graduate courses, research-based publications, interactive video courses, teacher-friendly training materials, and online resources—call SkyLight Professional Development today.

SkyLight specializes in three professional development areas.

Specialty #  1 — Best Practices

We **model** the best practices that result in improved student performance and guided applications.

Specialty #  2 — Making the Innovations Last

We help set up **support** systems that make innovations part of everyday practice in the long-term systemic improvement of your school or district.

Specialty #  3 — How to Assess the Results

We prepare your school leaders to encourage and **assess** teacher growth, **measure** student achievement, and **evaluate** program success.

Contact the SkyLight team and begin a process toward long-term results.

SkyLight Professional Development

2626 S. Clearbrook Dr., Arlington Heights, IL 60005
800-348-4474 • 847-290-6600 • FAX 847-290-6609
info@skylightedu.com • www.skylightedu.com